IMAGES
of America

PLANO

AN HISTORIC WALKING TOUR

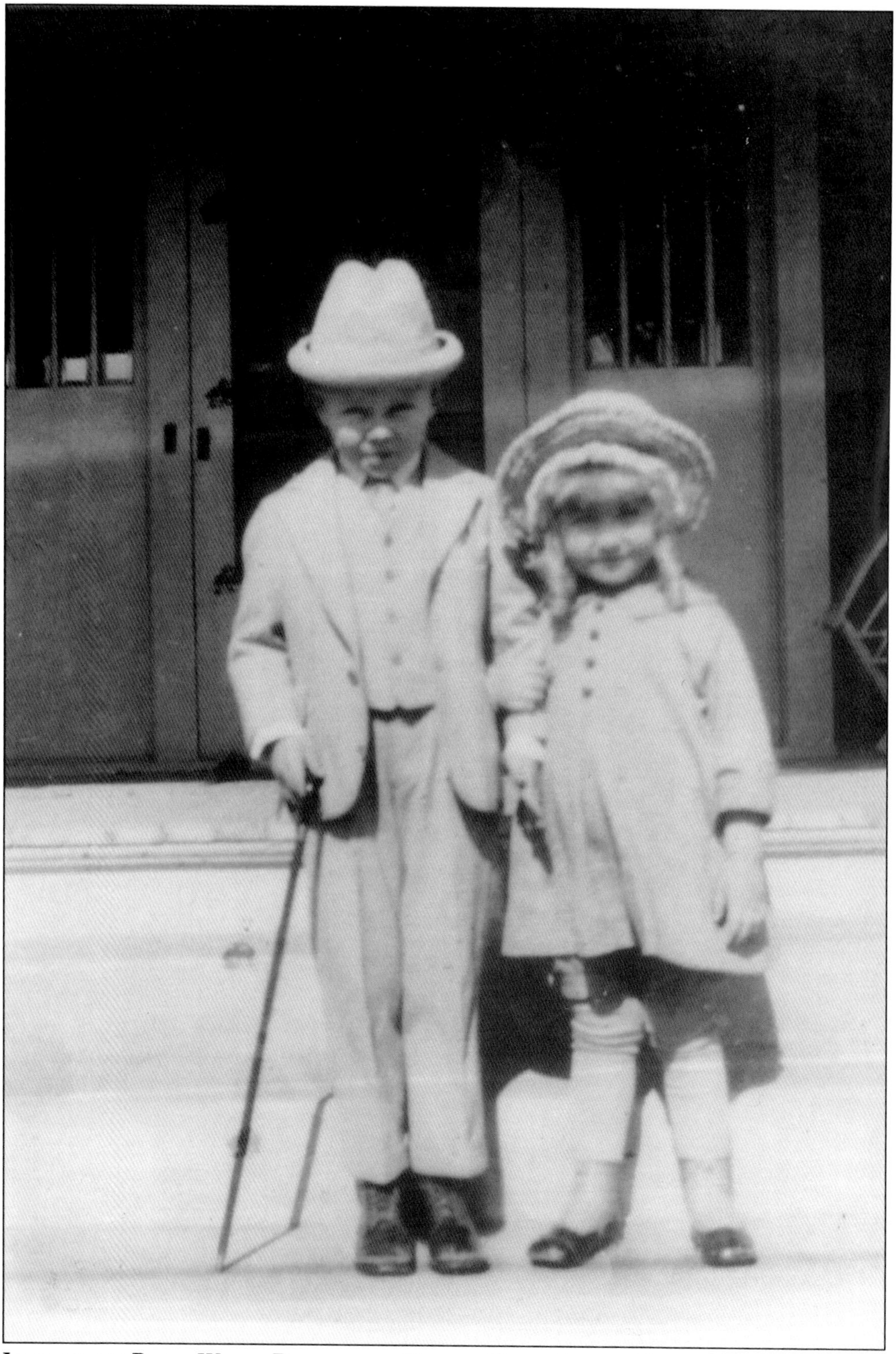

Jackson and Peggy Wyatt Ready for a Walk in Their Sunday Best.

IMAGES
of America

PLANO
AN HISTORIC WALKING TOUR

Nancy McCulloch

ARCADIA
PUBLISHING

ISBN 978-0-7385-0768-2

Published by Arcadia Publishing
Charleston, South Carolina

Printed in the United States of America

Library of Congress Catalog Card Number: 00-105512

For all general information contact Arcadia Publishing at:
Telephone 843-853-2070
Fax 843-853-0044
E-mail sales@arcadiapublishing.com
For customer service and orders:
Toll-Free 1-888-313-2665

Visit us on the Internet at www.arcadiapublishing.com

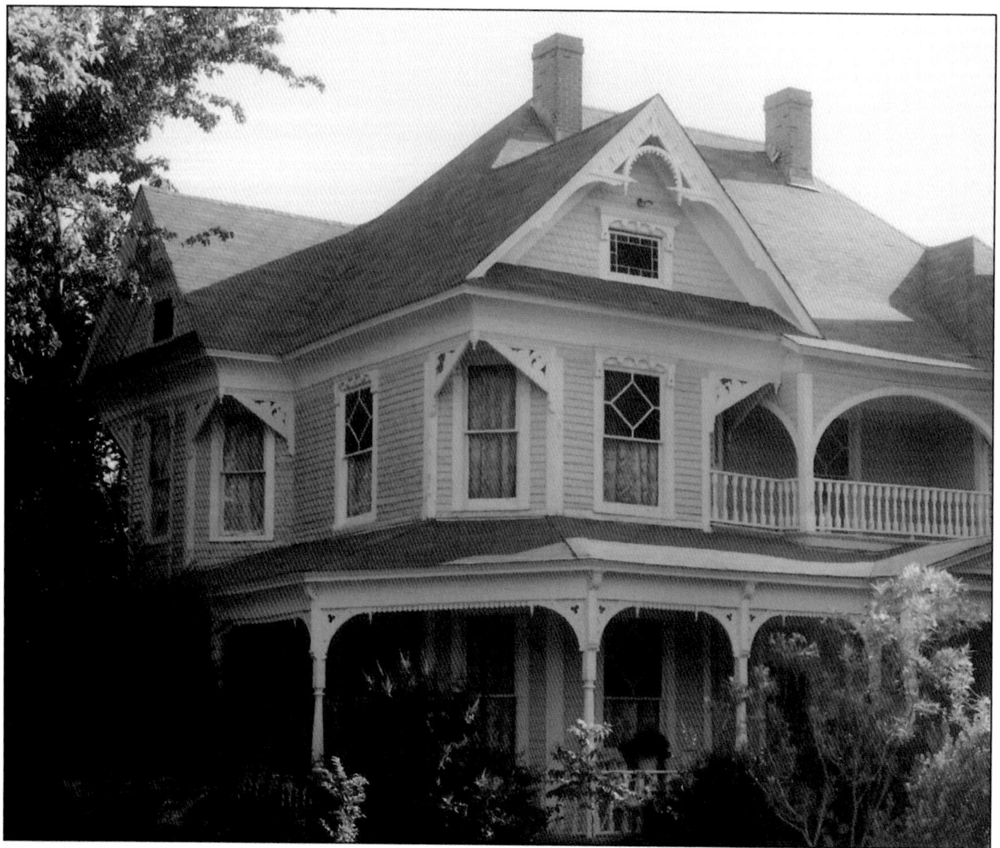

THE CARPENTER HOUSE.

Contents

Acknowledgments

I would like to thank the many people who have given their time and resources to help in the writing of this book: Peggy Mitchell, Dorothy Johnston, Joanne Haggard, Maxine Carpenter, Mary Katherine "Aunt Jel" Carpenter, Russell Carpenter, Betty Joy Riley, Elizabeth Thompson, Peggy Payne, Dorothy Iglehart, Doris Thompson, Michael Degate, Ouida Anderson, Emajean Hall, Dorothy Shaffer, Leslie Shelton, Donna Harrington, Rob Harrington, Sarah Haggard, Liz McKinnon, Jerry Haynes, Mary Muegge Sr., Mary Muegge Jr., Gladys Harrington, Dan Dudley, Janelle Malone, Pam Hatcher, John Proch, Helen Proch, Elta Chandler, Jack Nelson, Diane Nelson, Louise Scaling, Elizabeth Parks, C.J. Christie, Yvonne Cross, Gwen Workman, Alex Schell III, Shirley Schell, Penny Trosper, Bob Streiff, William Wells, and the staff at the Gladys Harrington Library. Without the help of all of you, the completion of this book would not have been possible. The longtime residents who have preserved the history of Plano in journals, letters, and photographs deserve a large amount of credit for the compilation of this book.

The support I received from my family and friends was invaluable. A big thank you to my daughters, Laura and Amy; my father, Robert Wharton, for his faith in me; my mother-in-law, Val McCulloch, for urging me to write this book; my father-in-law, Walter McCulloch; my neighbor, Adam Towber, for his excellent photography of some of the houses; John McGinnis for the use of his photocopy stand; and my sister-in-law, Sue McGinnis, for her idea to let me use John's photocopy stand. Last, but certainly not least, to my husband, Scott McCulloch, for giving his time and undying patience to help me copy photos, give suggestions, and just to act as a sounding board for ideas. I could never have done it without you, Scott.

Some of the photographs in this book are from the Frances Wells Collection, which can be found in the Gladys Harrington Library in Plano. Other photographs of houses are on file at the Gladys Harrington Library. The Mr. Peppermint photograph is courtesy of WFAA-TV and Belo, Dallas, Texas (All Rights Reserved)—these photos are so noted. The book *Plano, Texas, the Early Years* by Mozelle Jones Campbell, Maribelle McLaurine Davis, Betty Harrington Stranz, Frances Bates Wells, and Shirley Carter Schell was a useful reference. Most importantly, the bulk of the information and photographs in this book came from interviews with the longtime residents who were listed in the first paragraph.

This book encompasses many of the historic sites and buildings in Plano; however, there are many others that should be covered in future publications. This book is intended for the enjoyment of the citizens of Plano as well as visitors to the area. The preservation of historic structures and sites is an important element in commemorating the history of any locale.

Please keep in mind that the homes described in this book are private residences, and the owners' privacy should be respected.

Introduction

Early settlers were attracted to Plano, which was part of Peters Colony, in the mid to late 1800s because the fertile black soil of the area was excellent for growing crops. Some believed that the soil in the Plano area was the best in North Texas and others believed it to be the best in the country.

Many of the early settlers came from Kentucky and Tennessee. Settlers came from these two states since the headquarters for Peters Colony was located in Louisville, Kentucky, and Sam Houston described the benefits and the rich soil of the Plano area in a speech to the people of Tennessee. Since he had been governor of that state, his words carried particular weight. Farmers could plant two or three crops and be assured that at least one crop would survive and provide an income for the family. Many residents of Kentucky and Tennessee came to Plano in search of a new and better way of life. The population of Plano was 155 in 1870 and grew to 1,000 by 1886. Even as early as the 1800s, Plano gained a reputation for being a forward-thinking, upscale community with some of the most beautiful country homes in the area.

In many cases, the settlers' children grew up and intermarried. Therefore, many of these early families are related by marriage, and many of their descendants have fond childhood memories of Plano.

Plano's early settlers dealt with the normal problems of life in that era. Fire destroyed the downtown area in 1881 and again in 1895. After a rain, the roads could be so muddy that travel was impossible. The paving of the main street through downtown in 1925 was a noteworthy event in early Plano.

After World War II, modern housing developments began to be constructed within the city. When Central Expressway was opened in Plano in 1956, more housing developments were built. Growth continued gradually into the 1970s. In the 1980s, several businesses brought their headquarters to Plano to spur even more growth.

Today, Plano has about 230,000 residents. This growth has been gradual over the years. Plano has gained a worldwide reputation for its businesses and progressive nature. This development was a dream that began with the early settlers and has carried through to modern day.

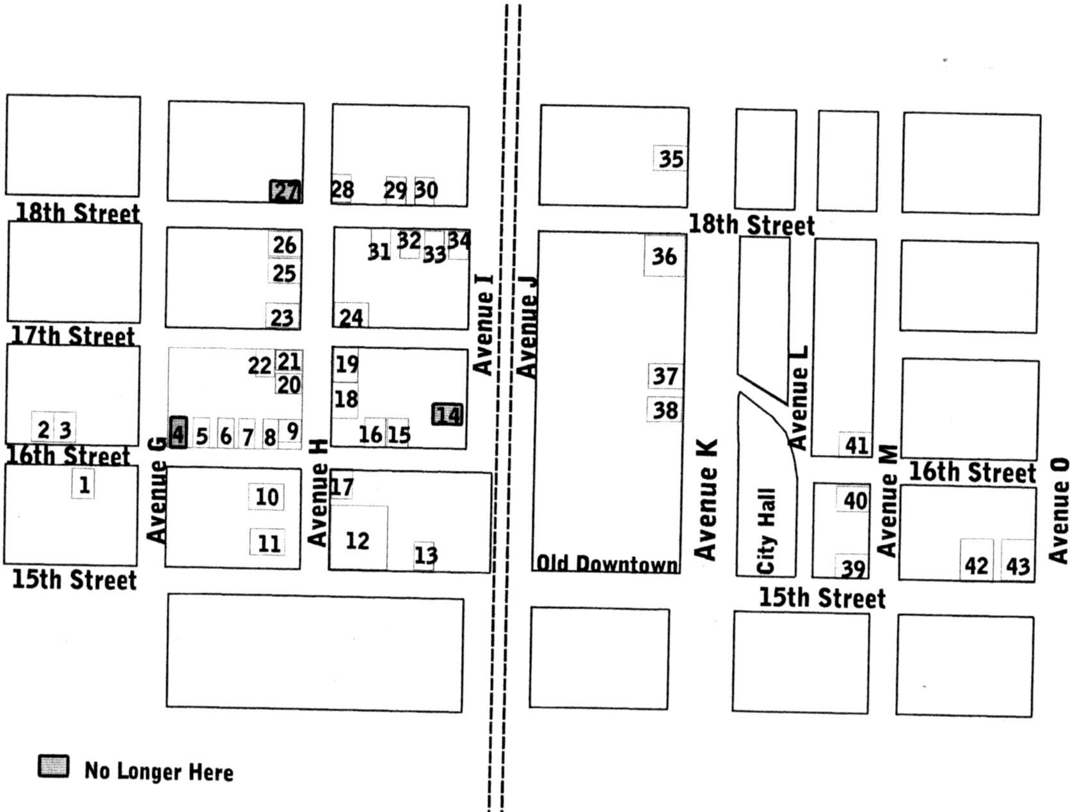
18th Street
17th Street
16th Street
15th Street
Avenue G
Avenue H
Avenue I
Avenue J
Avenue K
Avenue L
Avenue M
Avenue O
City Hall
Old Downtown
1 2 3 4 5 6 7 8 9 10 11 12 13 14 15 16 17 18 19 20 21 22 23 24 25 26 27 28 29 30 31 32 33 34 35 36 37 38 39 40 41 42 43
No Longer Here

One

Sites Around Historic Downtown

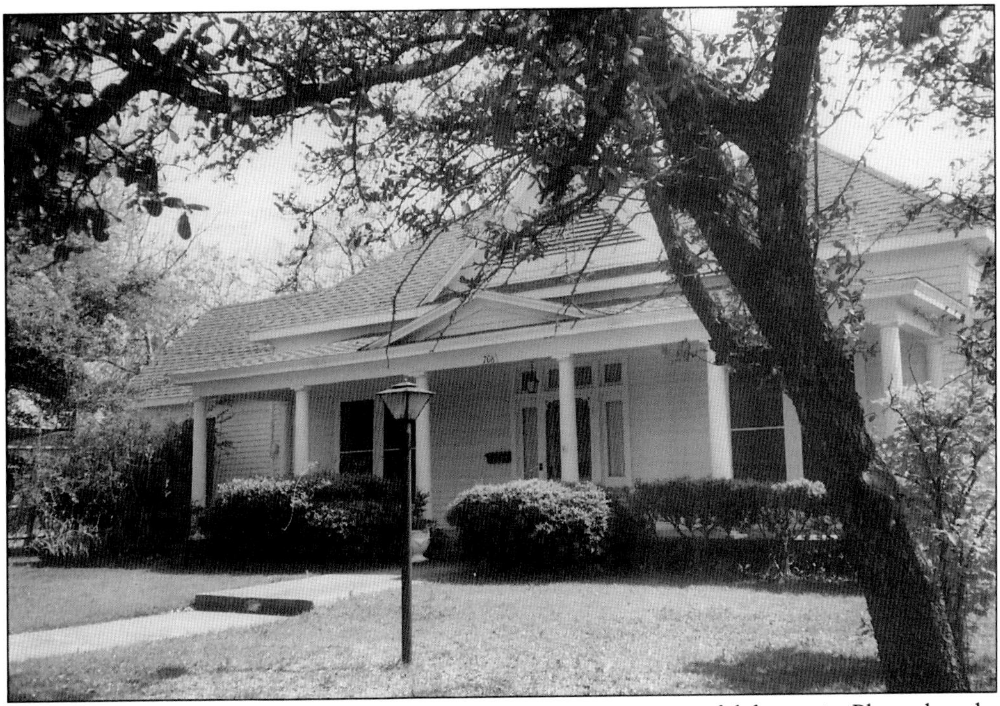

#1 W.J. Carpenter House. W.J. Carpenter, a prominent, successful farmer in Plano, bought this house a few years after its construction in the late 1800s. It was a working farm in the city. The family lived at this farm during the school year in order for the Carpenter's four sons to live near the school.

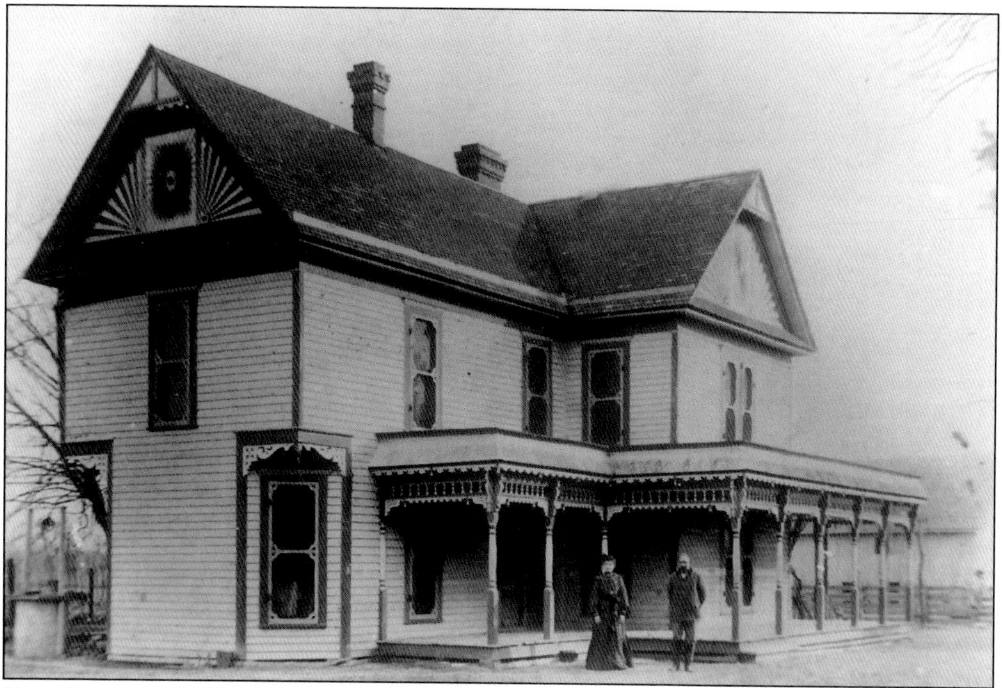

The Carpenter's Main Farmhouse. During the summer, the family lived at the main farm located between present-day Custer and Independence Roads, near Spring Creek Parkway. (Courtesy of the Frances Wells Collection.)

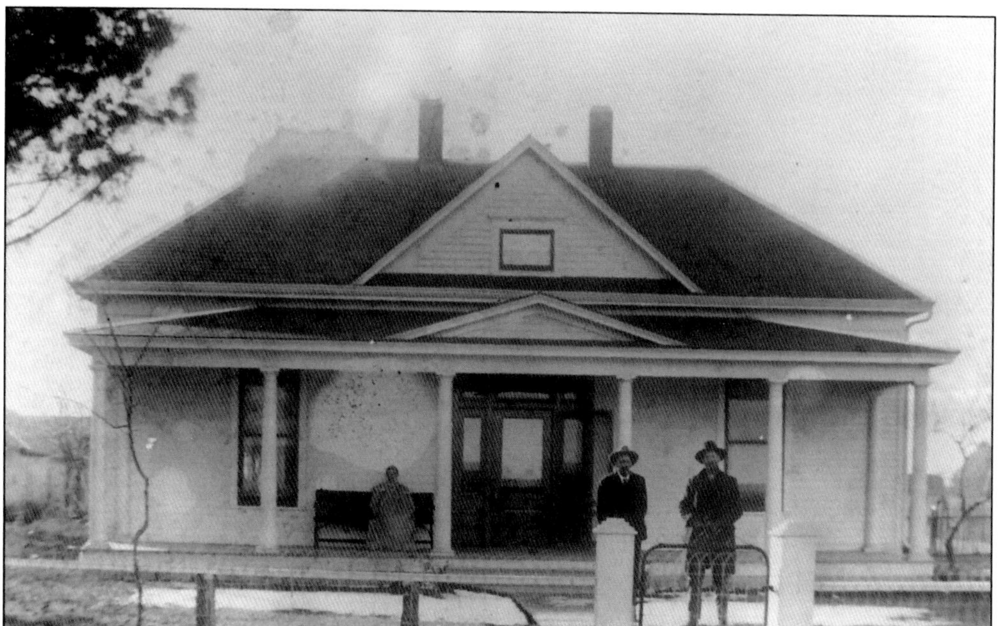

The W.J. Carpenter House in 1906. The farm in town consisted of 2.5 to 3 acres. The pasture extended to where Collin Creek Mall stands today. Mrs. Carpenter ran a dairy from the farm that was very well known in the area. The original farm buildings still stand on the property today. (Courtesy of the Frances Wells Collection.)

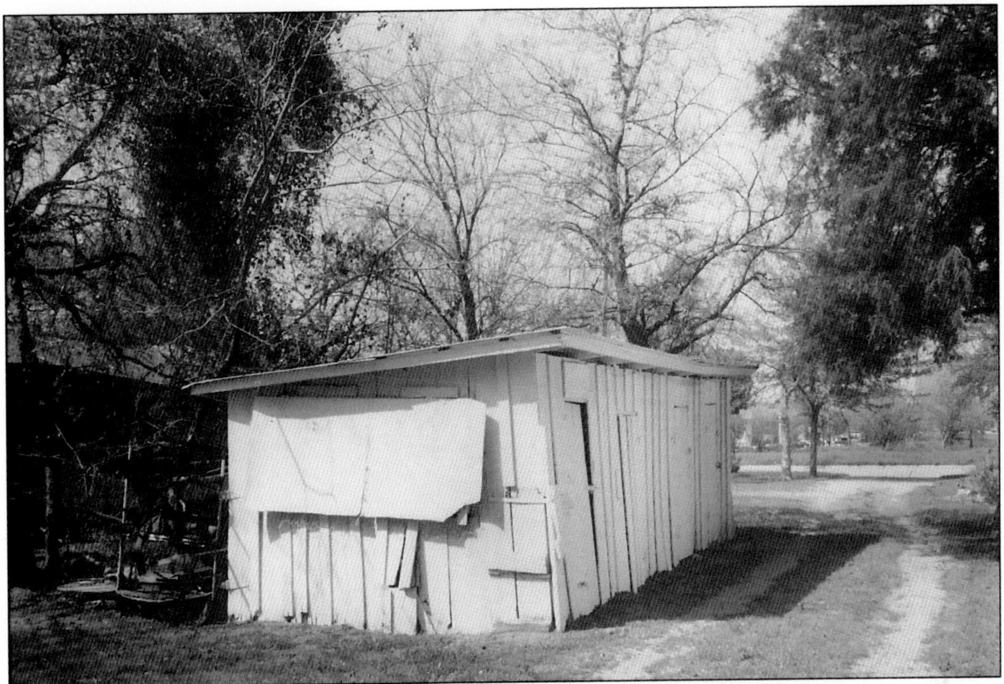

THE OLD SCHOOL OUTHOUSE. The outhouse from the nearby Plano School was relocated to the property when the school built indoor plumbing facilities. The Carpenter family used the building as both a chicken coop and storage area. Four doors still exist on the old school outhouse—one door each for boys, girls, men, and women.

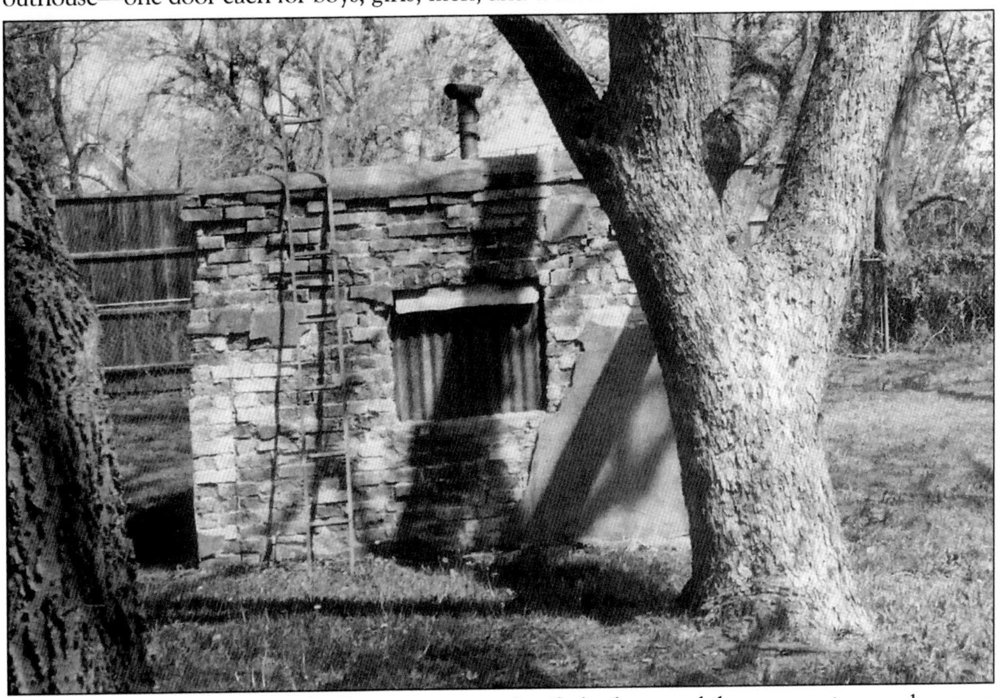

THE SQUAB HOUSE. During the Depression, the family built a squab house to raise squab, a type of pigeon raised for food.

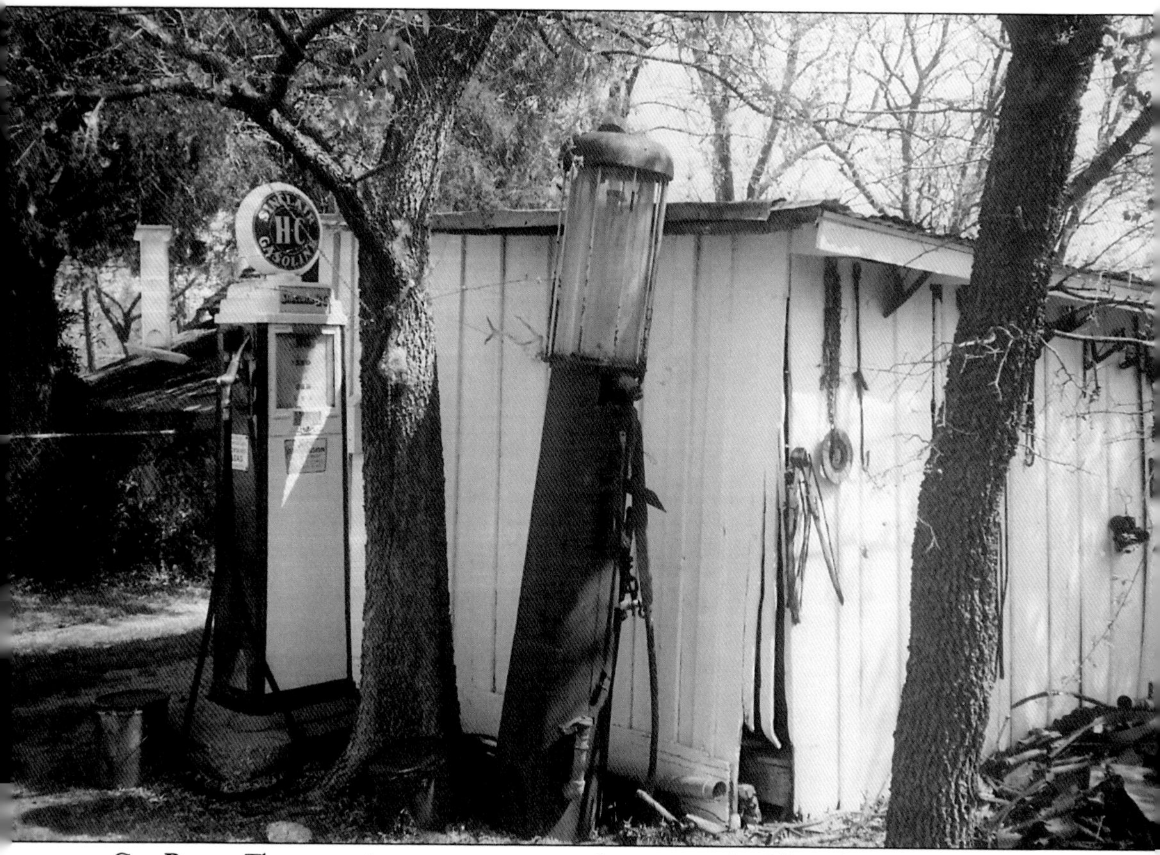

Gas Pumps. There remain two gas pumps on the property for filling the farm vehicles. One of the pumps is manual, and the other is electric. The electric pump was added to the property in the 1960s. The service man for the pumps convinced the Carpenters that they needed it, since it would register gas per gallon by the dollar. At the time, the Carpenters could not understand why that would ever be necessary since gas was going for about 30¢ a gallon at the time. In the 1970s, it was hard to imagine that gas would ever sell for over a dollar a gallon!

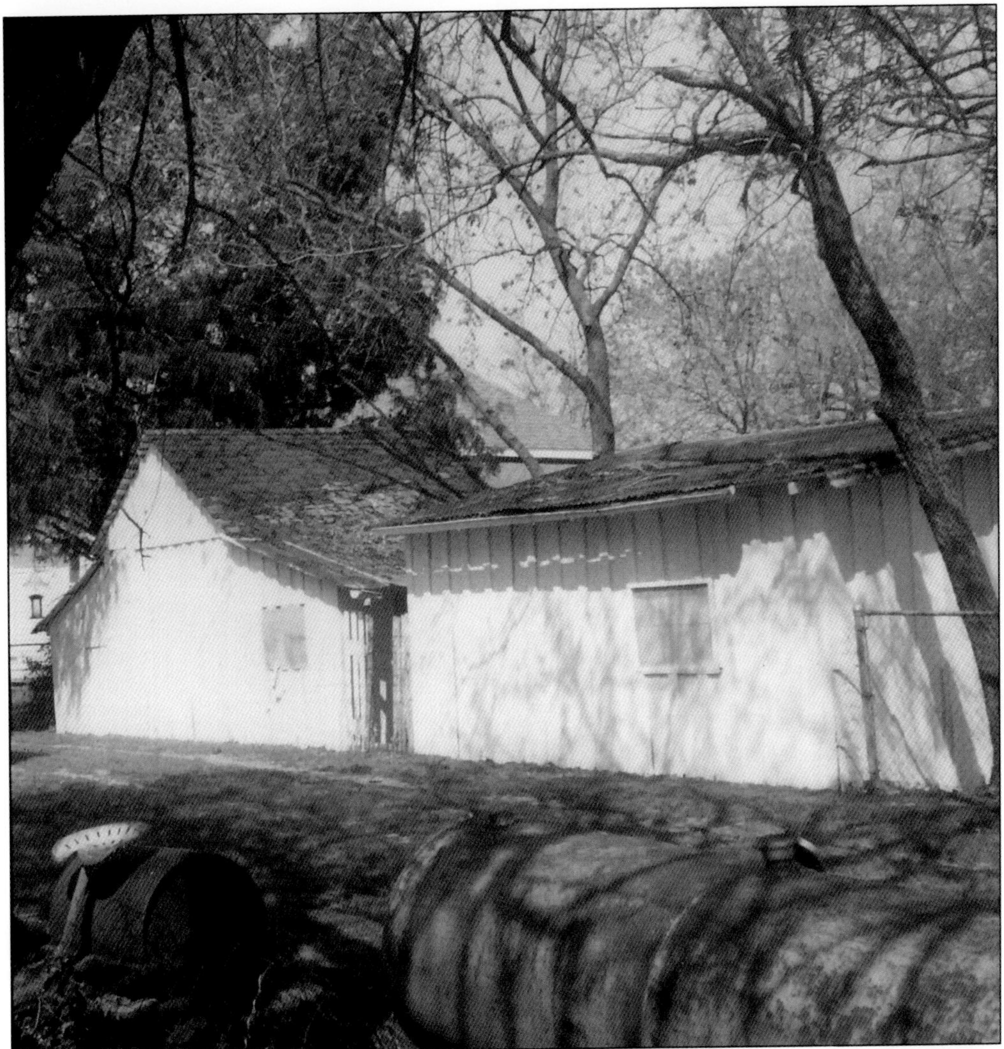

The Cob House on the Left; the Wash House on the Right. The cob house has three sections. One section has a special door where the family could throw in the corncobs left over from making food for the hogs. The cobs were soaked in kerosene. Another section provided storage for coal. The kerosene-soaked cobs and the coal were used in combination to make fires for cooking. The section on the very end was the place in which meat was smoked, cured, and stored.

The wash house was used for washing clothes and slaughtering hogs. The building has a dirt floor. When clothes were washed in the house, water was boiled over a fire in a large iron pot just outside the house, then it was carried in and poured into the washing machine. A gasoline engine agitated the clothes. When the wash cycle was complete, the hose was placed out of the window for the water to drain, and the clothes were run through the ringer.

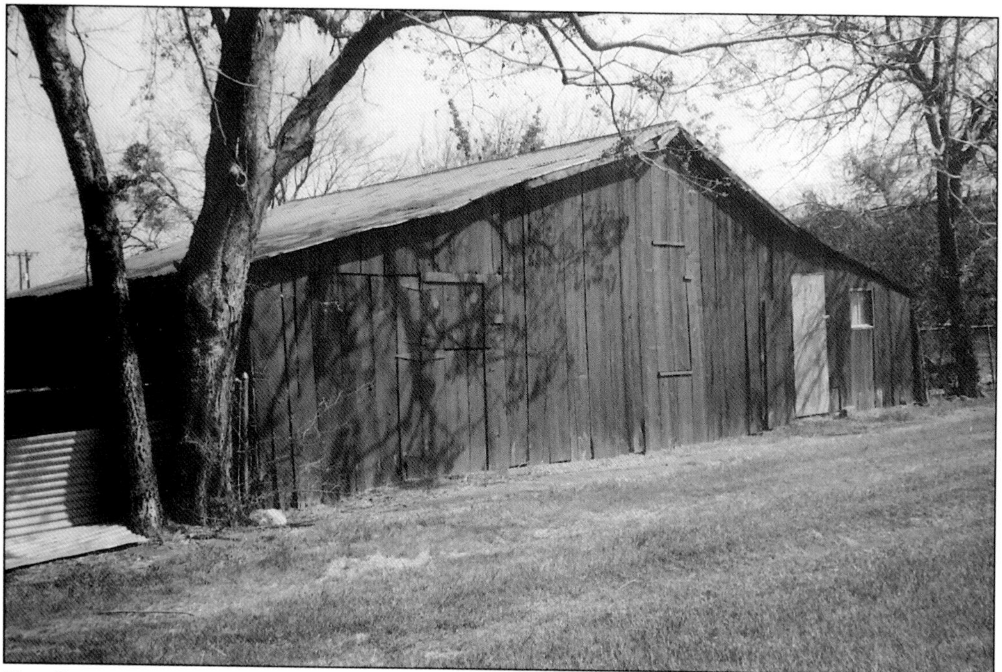

The Barn.

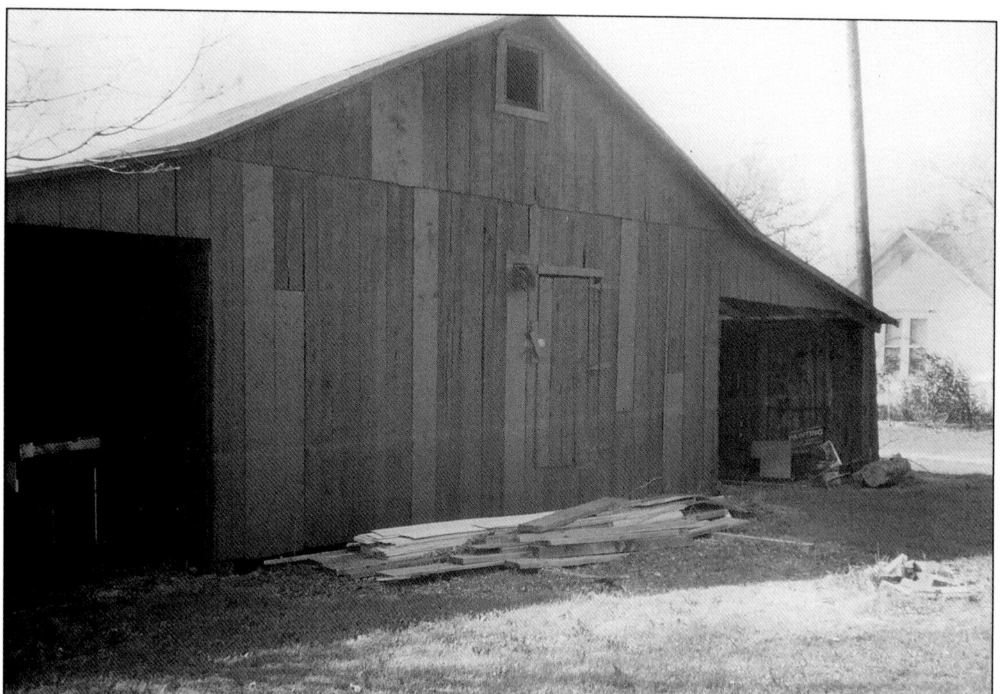

The Granary. W.J. Carpenter had the granary constructed. The grain grown on the farm was shelled and placed in bags, which were then dragged across the floor to be stacked. This made the floor slick, thus becoming an ideal rollerskating rink for the children.

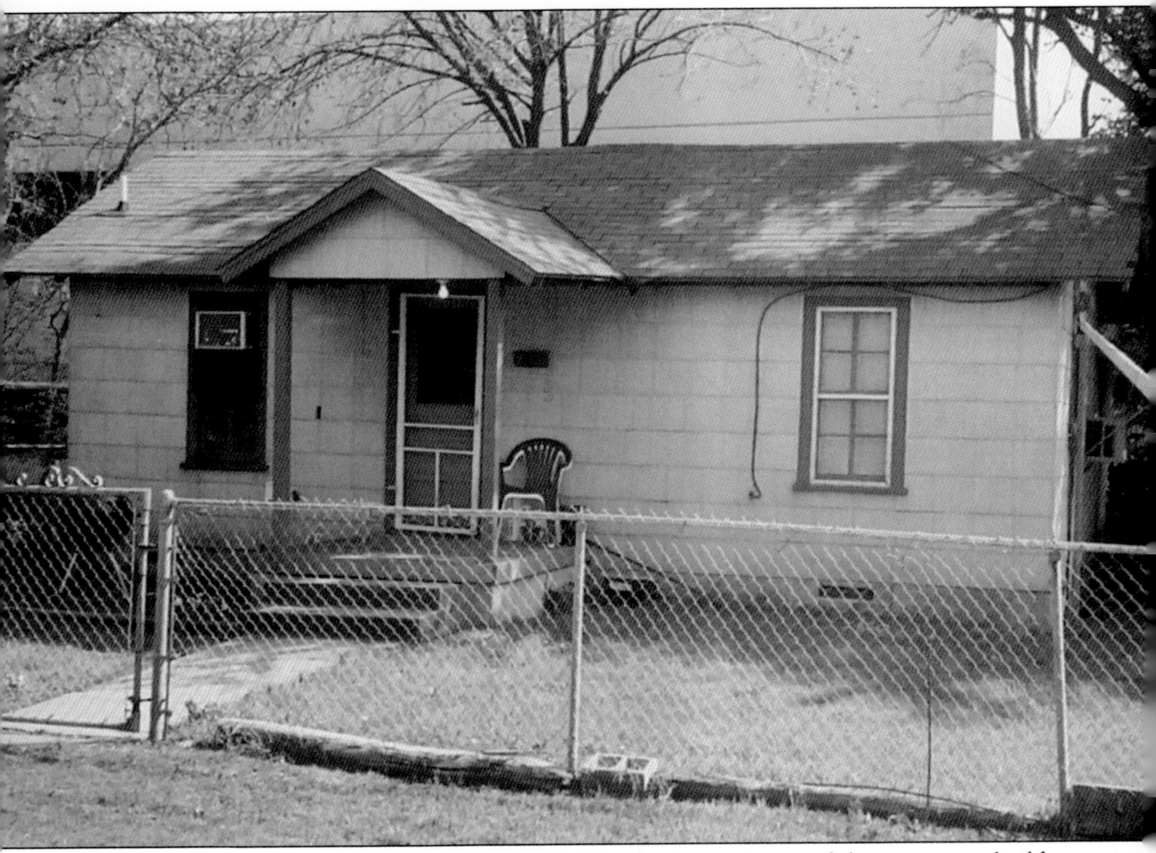

The Shack. There was enough lumber left over from the construction of the granary to build a small house. Mr. Carpenter did just that, with the intention of hiring a family to live in this small house and help out on the farm. However, before he could do so, his three oldest sons claimed the house. The boys called it the "shack" and began a club called the Ten Tough Tamales. Children from Wylie, Richardson, and Allen went to Plano schools in order to graduate from an accredited school. Some of these children joined the club and stayed in the shack, since traveling from these nearby towns was difficult. The name of the group grew to the Twelve Tough Tamales, and finally became the Twenty Tough Tamales.

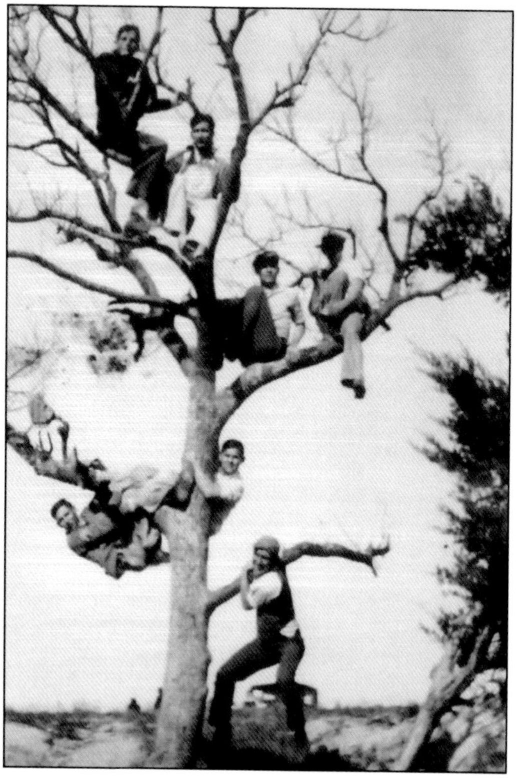

Tough Tamales. Pictured from left to right, they are: Bert "Buddy" Carpenter, Clint Carpenter, Willie Carpenter, John Beverly, unidentified (wearing hat), Lois "Esse" Howard, and Jack Miller. The members paid dues, followed club rules, and conducted regular meetings every Sunday. They performed good deeds in the community but preferred to keep them quiet. They were known for the exhaust whistle which they put on a car to be heard throughout the town.

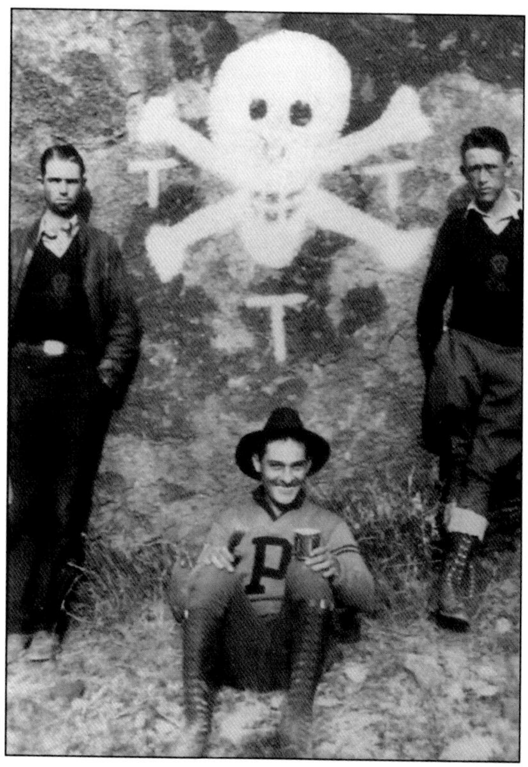

Tough Tamales Painted Club Emblem Near Big Ben National Park. They are, from left to right: Norton Fortner, Ben O. Carpenter, and H.D. Boggess. The Tamales wanted to be thought of as tough. They wore black shirts with "T.T.T." written on the back, and their emblem, a skull and crossbones, on the front. The Tamales liked to play pranks on Halloween night. People would awaken to find items hung from trees or porch swings switched around.

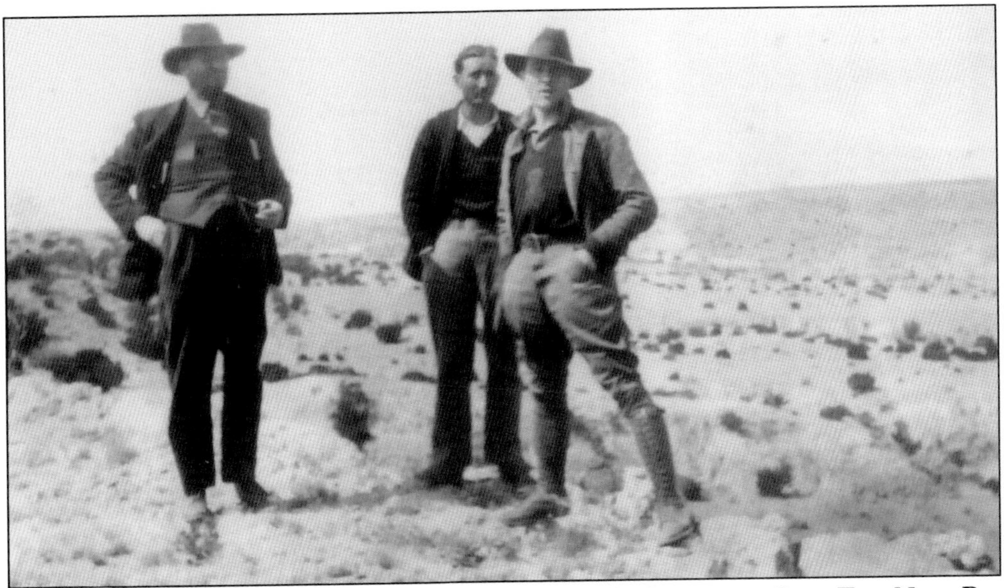

Bert B. Carpenter Sr., Willie Carpenter, and Ben O. Carpenter On a Trip Near Big Bend National Park. Mrs. Carpenter made breakfast every morning for all of the boys who stayed in the shack. She never knew from one day to the next how many spent the night in the shack or how many would show up for breakfast the next morning. Every breakfast she prepared for the Tough Tamales included about two dozen eggs.

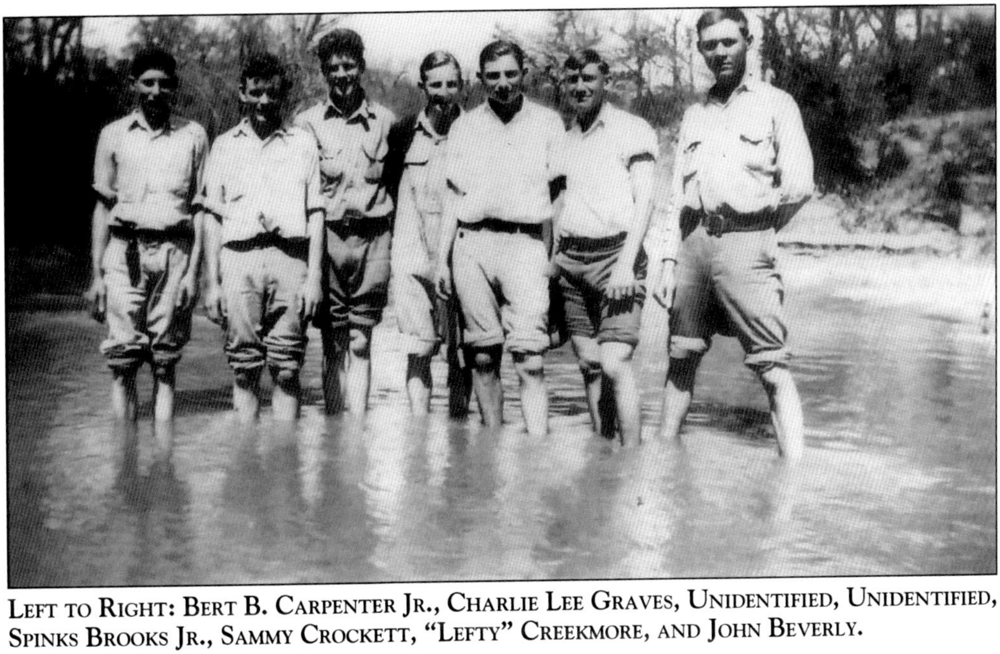

Left to Right: Bert B. Carpenter Jr., Charlie Lee Graves, Unidentified, Unidentified, Spinks Brooks Jr., Sammy Crockett, "Lefty" Creekmore, and John Beverly.

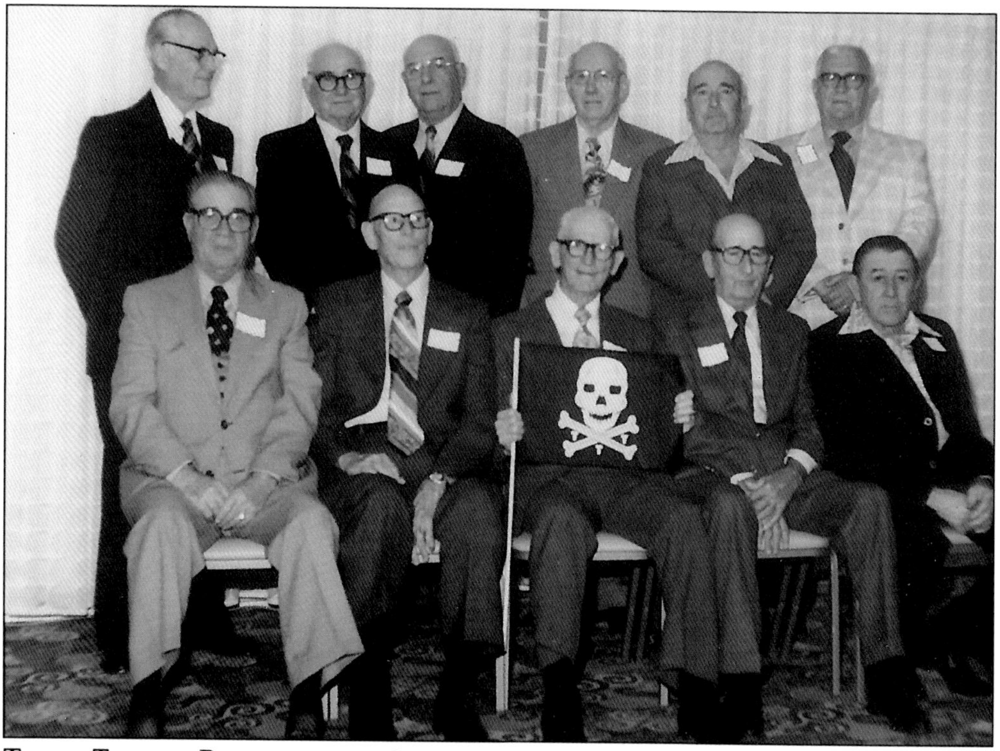

Tough Tamales Reunion in the Late 1970s. They are, from left to right: (front row) Reedy Dunn, unidentified, E.A. Sigler (their school teacher), Willie Carpenter, H.D. Boggess; (top row) Claude Creekmore, Sam Crockett, John D. Wells, Bert "Buddy" Carpenter, Elzie Carpenter, and Lois Howard.

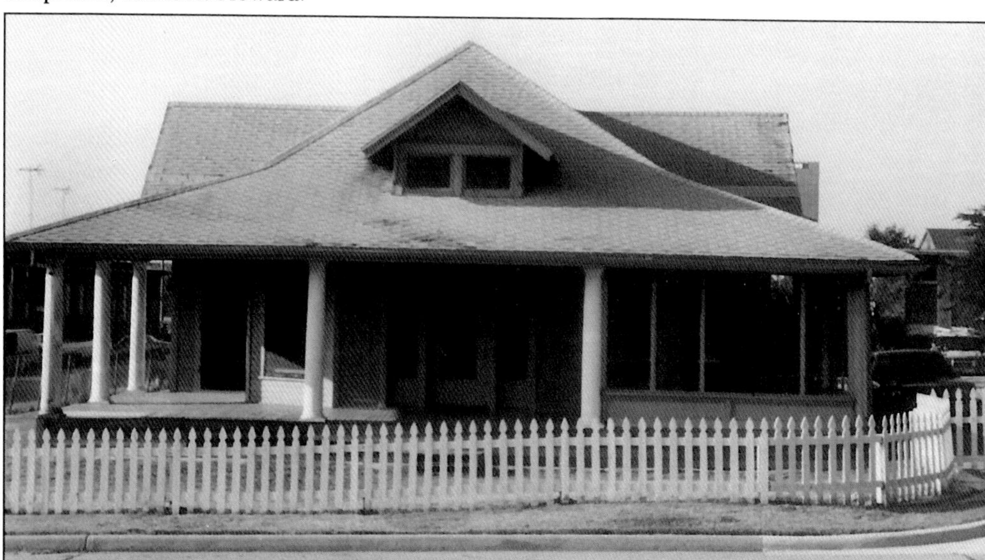

#2 Wetsel House. Andrew Wetsel lived in this house. He was a furniture maker and undertaker. Furniture making and the manufacture of caskets for undertaking were a common combination during this era. Andrew Wetsel's furniture and undertaking store was in operation in the late 1800s.

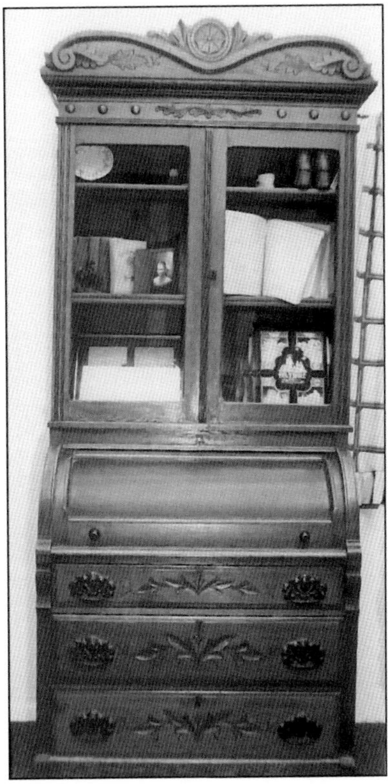

DESK MADE BY ANDREW WETSEL. The furniture that Wetsel made is still found in homes and buildings in the Plano area today. (Courtesy of the Frances Wells Collection.)

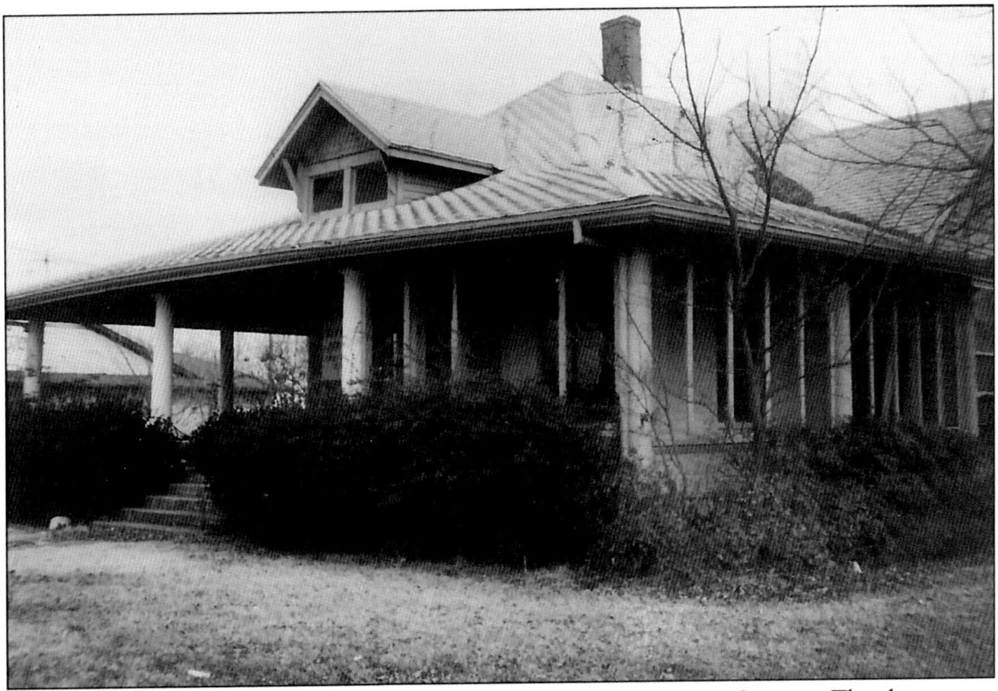

THE WETSEL HOUSE AT ITS ORIGINAL LOCATION ON EAST 16TH STREET. This house was originally located at 607 East 16th Street and was moved to this location in the late 1980s.

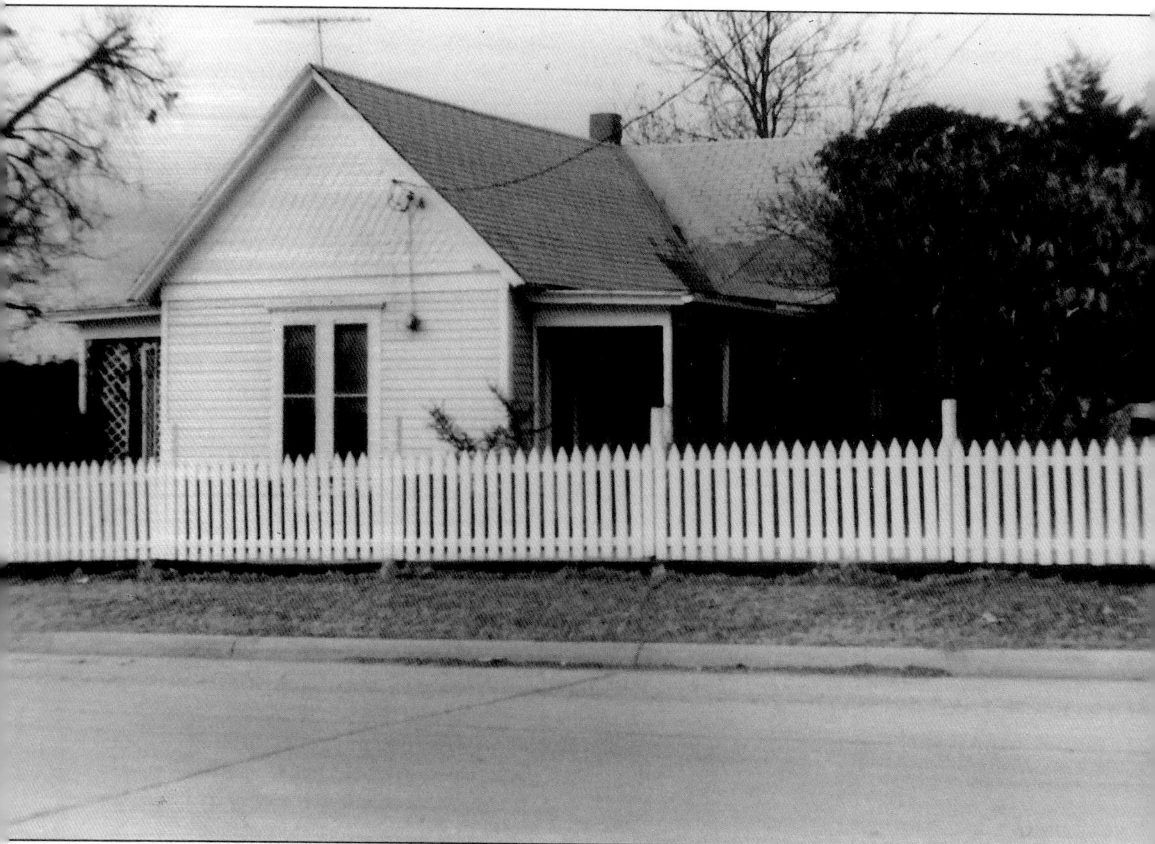

#3 The Mitchell House. This house was built around 1891. Later, Walter A. and Beulah Allen Mitchell purchased it around 1933. The house has been owned by the Mitchell family ever since. It is believed that the Bass family originally built the house. The Mitchells had five children who all graduated from Plano High School.

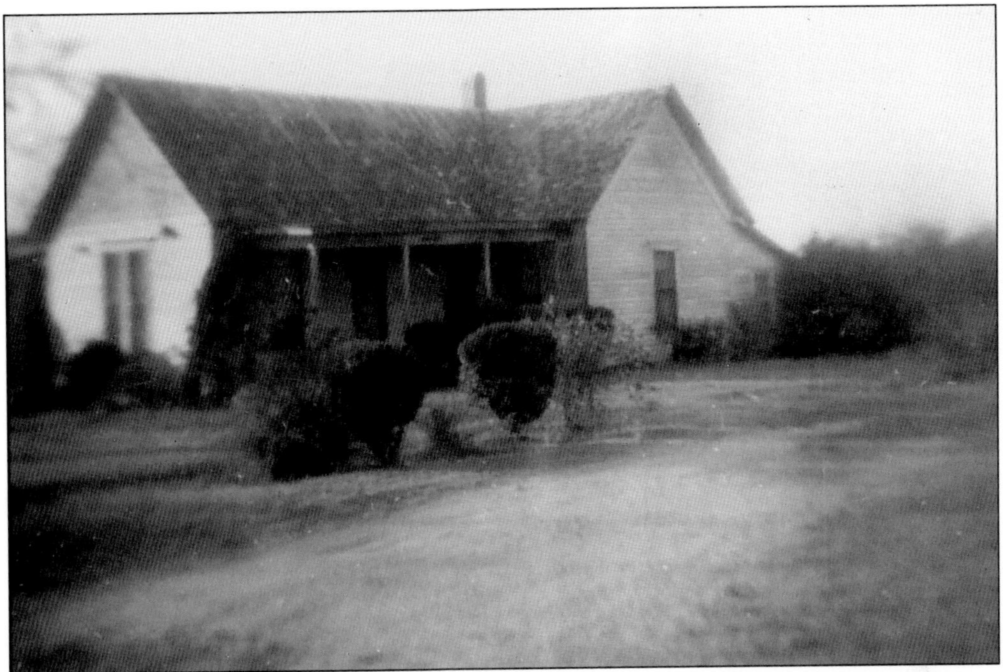

THE MITCHELL HOUSE IN THE 1940s. When the family moved in, there were cotton fields and land surrounding them to the west and north.

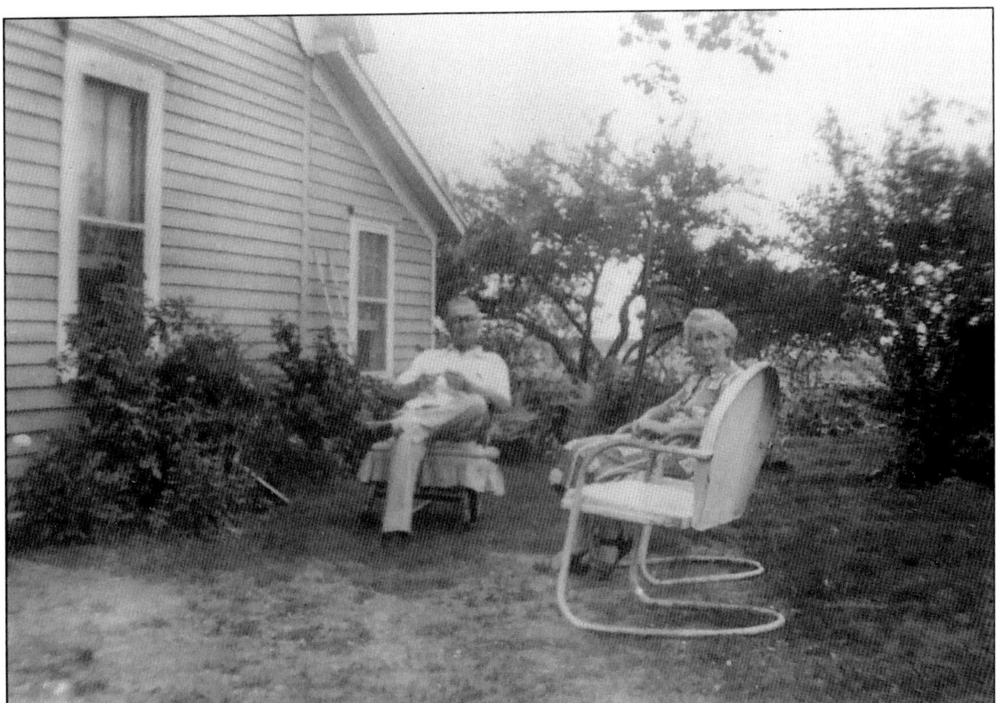

WALTER AND BEULAH MITCHELL ENJOYING THEIR YARD AROUND 1945.

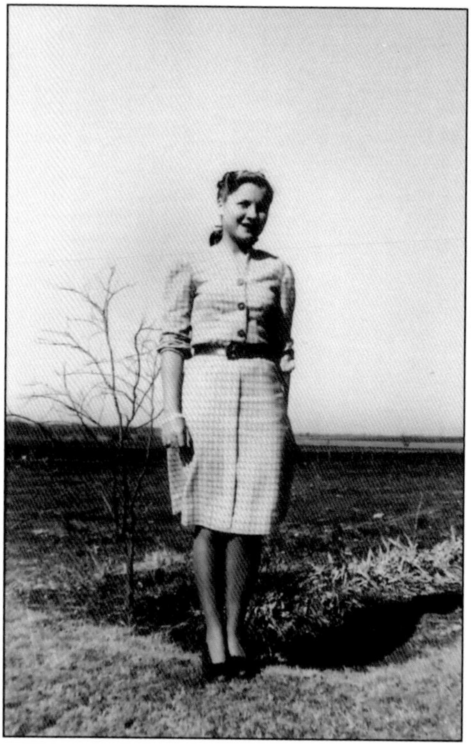

PEGGY MITCHELL AROUND 1948. The west view of the house is visible behind Peggy in this picture. There was also a clear view of Spring Creek at the time.

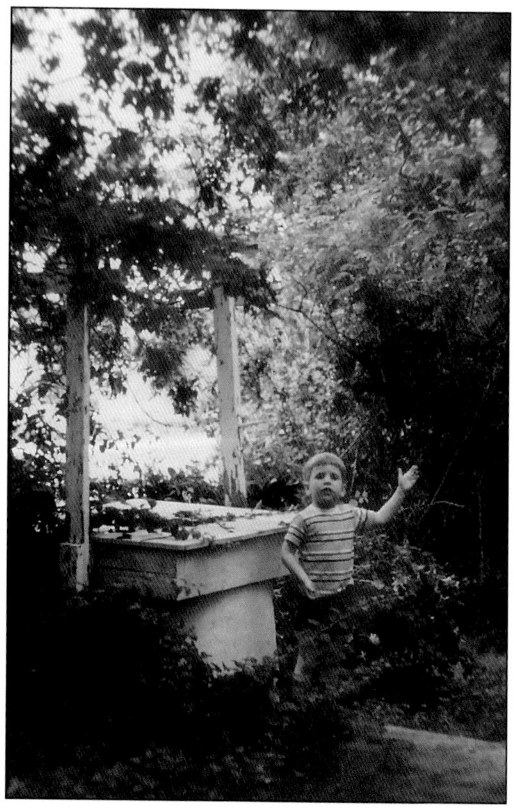

ROBERT MITCHELL AT THE WELL DURING THE MID-1970S. As a part of renovation, the Mitchells covered the well with a gazebo. Peggy and Dorothy, daughters of Walter and Beulah, remember washing their hair on the porch with the well water.

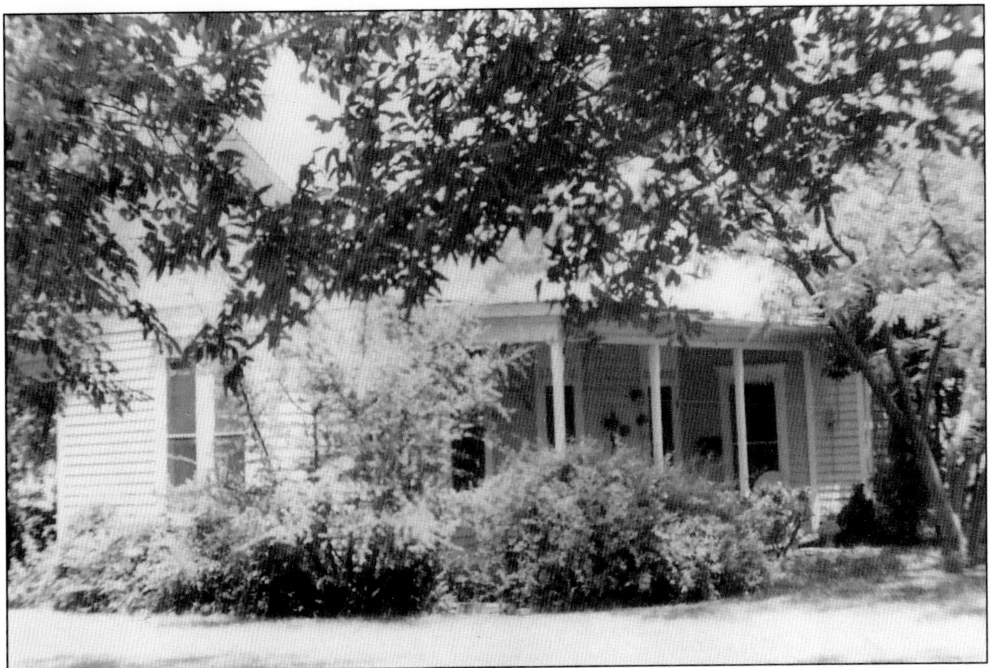

The Mitchell House in the 1970s. In the mid-1940s, Mr. Mitchell renovated the house. From 1986 to 1988, the Mitchell sisters, Peggy and Dorothy, along with Dorothy's husband, Robert Johnston, completed another major renovation of the house. They raised the house over a foot by adding a new foundation as well as adding a room onto the back of the house.

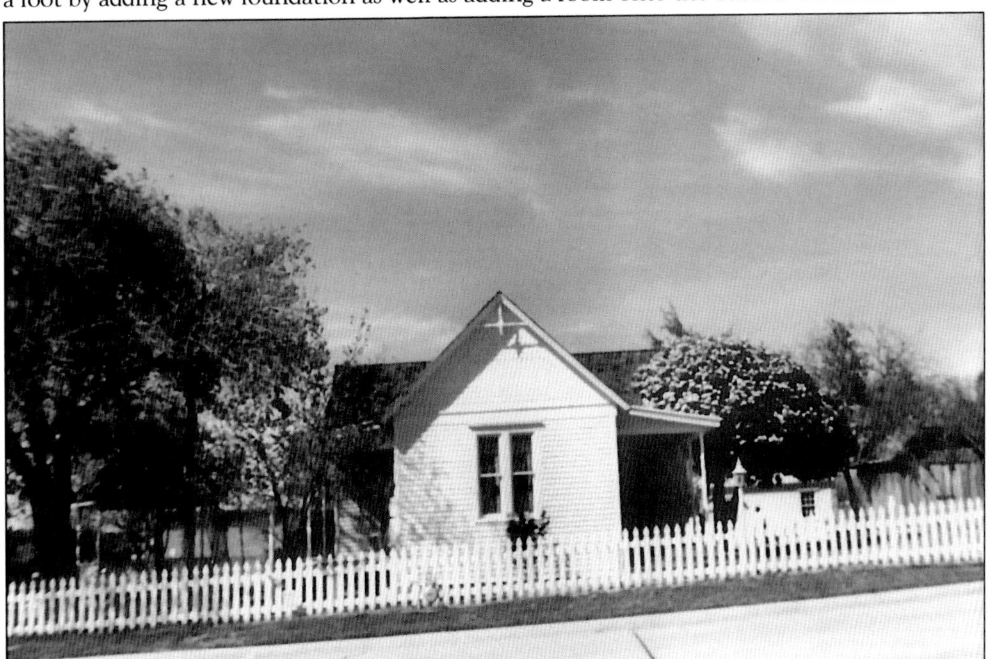

The Mitchell House With View of Porches. The house has identical porches on each side. The addition matches the south gable. From an aerial view, the house appears to take on the shape of a cross.

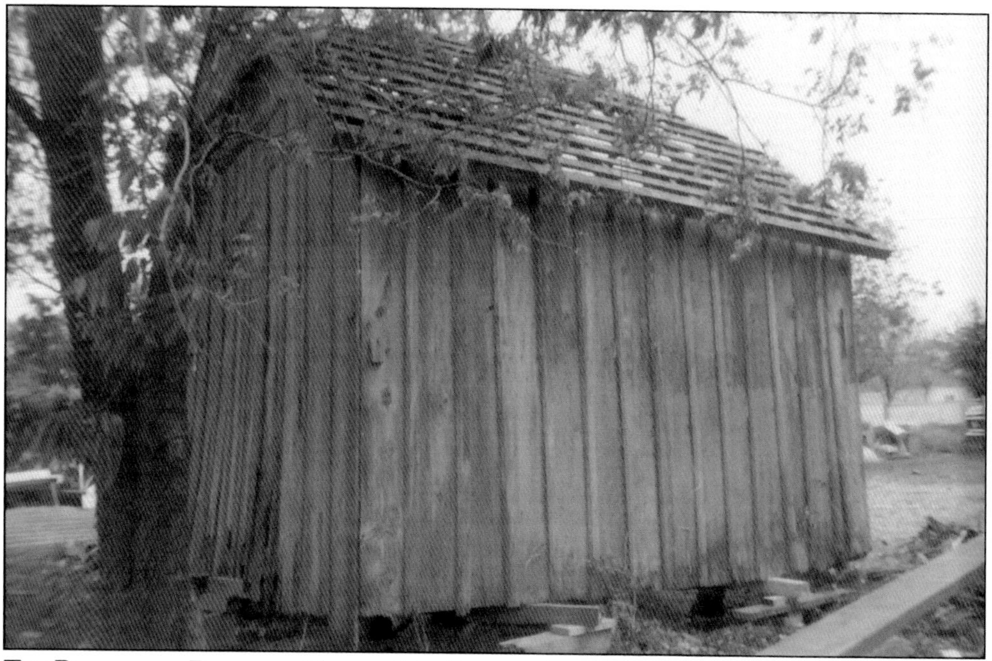

The Blacksmith Building. The small building on the east side of the property appears to have been used for blacksmithing and seems to be older than the house itself. The family has found old horseshoe nails under the building. Traces of the original red paint on this building are still visible on it today. A new foundation and roof were added to the blacksmith building during the renovation in the 1980s.

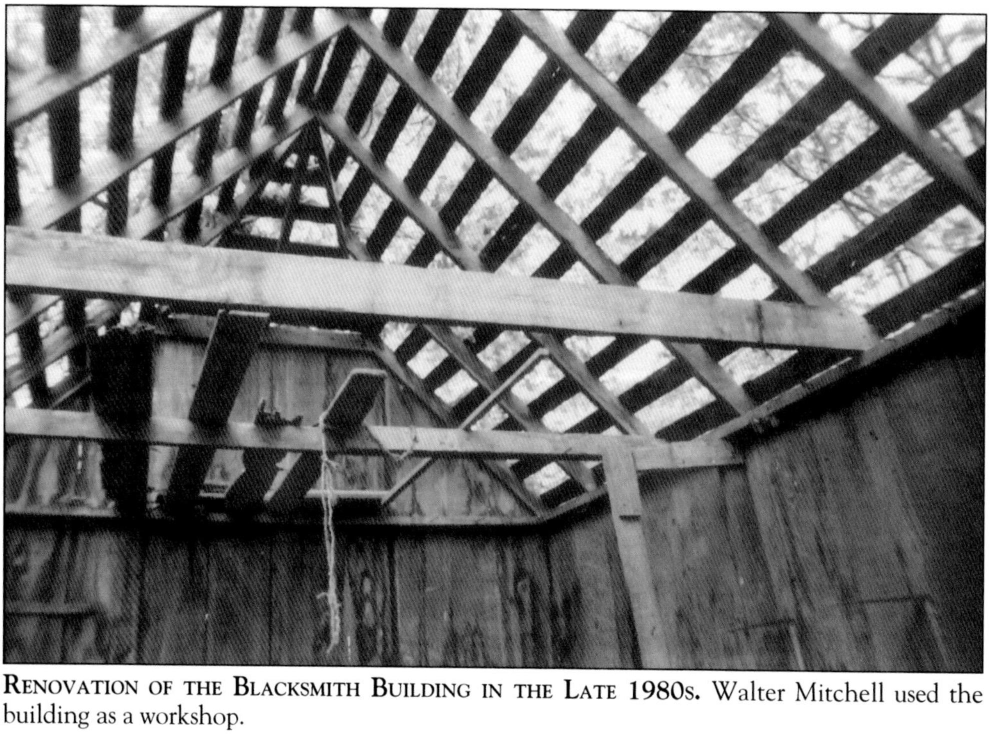

Renovation of the Blacksmith Building in the Late 1980s. Walter Mitchell used the building as a workshop.

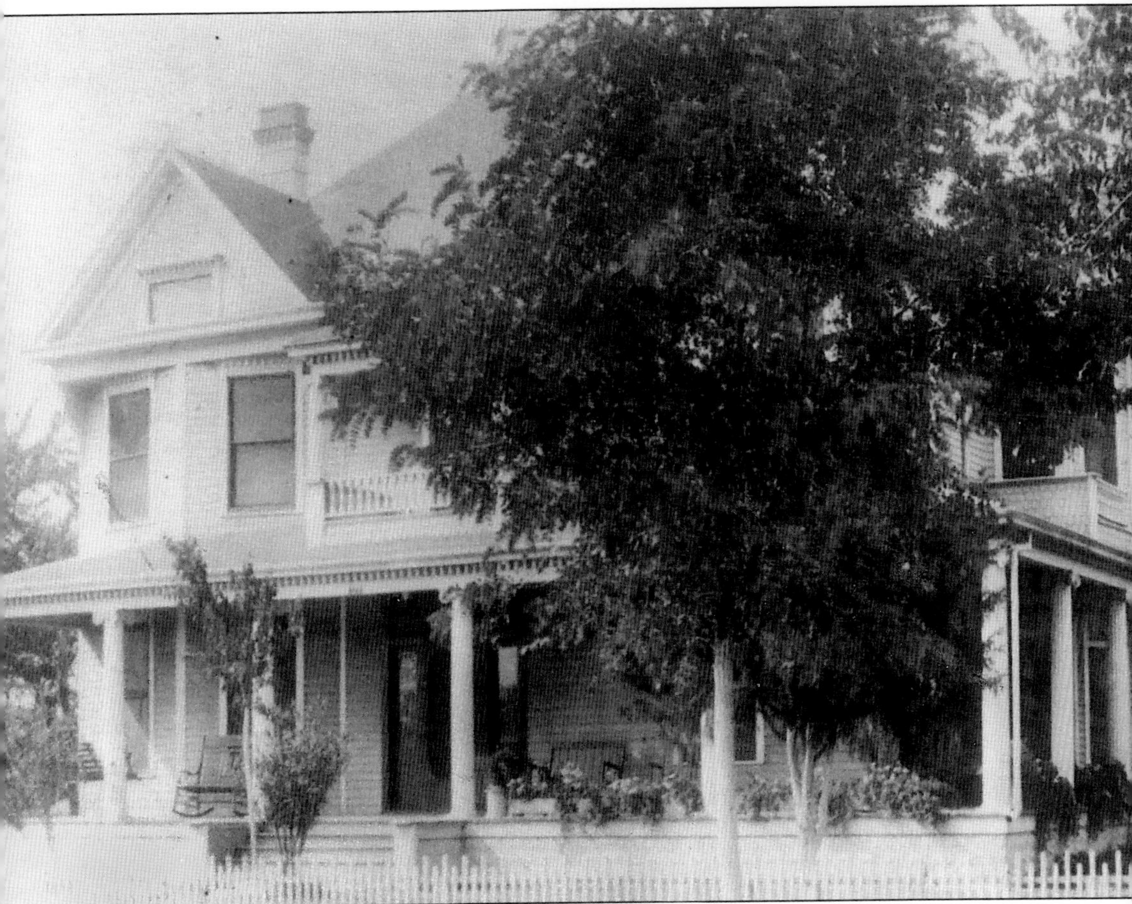

#4 The Shepard House. J.W. and Molly Shepard built this house around 1904. It was torn down in the mid-1900s sometime after the Shepards passed away. It was located on the northeast corner of 16th Street and Avenue G.

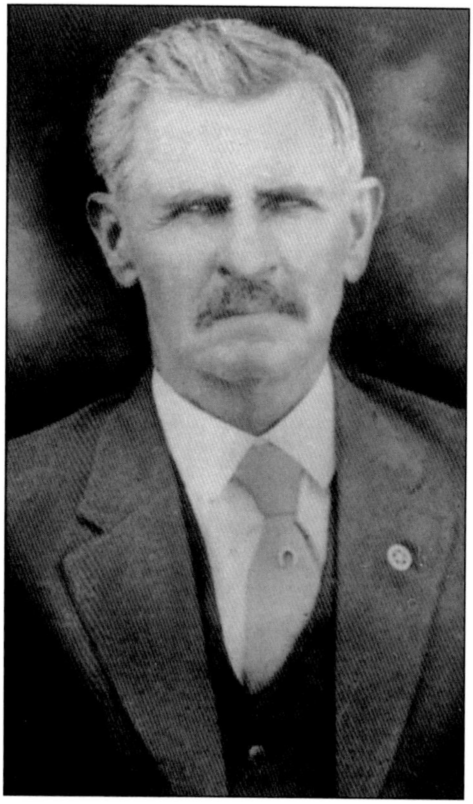

JOSEPH WILLIAM SHEPARD. (Courtesy of the Frances Wells Collection.)

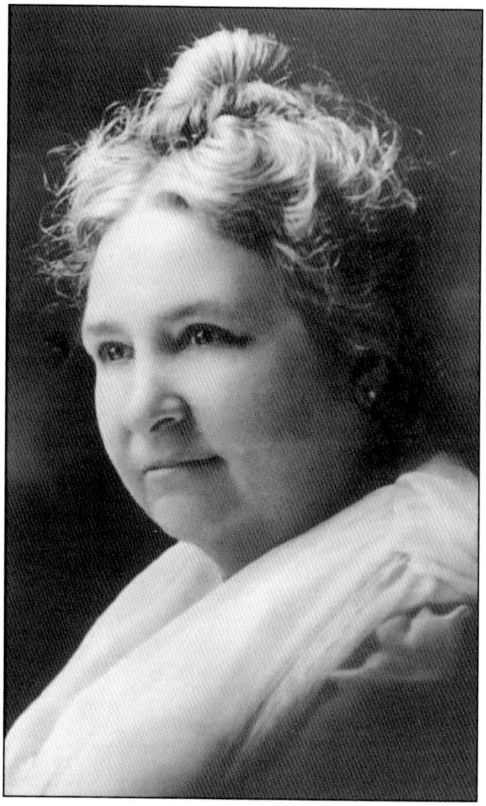

MOLLY HAGGARD SHEPARD. (Courtesy of the Frances Wells Collection.)

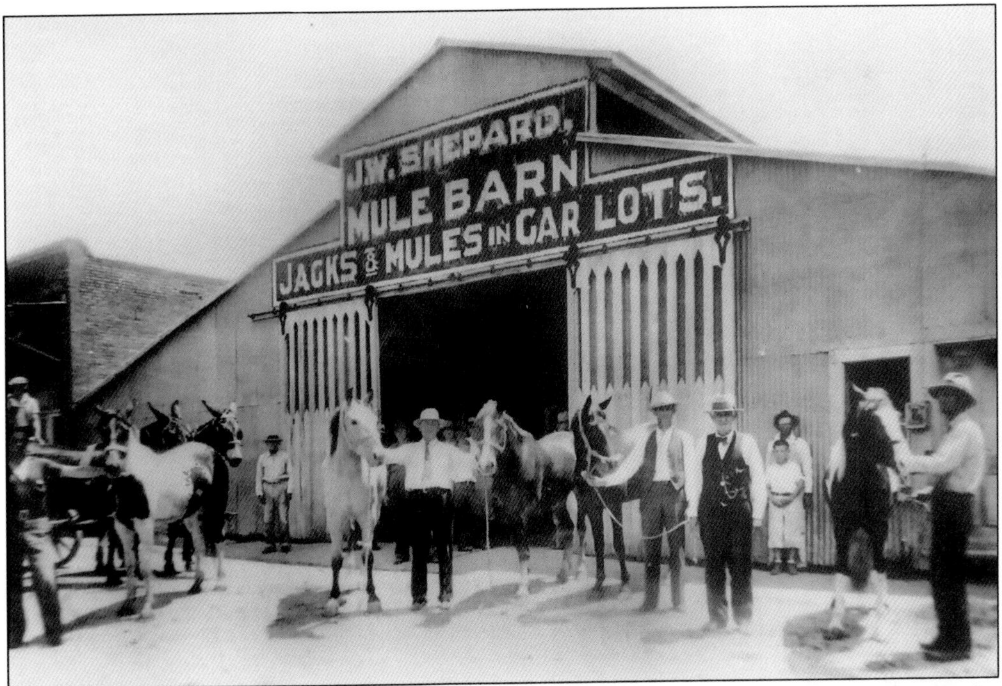

J.W. Shepard's Barn-Raised Mules. Plano gained a reputation all over the country for the outstanding mules raised in the area. J.W. Shepard raised and sold some of these mules. Around 1896, he helped to establish Trades Day in Plano. (Courtesy of the Frances Wells Collection.)

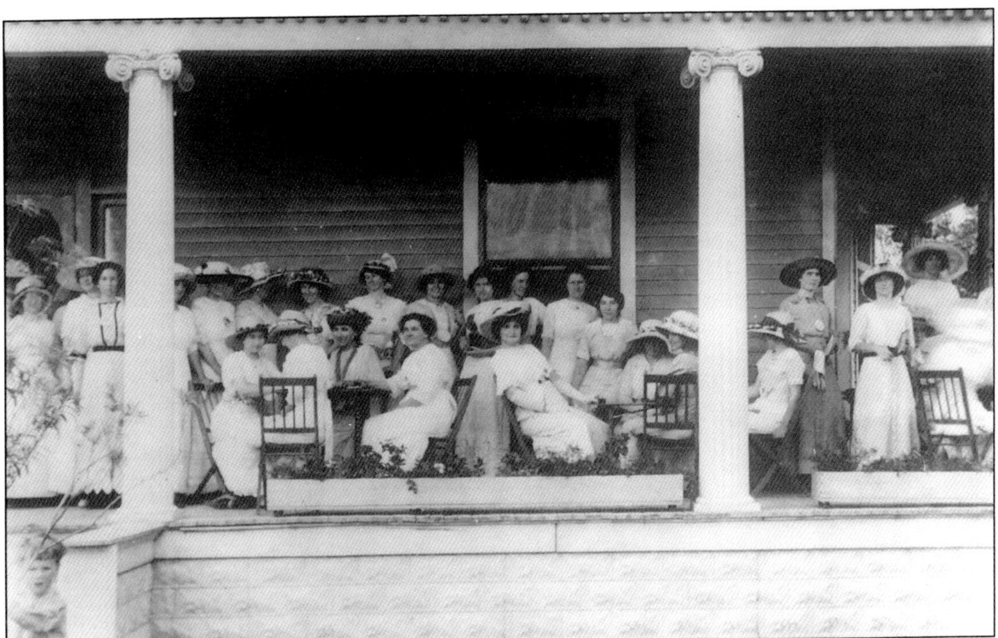

A Summer Afternoon at the Shepard's House. (Courtesy of the Frances Wells Collection.)

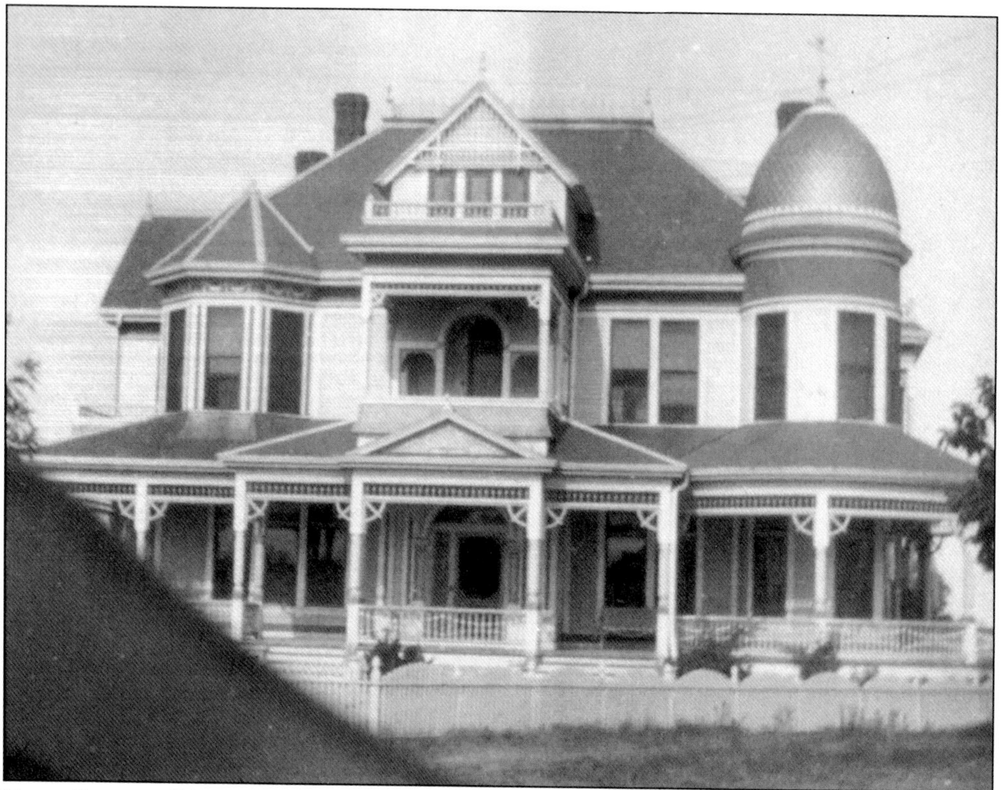

First Shepard House. It is believed that this house may have been the first structure built on the property. It may have been destroyed by fire and replaced by the house which was built around 1904.

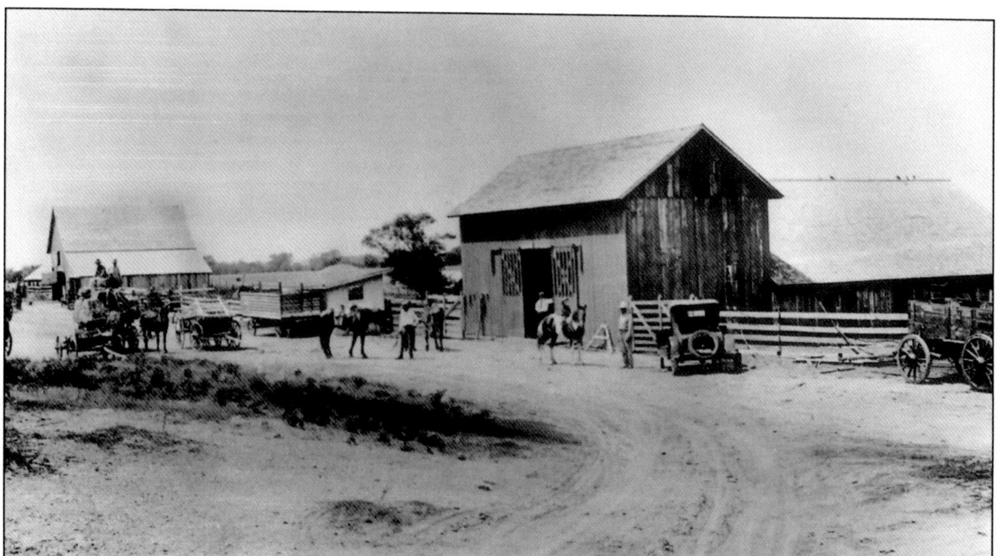

The Shepard Ranch, 1925. The family had a ranch near the corner of present-day Park Boulevard and Preston Road near the housing development of Old Shepard Place. (Courtesy of the Frances Wells Collection.)

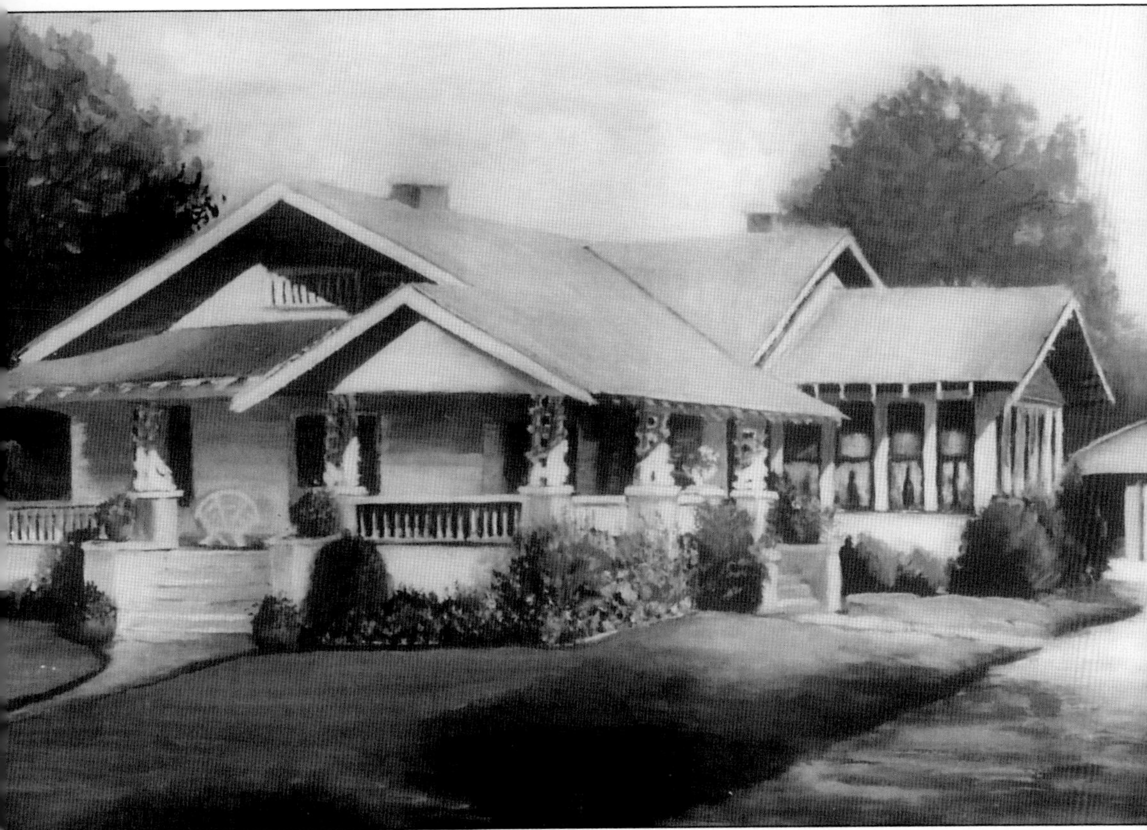

#5 Wyatt-Sandifer House. This house was built in 1910. Dr. S.B. Wyatt purchased the house in 1911 and moved in 1912 when he married Frances Jackson. The family lived here until they traded houses with the R.W. Sandifers in 1935. This house, along with the Wyatt Hatchery, was part of the trade for the Sandifer's home located on Avenue K and 18th Street.

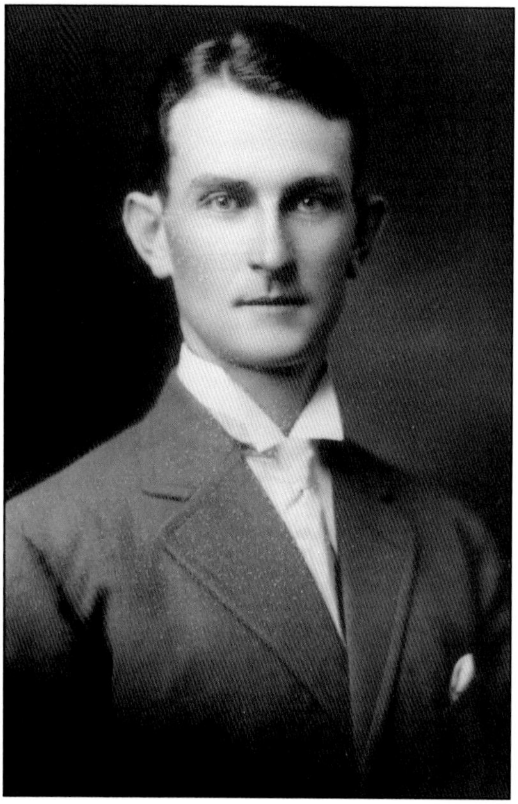

Dr. Slater Benjamin Wyatt.

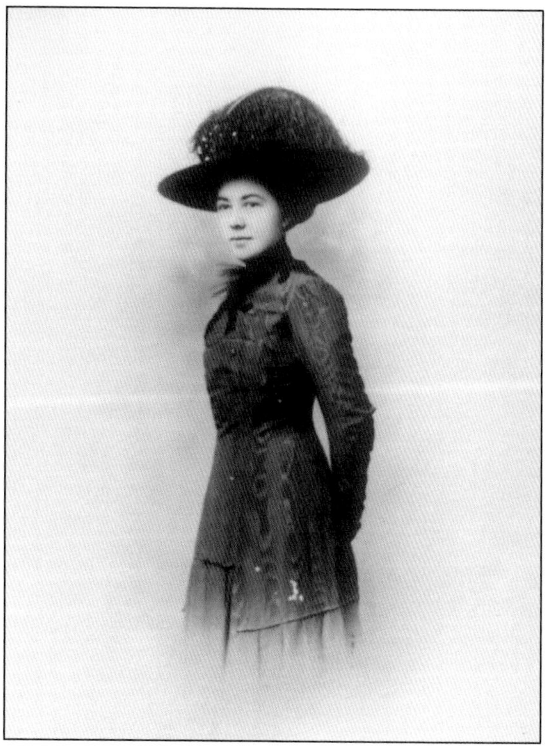

Frances Jackson Wyatt.

Jackson, Dorothy, and Peggy Wyatt Around 1926. The couple had three children—Dorothy, Jackson, and Peggy.

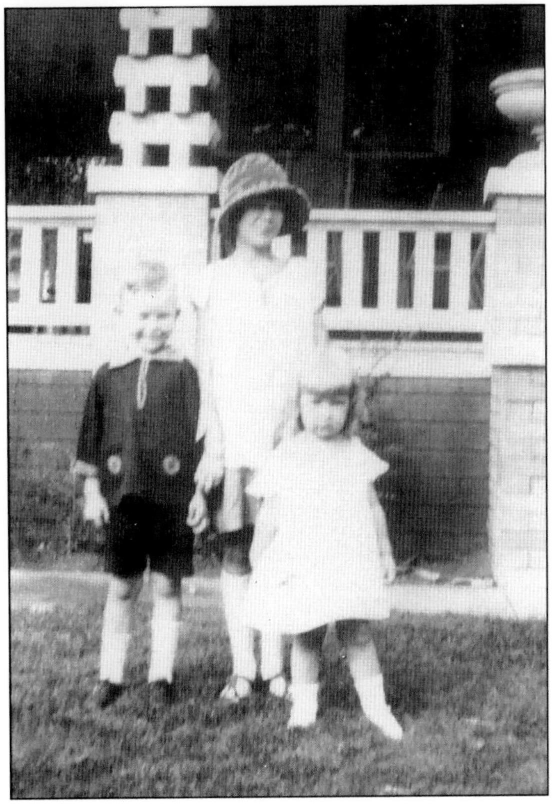

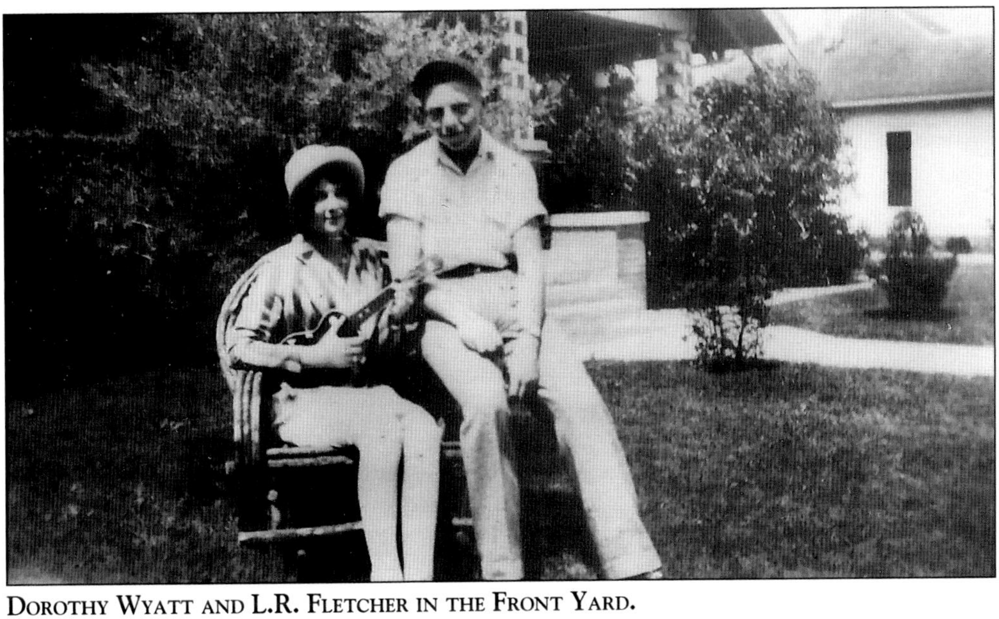

Dorothy Wyatt and L.R. Fletcher in the Front Yard.

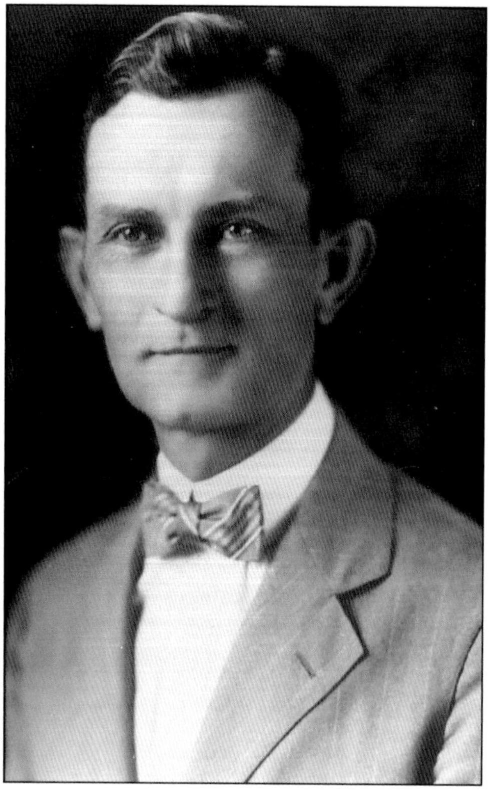

Dr. Slater Benjamin Wyatt Around 1905. Dr. Wyatt graduated from the first class of Baylor Medical University in Dallas in 1905. He practiced medicine in Plano for about 48 years and started the first hospital in Plano, which was located on present-day Avenue K. Dr. Wyatt was honored as one of "Plano's One Hundred Heroes."

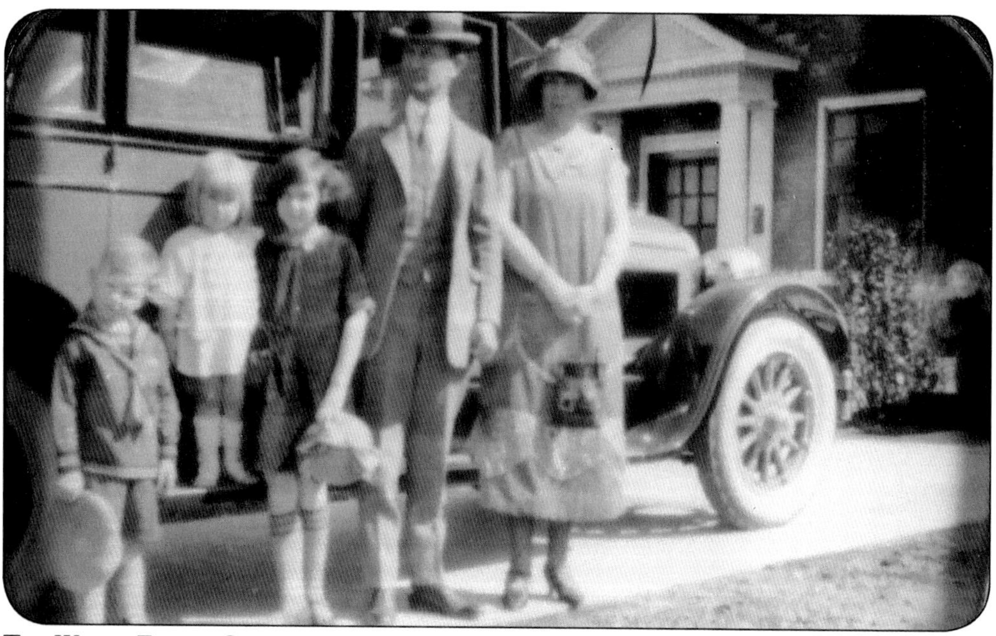

The Wyatt Family Out for a Drive Around 1924.

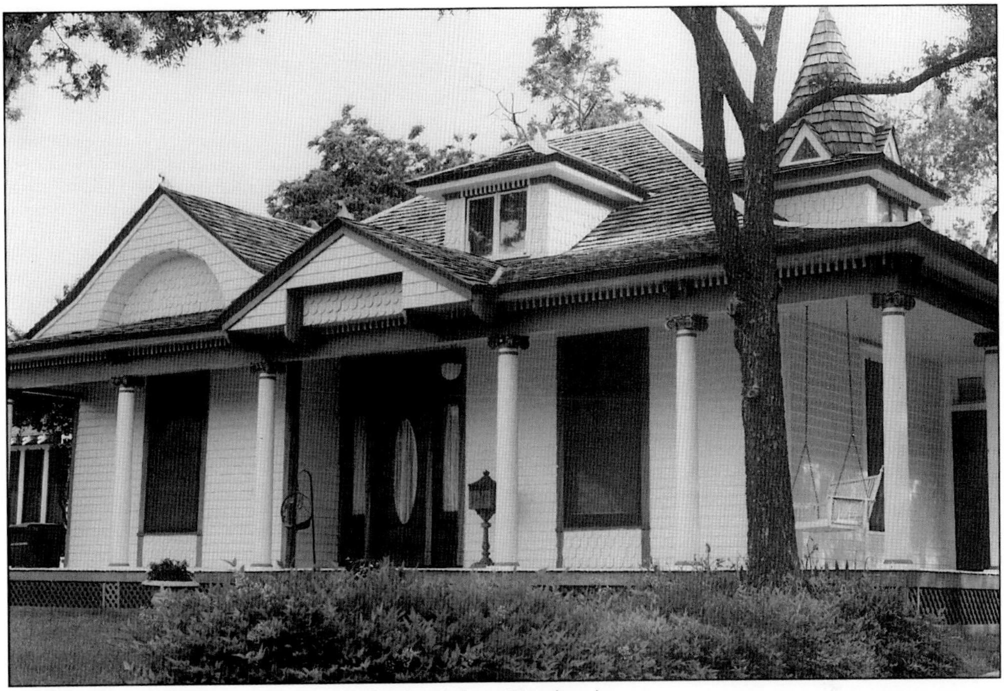

#6 Dr. Beaty House. (Photography by Adam Towber.)

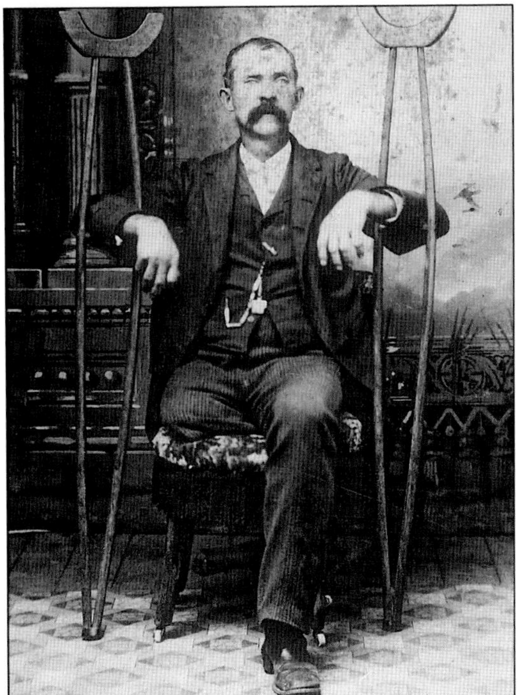

Dr. Henry Beaty. Dr. Henry Madison Beaty and Mary Ella Austin Beaty moved their family to Plano in 1880. Dr. Beaty lost a leg in the Civil War while serving for the Confederacy. After the war, he studied medicine in Tennessee and Kentucky.

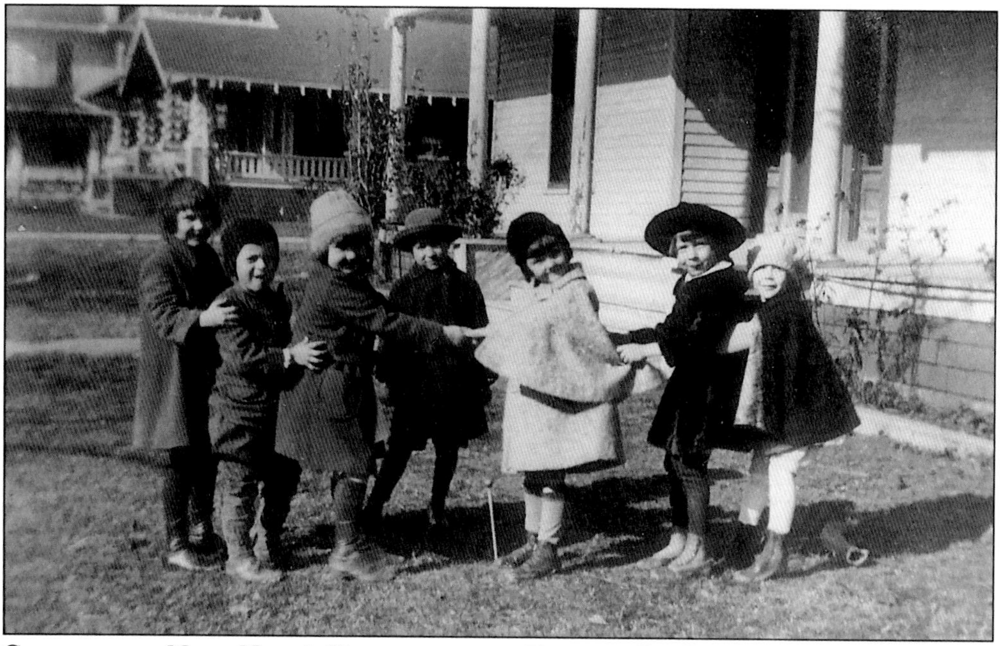

CLASSMATES IN NONA HORN'S KINDERGARTEN IN FRONT OF DR. BEATY'S HOUSE, 1922. From left to right, they are: Mary Sue Thompson, S.J. Mathews, Dorothy Stogner, Bowman Bryan, George Bowman Jasper, Pauline Wilson, and Edwina Harrington.

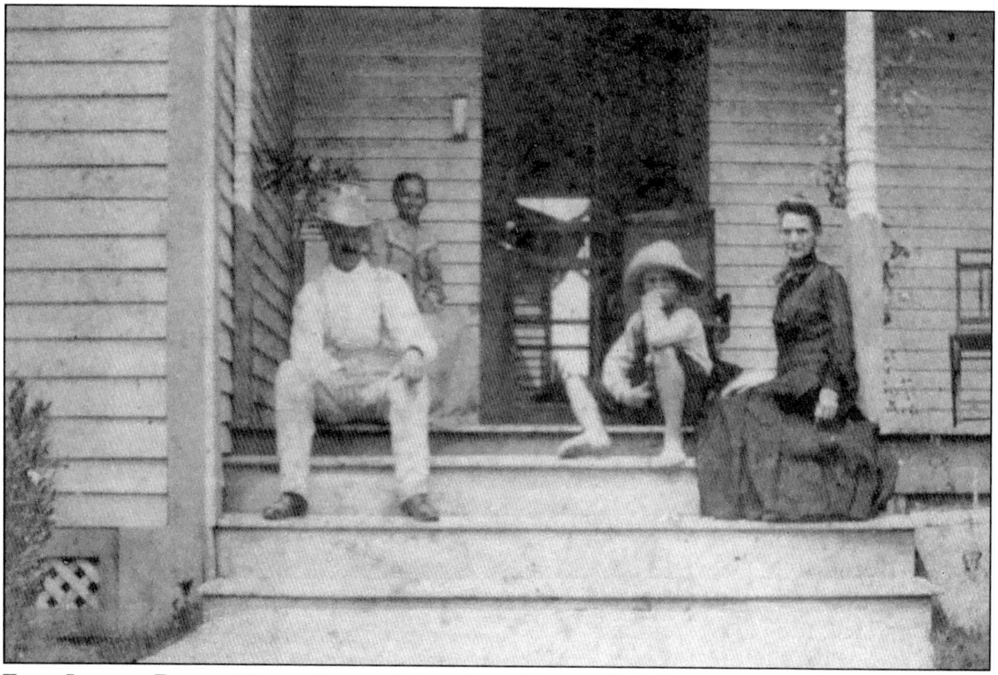

FROM LEFT TO RIGHT: HARRY BEATY, MARY ELLA BEATY, SAM STOGNER, AND GEORGIA BEATY. Dr. Beaty went into the drugstore business with Thomas L. Hood and George W. Kennedy. In 1888, he bought a storefront in downtown Plano and practiced medicine in the rear of the store while his sons, Harry Beaty and Wilkes Booth Beaty, ran the store. This was a common practice for physicians in those days.

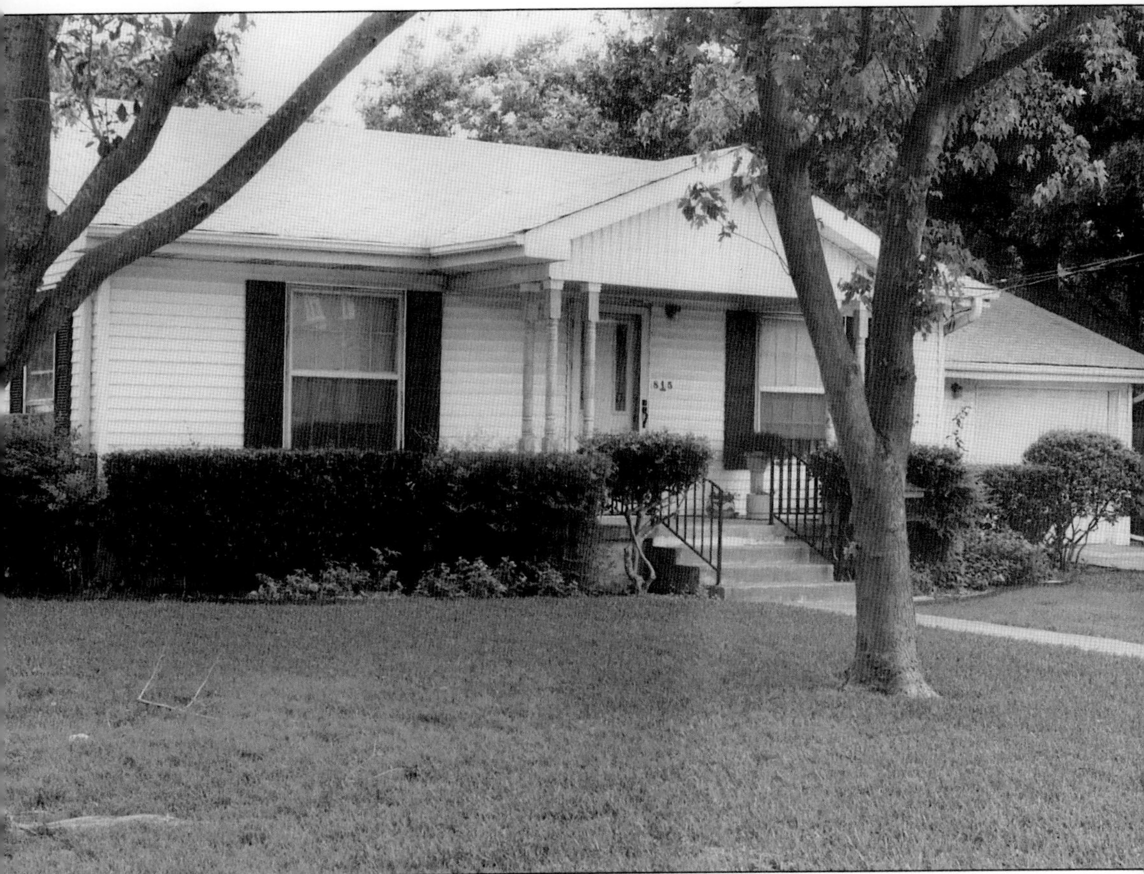

#7 Bertha Haggard Home. Bertha Haggard and her seven children moved to this property in the early 1930s when she traded a small farm for it. The original house burned around 1953, and the house that is on the property today was constructed in its place. Before moving to this property, Bertha and her husband Emmitt lived on the land grant that was given to Emmitt's grandparents, John Berryman and Martha Cook Martin. They lived in the house that Mr. Martin had built.

Bertha's family was among the many pioneer families of the area. Her parents, John Marshal and Maude Salmon Daffron, bought the old Huffman place located between present-day Yeary Road and Park Boulevard just west of Preston Road. Pictures of this family and the home they lived in can be found in the last chapter of this book. (Photography by Adam Towber.)

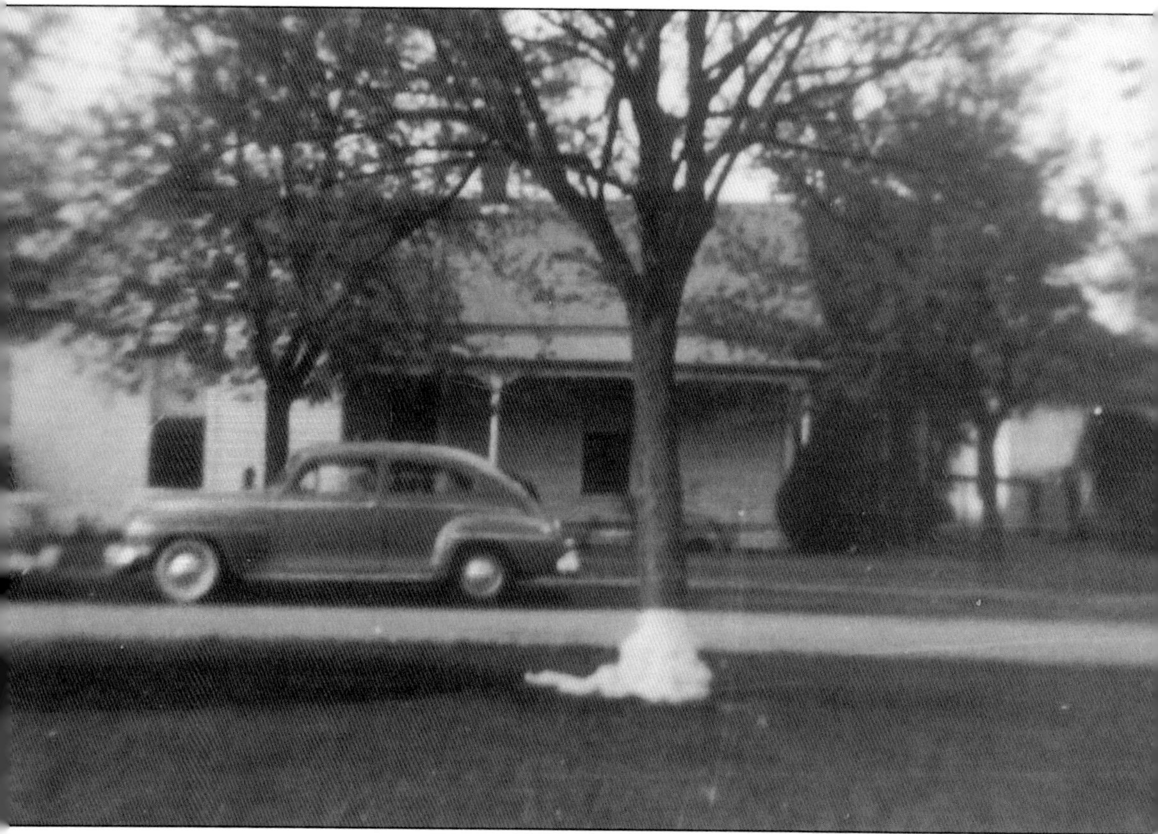

Original House in 1930s. Since the Depression was in full swing, and there were not many jobs when she moved to this house, she did not work for a while. After a time, she worked for Dr. Wyatt tending to patients at night. Later she went to work every day at Dr. Wyatt's private hospital for $1 a day. She then went to work at the school library under a government-sponsored program. At the high school, her oldest grandson, W.D. Wiser Jr., called her "Mama," and the name "Mama" Haggard became legendary for Bertha.

During World War II, she worked at the hospital in McKinney and then at St. Paul Hospital, where she retired after 18 years of service.

BERTHA HAGGARD. This picture of Bertha was taken outside of the original house.

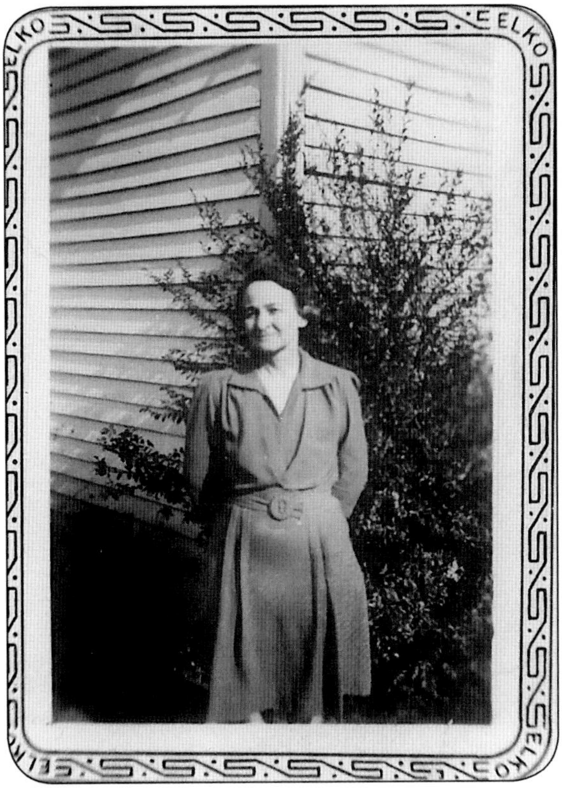

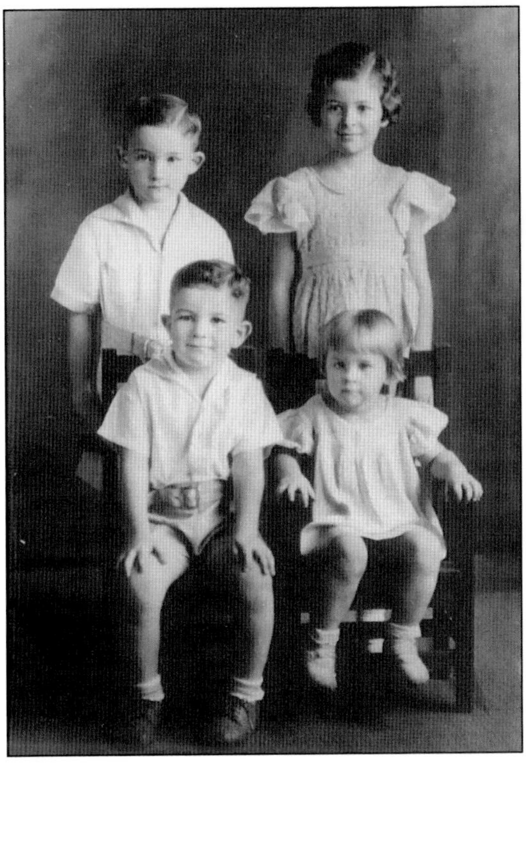

THE YOUNGEST HAGGARD CHILDREN. From left to right, they are: (front row) Jack and Joanne, (top row) Thomas and Virginia. Bertha's children pitched in to do odd jobs such as hoeing, picking cotton, mowing yards, delivering milk and newspapers, and babysitting.

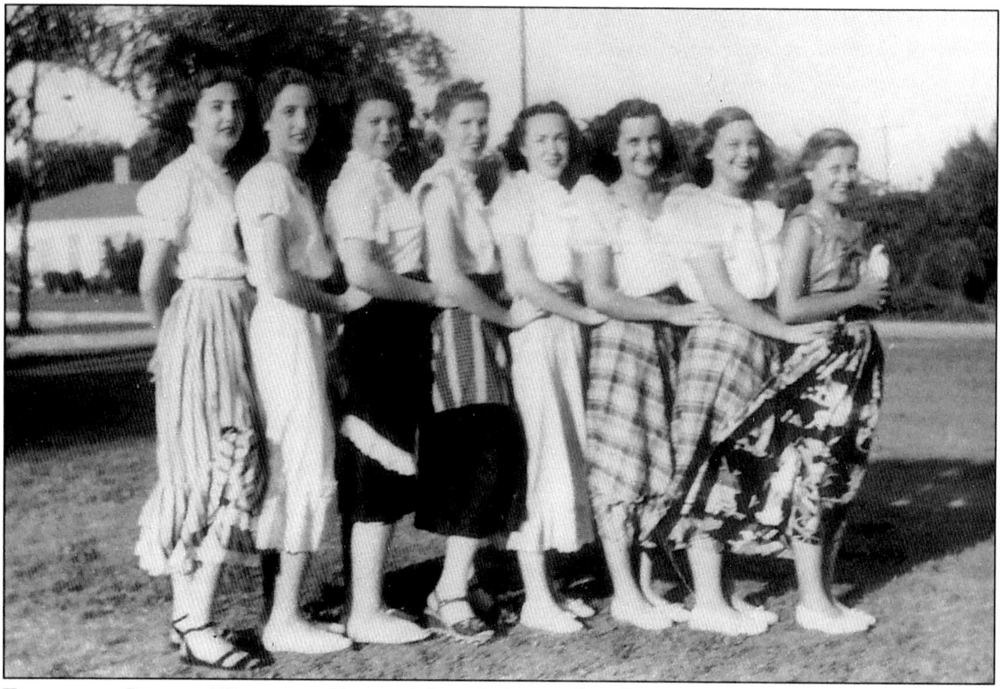

FRIENDS OF JOANNE HAGGARD. Pictured from left to right, they are: Betsy Brent, Alice Dupree, Annette Williams, Joyce Skaggs, Bobbi Allen, Pebba Montgomery, Joanne Haggard, and Peggy Mitchell in May 1948. Bertha always allowed her children to have friends over and set a place for them at the table when they came to visit.

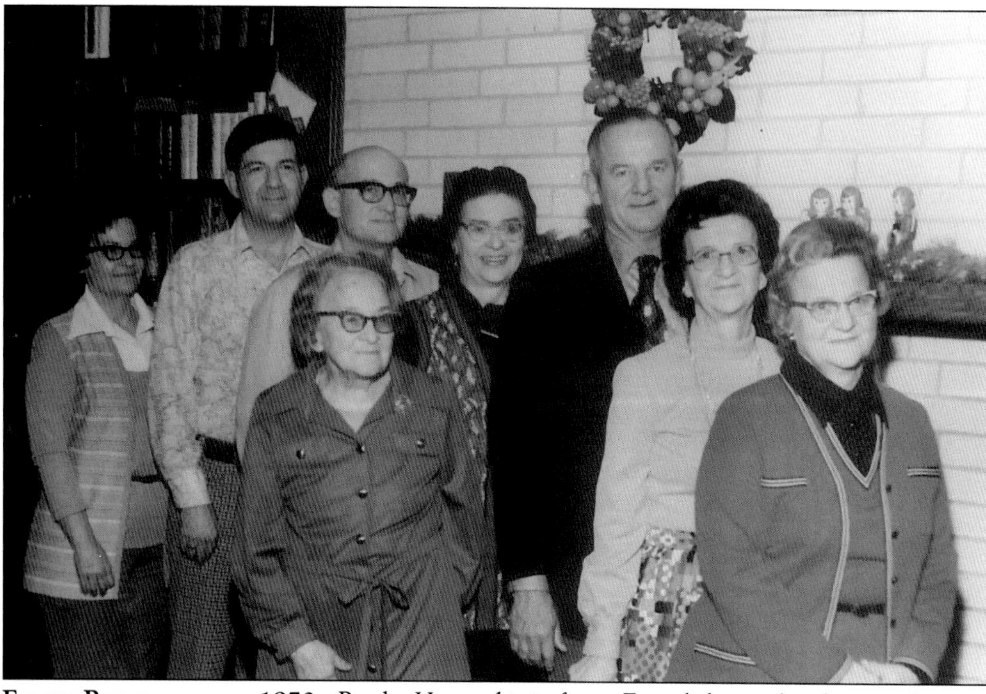

FAMILY REUNION IN THE 1970s. Bertha Haggard is in front. From left to right, they are: Joanne, Jack, Thomas, Virginia, William, Gladys, and Geneva.

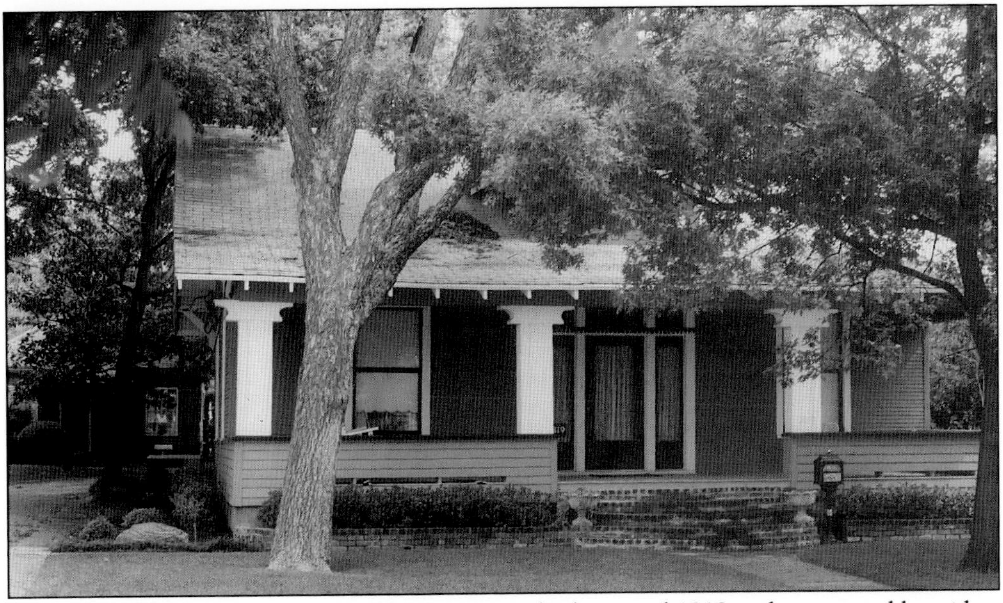

#8 Palmer-Harrington House. This house was built around 1912 and was owned by widow Mattie Palmer. Mattie died in 1918. Around 1920, her brother, J. Frank Harrington, purchased the house and lived in it. Frank had four sons—Francis, John Mack, Bennett, and Michael. Frank Harrington served in the state legislature in the 1920s and was the attorney for the Southern Pacific Railroad. J. Frank Harrington was later elected to office as county judge.

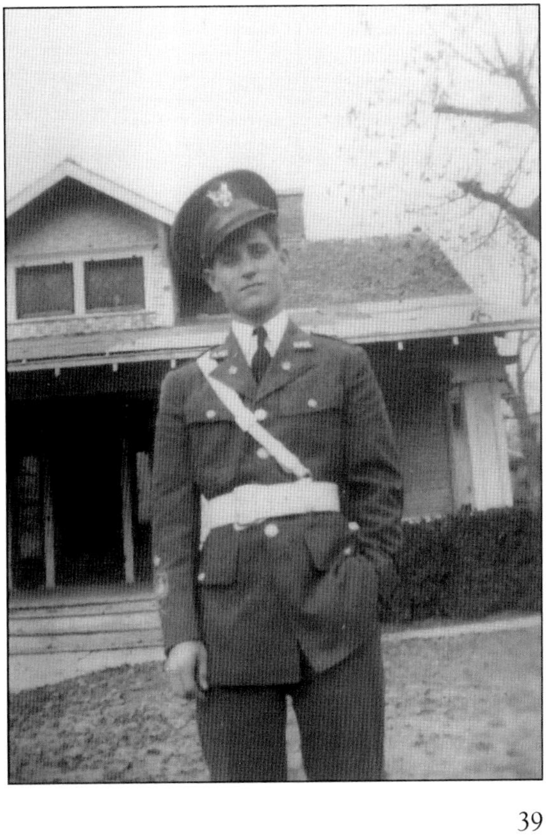

Mike Harrington on a Visit Home from Texas A&M University in 1940.

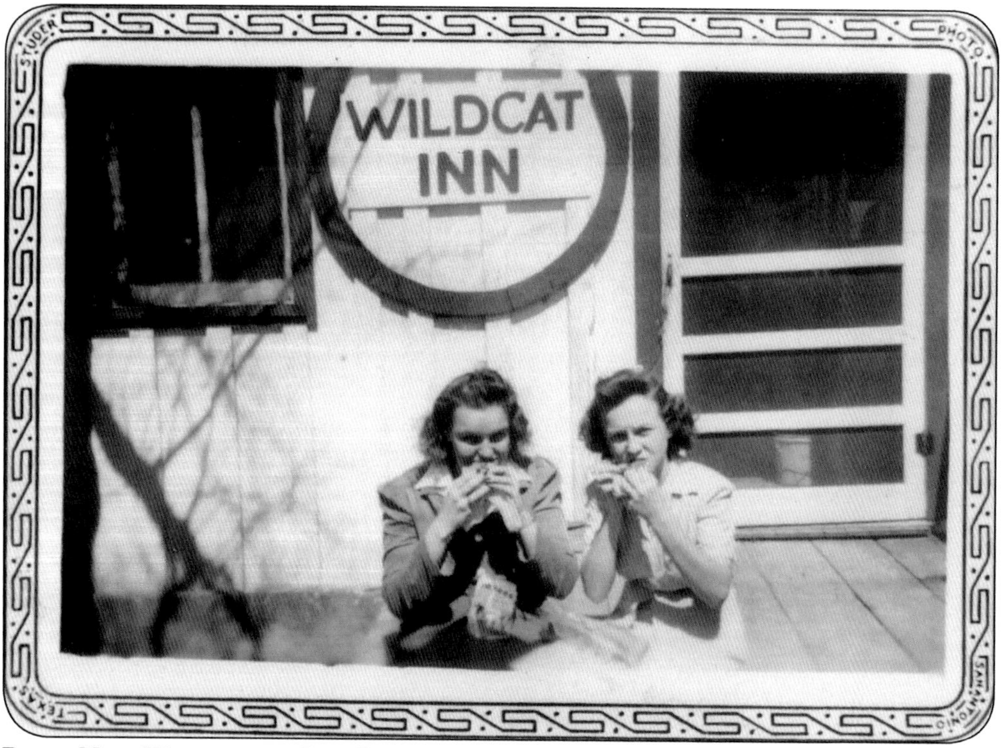

Bobby Nell Watkins and Dot Barnes at the Wildcat Inn. During the early 1940s, the Wildcat Inn was located between this house and Bertha Haggard's house next door. Since the Plano School across the street did not have a cafeteria at that time, the Wildcat Inn cooked and served hot dogs and hamburgers on a made-to-order basis for the students.

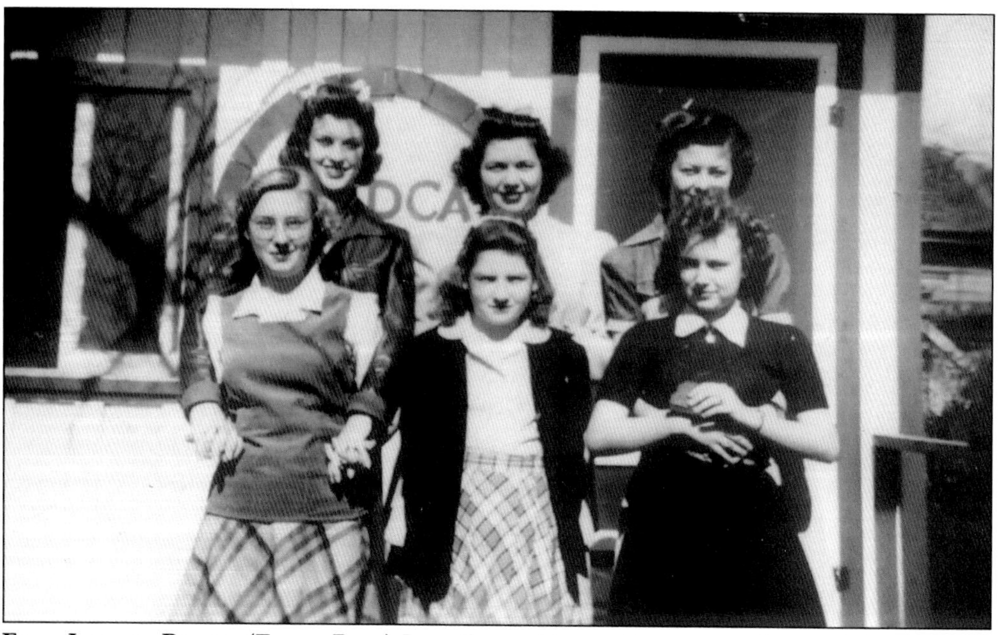

From Left to Right: (Front Row) June Rush, Marty Batchelor, Nancy Miller, (Top Row) Doris Ann Graves, Estelle Cooper, and Virginia Haggard at the Wildcat Inn.

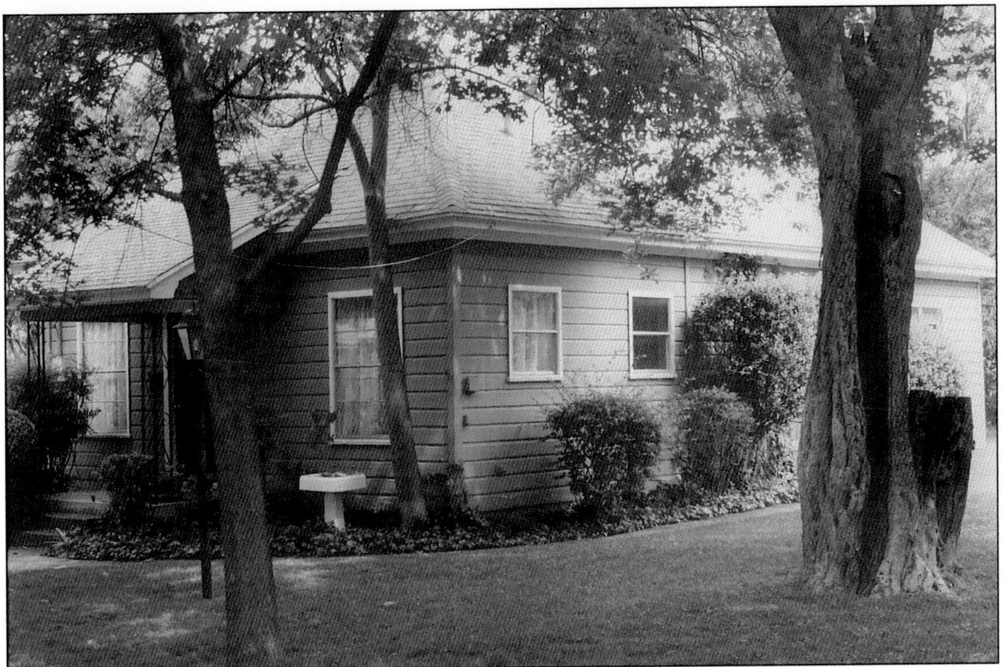

Happy Time Kindergarten Building. During the late 1950s and 1960s, Mrs. Walker lived in the house. She started Happy Time Kindergarten in the small structure on the west side of the house, towards the back of the main house.

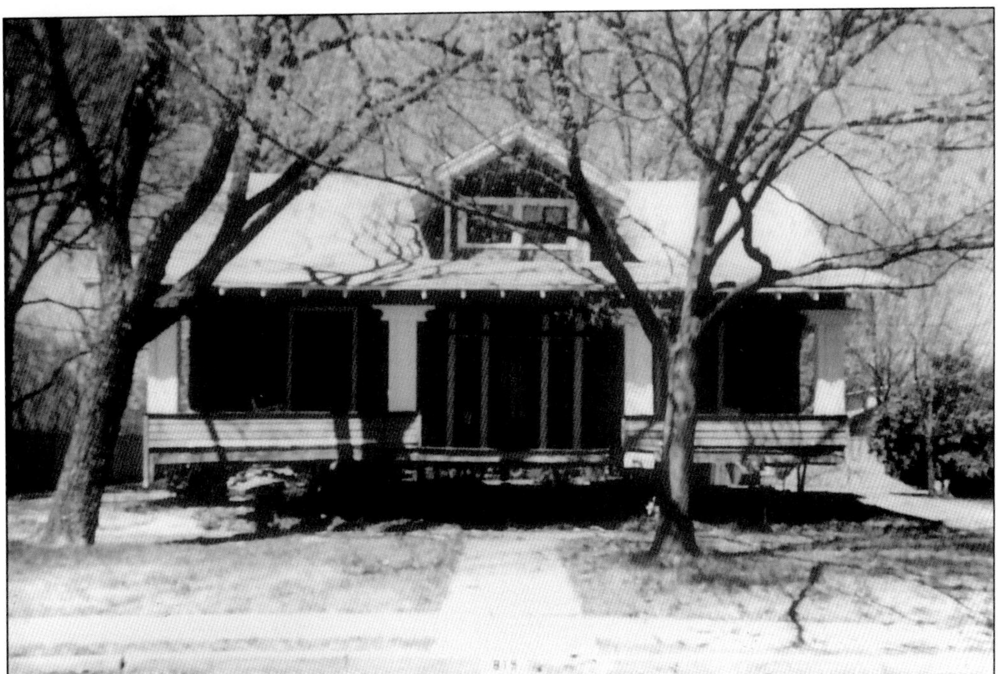

Remodeling the Palmer-Harrington House. The house has been remodeled in recent years. The front porch steps came from an old school house in Durant, Oklahoma, and the bricks are approximately the same age as the house.

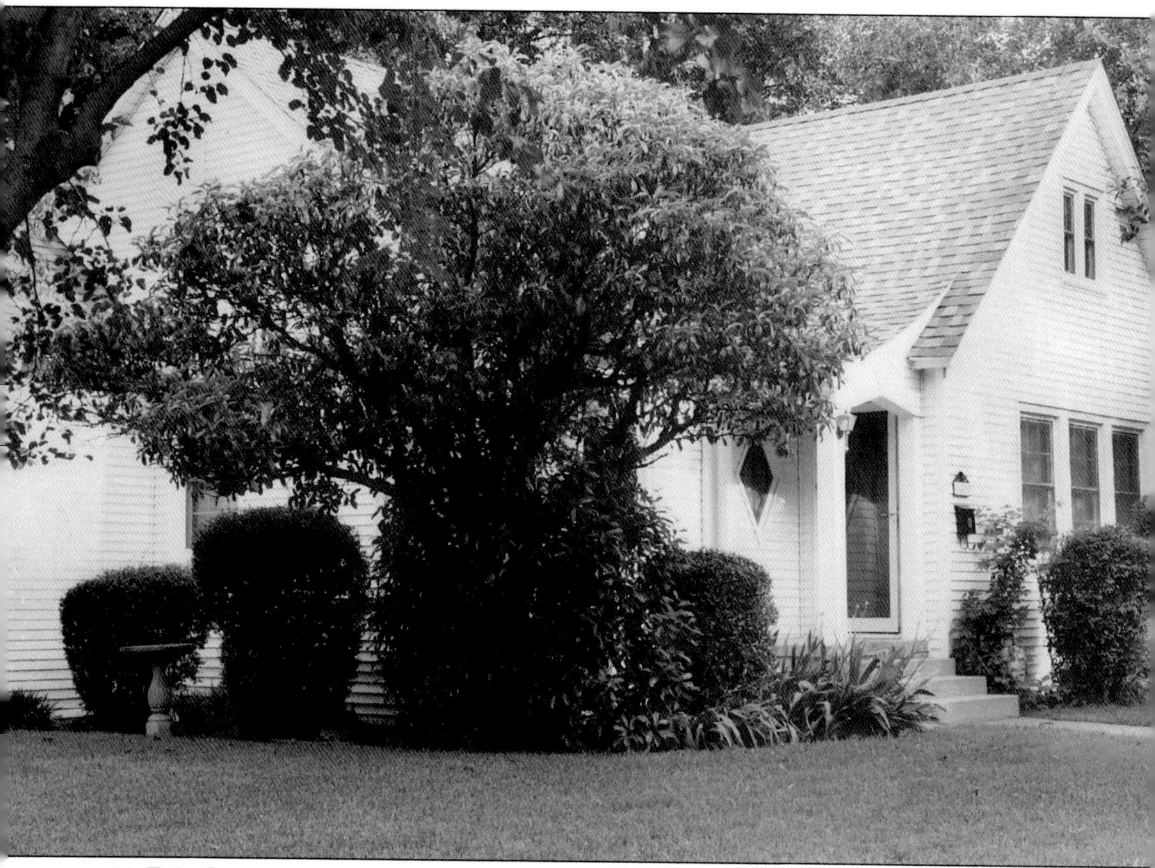

#9 E.A. Sigler House. E.A. Sigler became principal of the high school in 1921. The school had lost its accreditation in biology, chemistry, physics, and general science in 1920. In addition to serving as principal, Mr. Sigler taught these subjects, and the accreditation was restored. He also coached all of the sports at the school.

In 1927, Sigler became superintendent and served in this capacity until he became director of business services in 1961. He retired from his service to the Plano schools in 1968. (Photography by Adam Towber.)

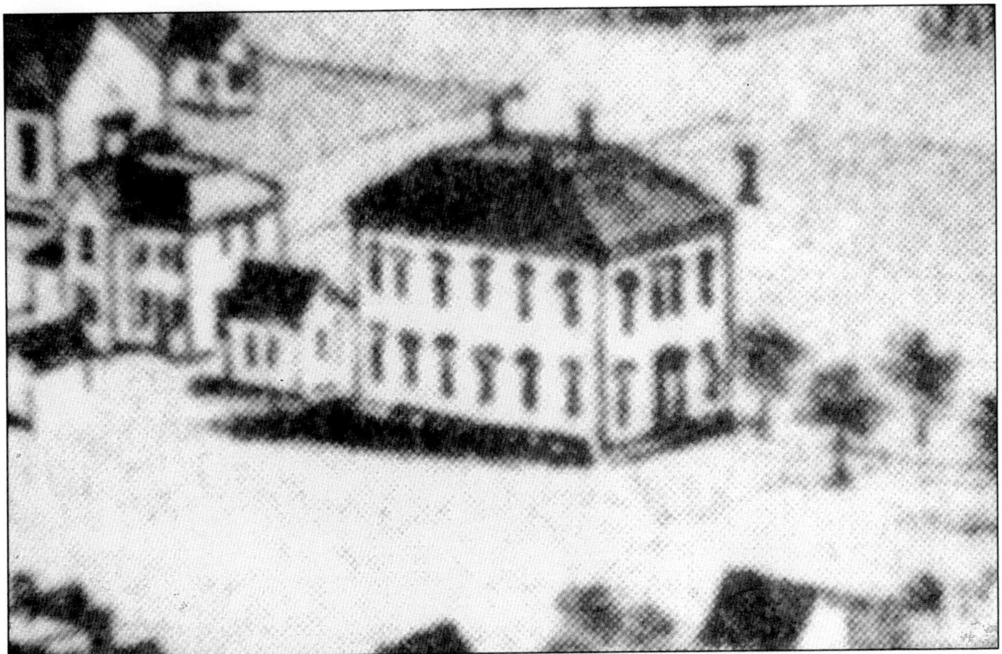

#10 Plano School. The Plano Institute was established by Professors Mister and Harris and was built in 1882. In 1891, voters determined that the City of Plano should control the schools. A special tax was also voted, which allowed the city to buy the school from the professors. The building burned in 1894 and was replaced by a second larger building which was also destroyed by fire in 1903. (Courtesy of the Frances Wells Collection.)

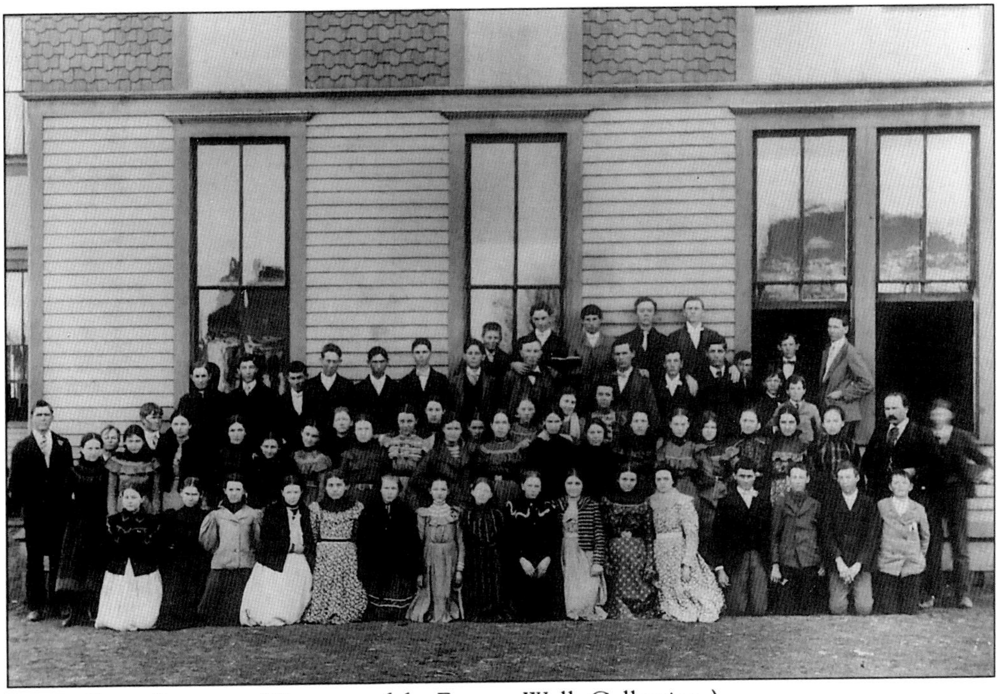

Plano Class Picture. (Courtesy of the Frances Wells Collection.)

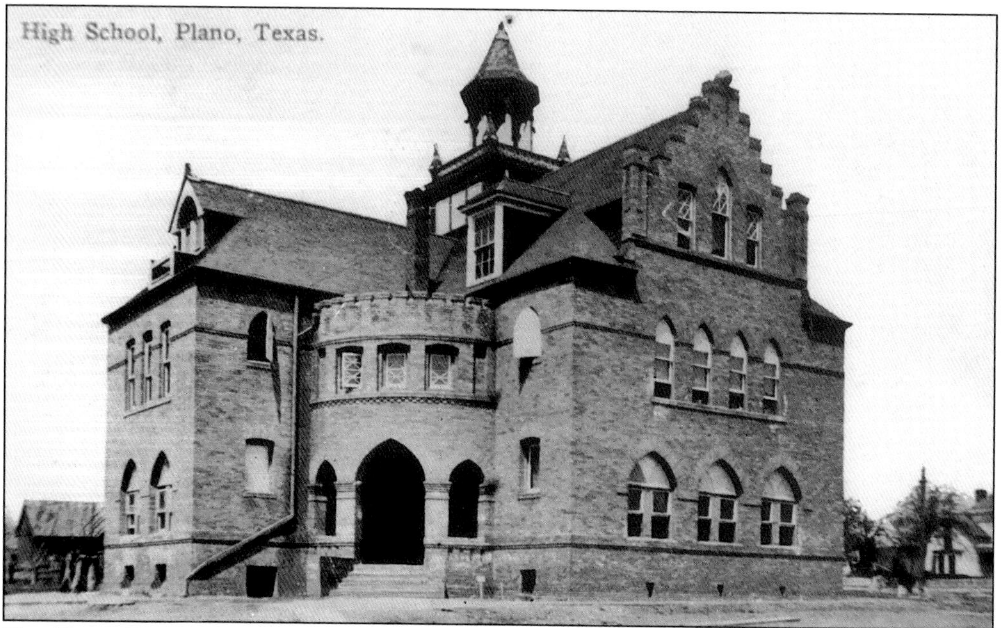

THE THIRD PLANO SCHOOL BUILDING.

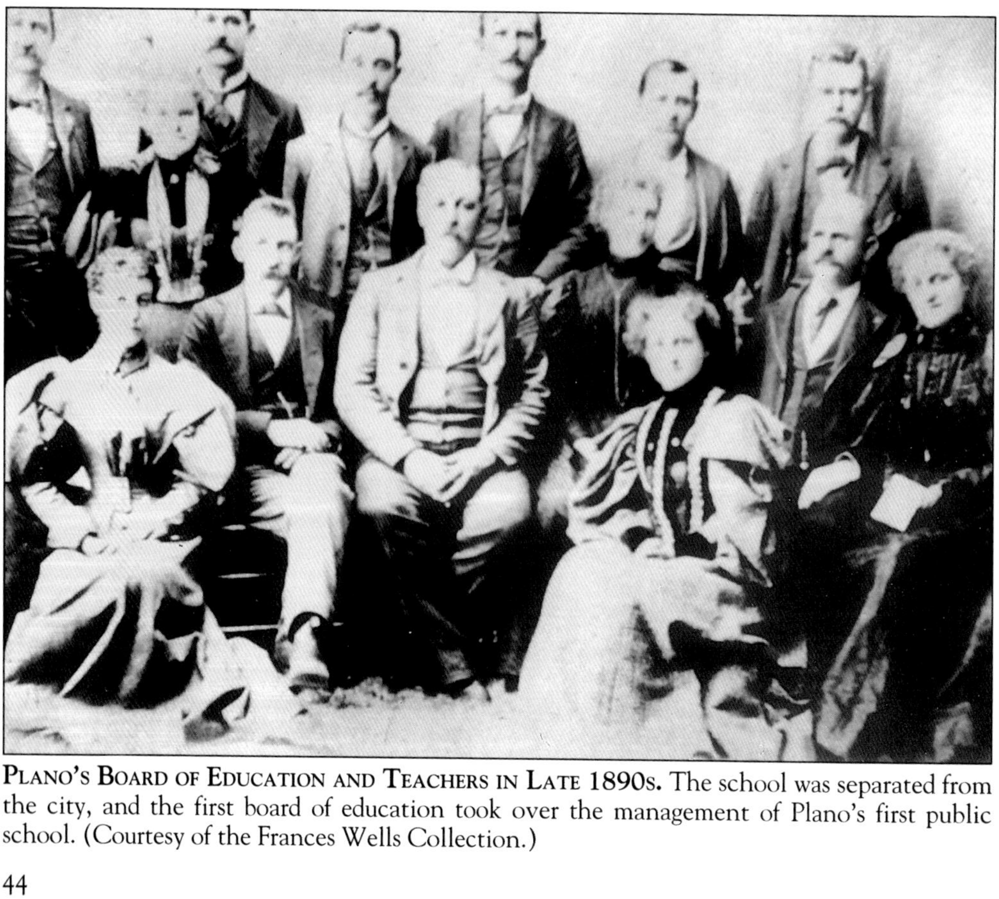

PLANO'S BOARD OF EDUCATION AND TEACHERS IN LATE 1890S. The school was separated from the city, and the first board of education took over the management of Plano's first public school. (Courtesy of the Frances Wells Collection.)

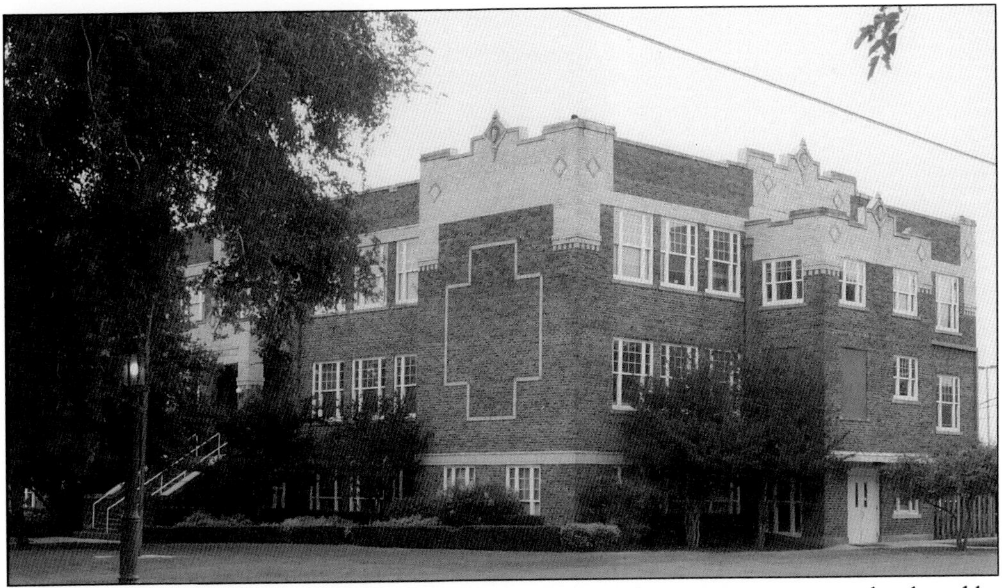

Fourth School Building. In 1923, a bond issue was passed to construct a new school, and by 1924, the fourth school building was completed.

The children who attended the school and lived in the surrounding neighborhood would wait for the first bell to ring before leaving for school, and would run to make it to class before the second bell rang.

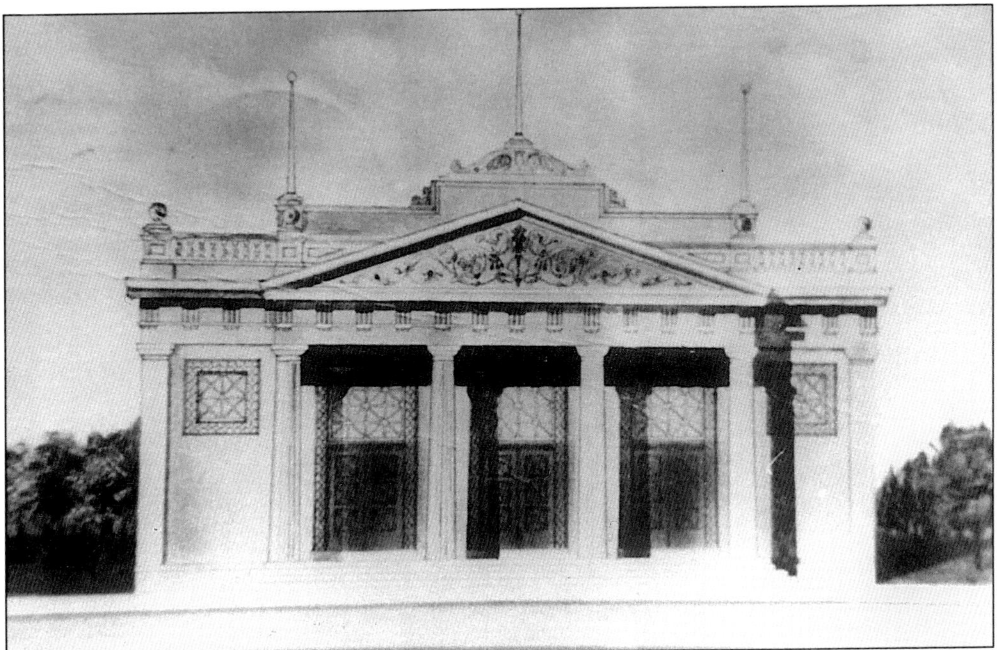

The School Auditorium. The auditorium was built as a WPA project during the Depression. (Courtesy of the Frances Wells Collection.)

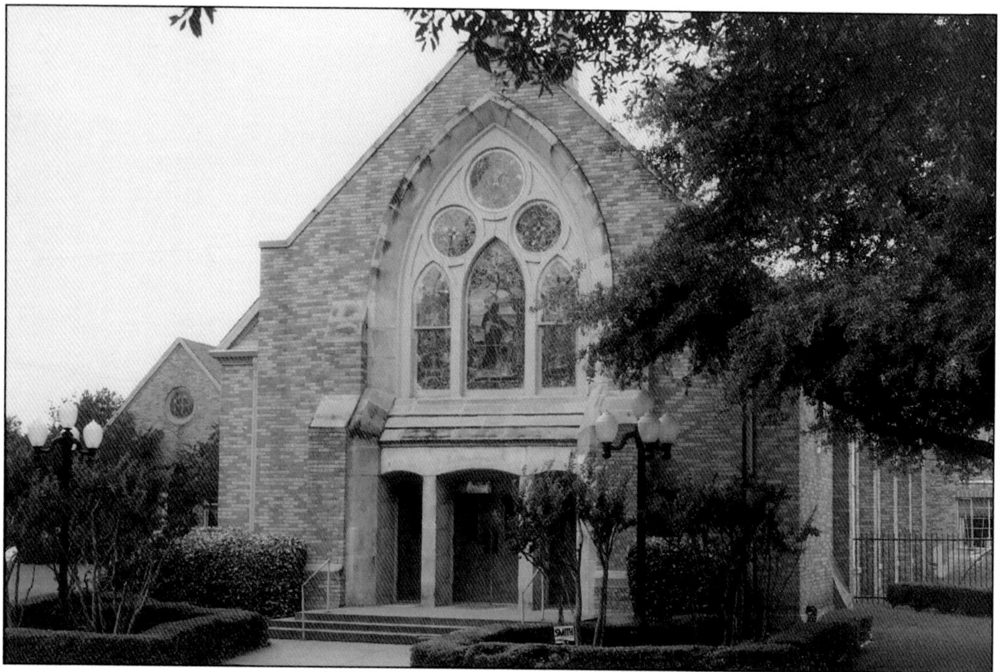

#11 First Christian Church.

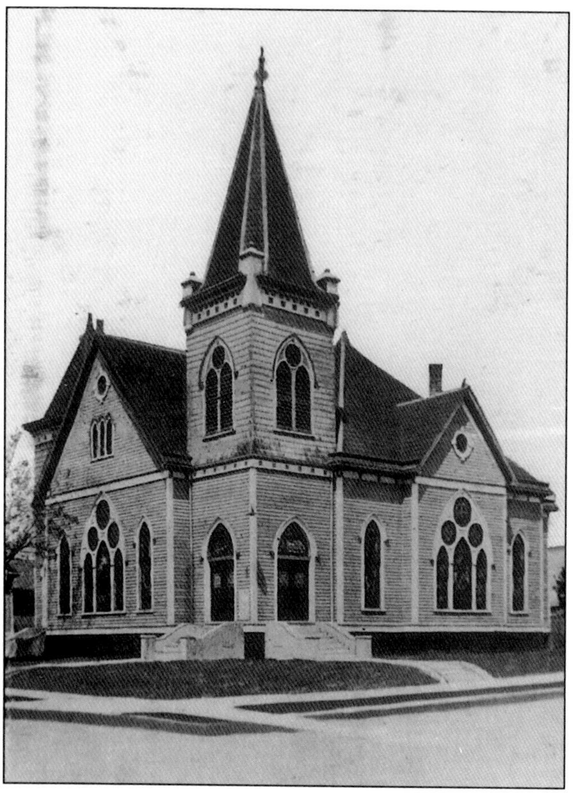

The First Christian Church Built in 1899. The first site for this church was in a meeting house located near present-day Alma Street and Park Boulevard near Spring Creek. The church was organized on March 11, 1860, and its first building was built at 16th Street and Avenue G in 1873. In 1898, it was moved to its present location at 15th Street and Avenue H, and the building was completed in 1899.

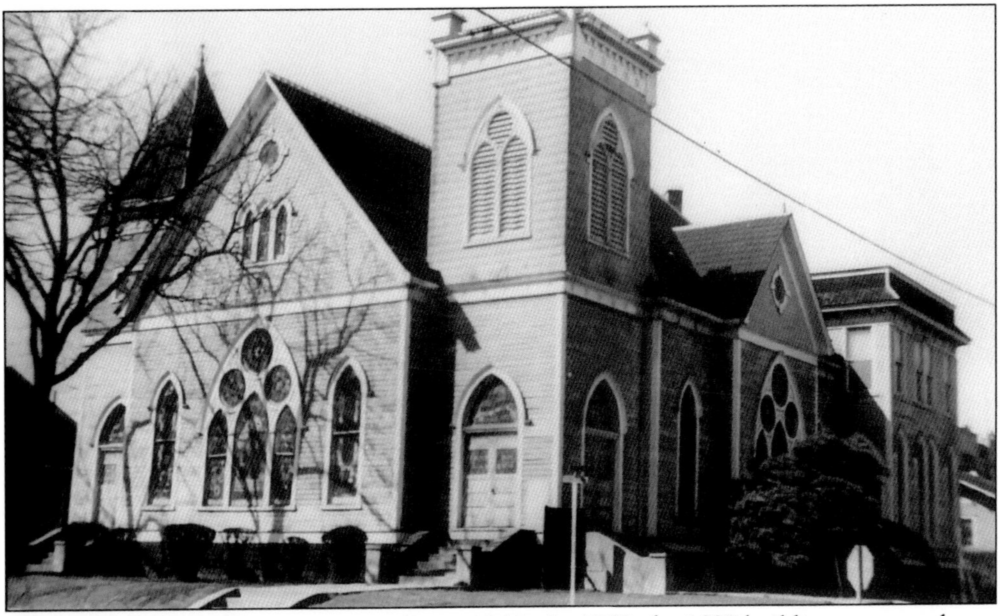

THE 1899 CHURCH BUILDING IN THE LATE 1940S. In 1950, the 1899 building was torn down, and the current building was completed in 1951.

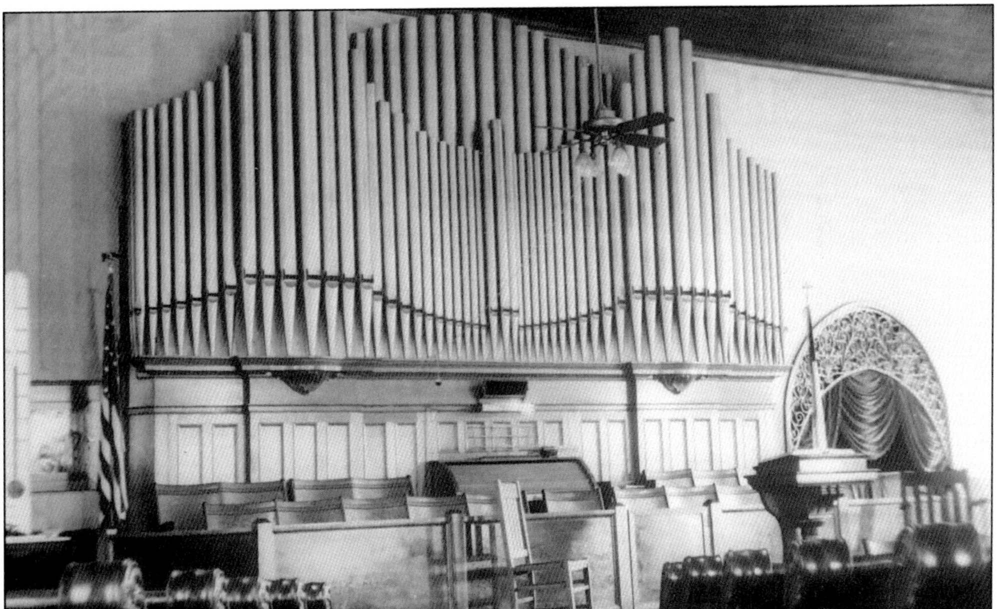

THE ORGAN FROM THE 1899 BUILDING. Elements from both the 1873 and 1899 buildings were used within the current building. These include the bell, the stained glass windows, and the organ. It is believed that the bell is the only one in Plano on a belfry. It is inscribed with the following: "Christian Church of Plano, Texas, Given by Merchants of Troy, New York, 1873."

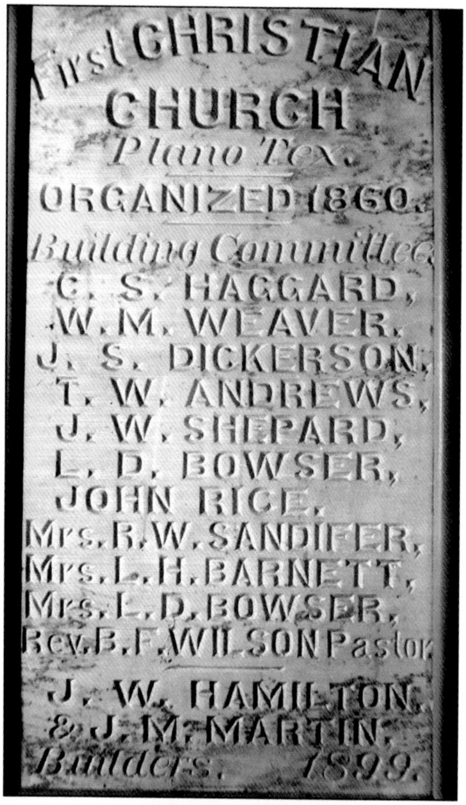

Cornerstone from the 1899 Building. Meetings for organizing Add-Ran College took place in this church. Add-Ran College was established to provide a college of Christian brotherhood for Texas. It was located in Thorpe Springs and was later moved to Fort Worth, where it became known as Texas Christian University.

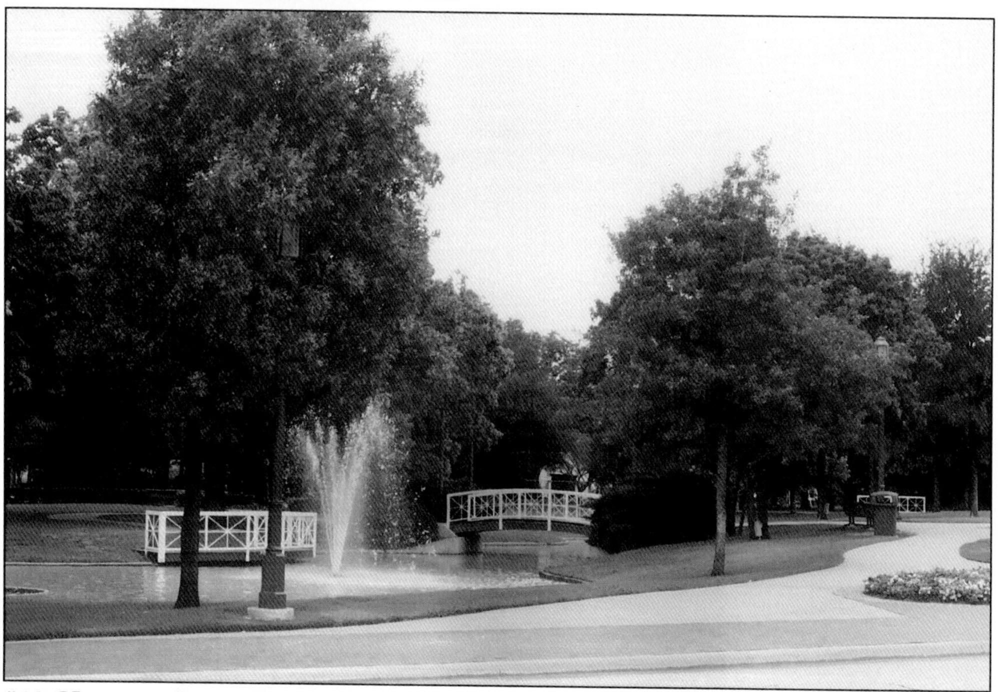

#12 Haggard Park. Emma Bishop, in memory of her parents, C.S. and N.K. Haggard, dedicated Haggard Park in 1928. The park is currently a popular location for events.

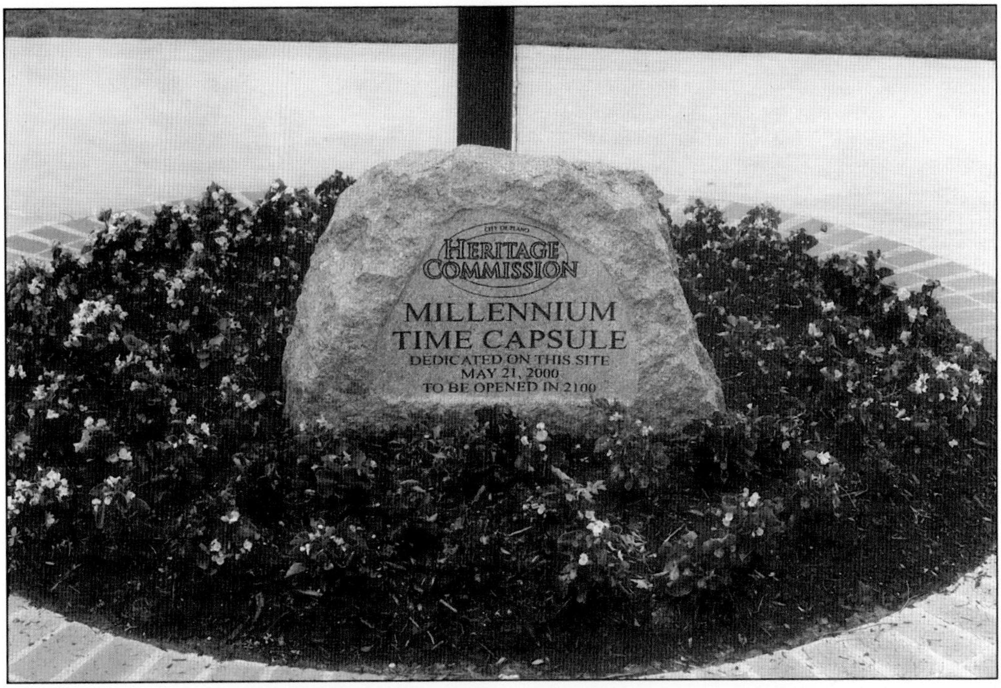

MILLENNIUM TIME CAPSULE MARKER. In 2000, a millennium time capsule was dedicated and placed under the flagpole near the Interurban Station. The time capsule will be opened in the year 2100.

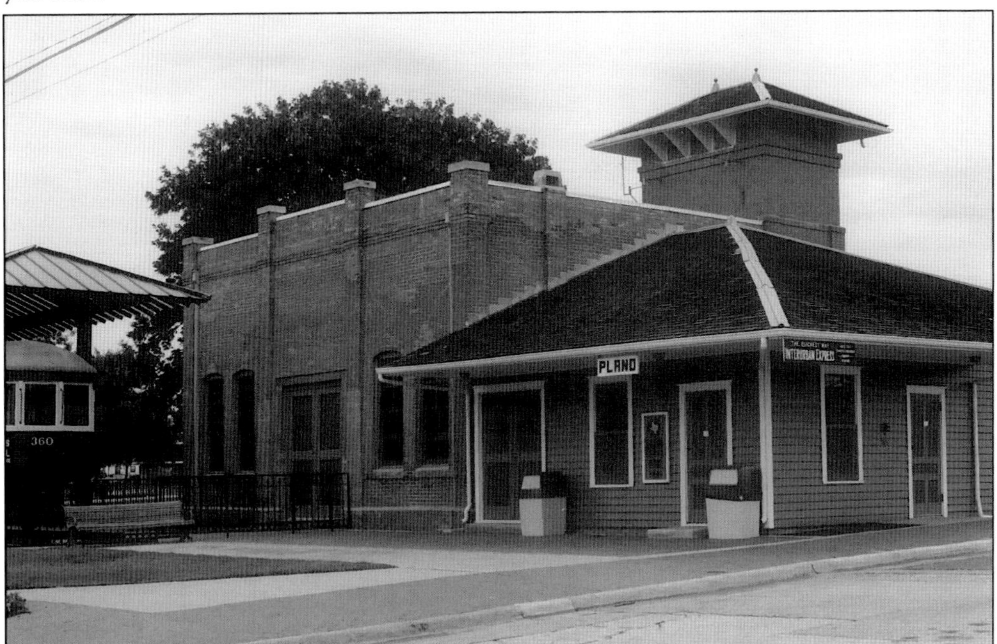

#13 INTERURBAN STATION. This is the only remaining station from the Sherman-Dallas segment. The Interurban Station served as a depot from 1908 until 1948. The trip from Plano to Dallas took about 25 minutes. With the ownership of cars and the availability of buses, the Interurban ceased its service in 1948. The building now serves as a museum.

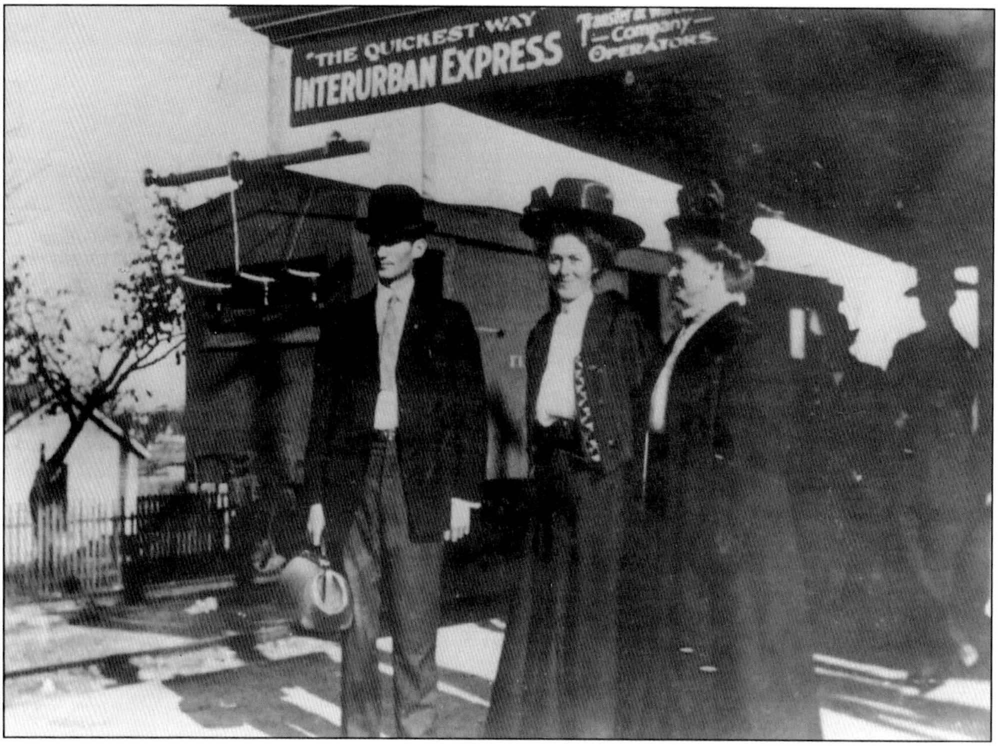

AT THE INTERURBAN STATION—C.C. ALLEN COURTING EFFIE HUGHELEY. (Courtesy of the Frances Wells Collection.)

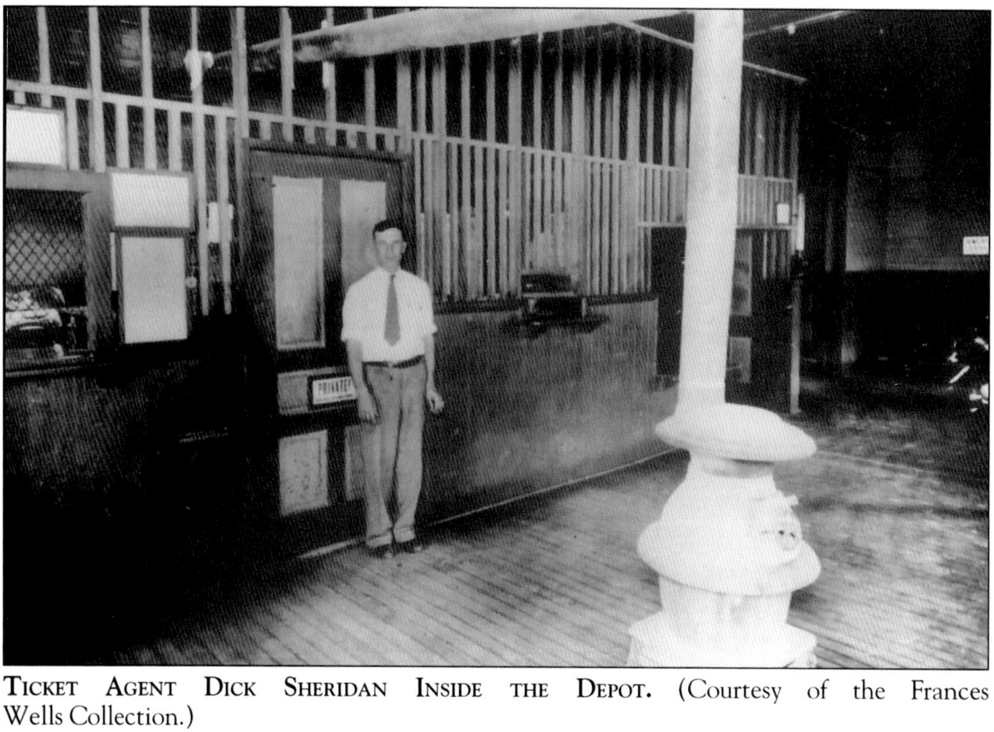

TICKET AGENT DICK SHERIDAN INSIDE THE DEPOT. (Courtesy of the Frances Wells Collection.)

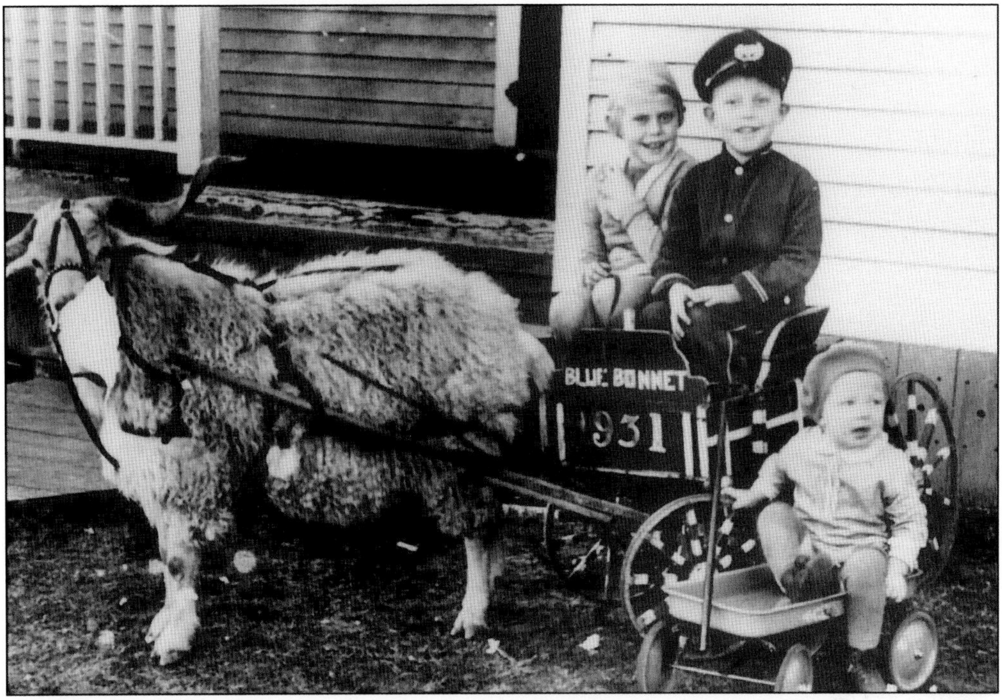

#14 Haynes House. They are, from left to right: Mary Louise, Jerry, and Hal Haynes in 1932. Fred Elmore Haynes and Louise Ernestine Schimelpfenig Haynes and their children lived in a house at this approximate location on what is now Avenue I between 16th and 17th Streets. The house has since been torn down. The family lived there from 1930 to 1942, in a two-story white frame house built in 1920 by Louise's father, Fred Schimelpfenig, as a rental house.

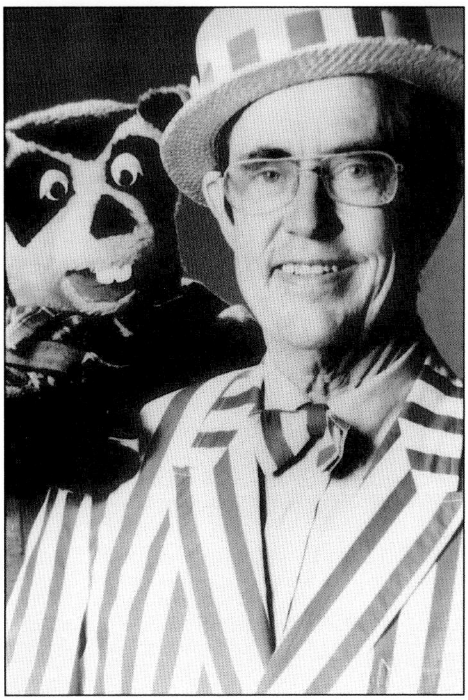

Jerry Haynes as Mr. Peppermint. The couple's son, Jerry, became known as "Mr. Peppermint," a popular children's personality on WFAA, a Dallas television station.

Fred Haynes always enjoyed poetry. Jerry's father would pay him 50¢ to memorize poems and recite them in front of the family. From this experience, Jerry became interested in acting. (Mr. Peppermint photograph courtesy of WFAA-TV and Belo, Dallas, Texas. All Rights Reserved.)

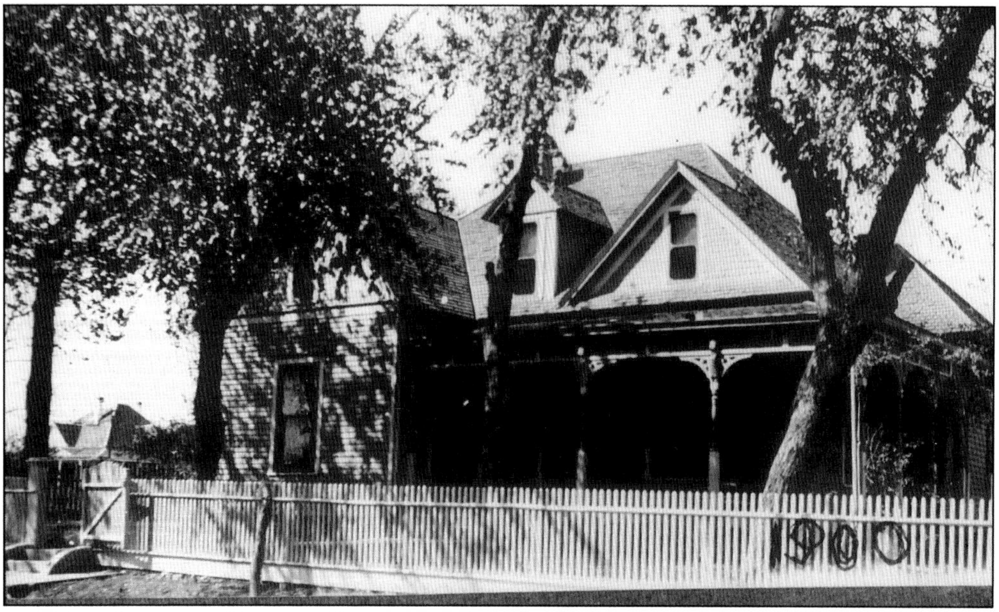

#15 THE ELIZABETH SMOOTH HOUSE IN 1900. Elizabeth "Granny" Smoot lived in this house with her son, John, and Mattie Hulse. John was a doctor at Baylor Hospital in Dallas and later taught at Baylor Medical College.

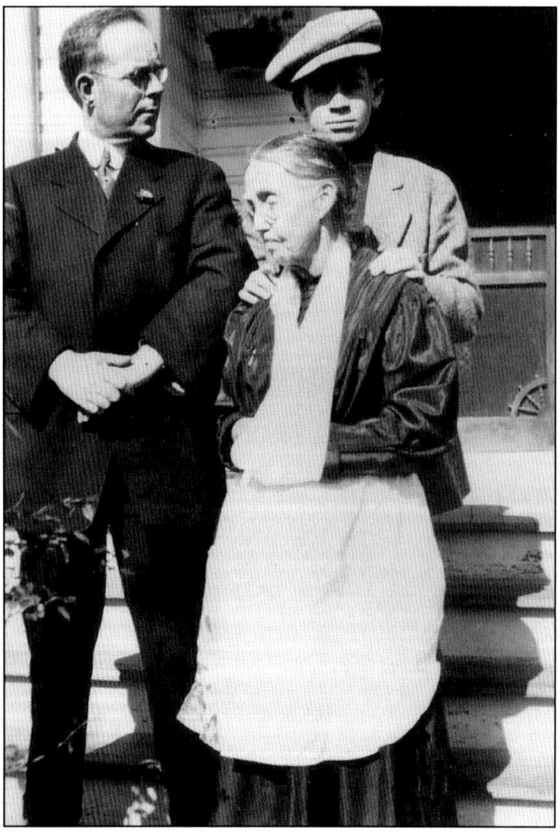

LEFT TO RIGHT: DR. JOHN SMOOT, GRANNY SMOOT, AND DR. SMOOT'S SON BRAGG STANDING IN THE BACK.

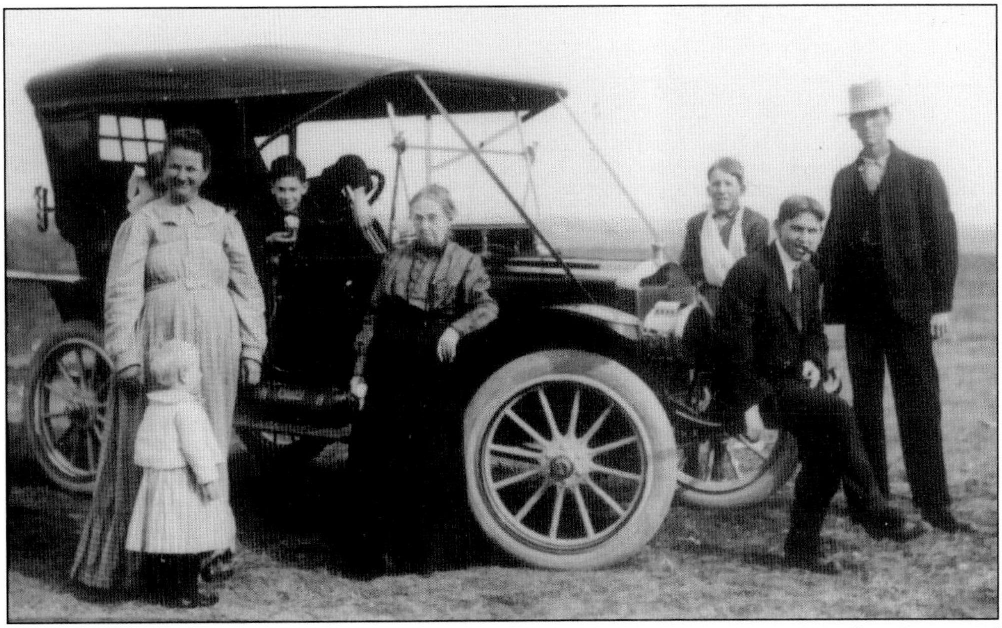

Granny Smoot's Farm. Bragg Smoot is inside the car, Granny Smoot is pictured in front, and Dr. John Smoot is sitting on the front of the car (others were hired hands and their names are unknown). Granny Smoot maintained a farm just outside of Plano. She is pictured here on the farm with her son, grandson, and the hired hands that helped run the farm.

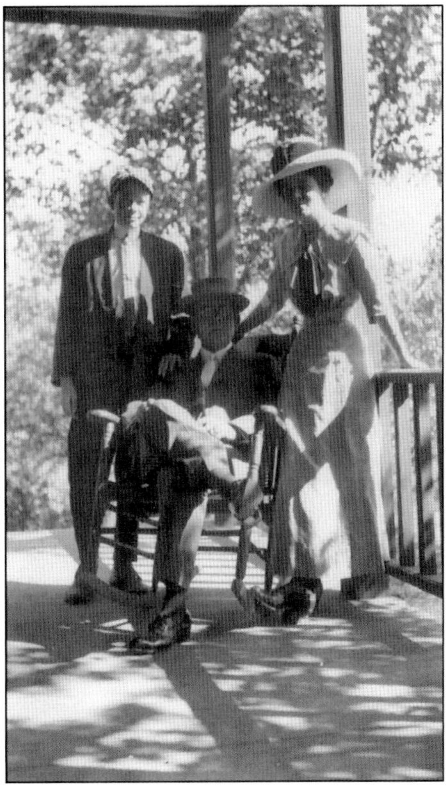

Left to Right: Bragg Smoot, Dr. John Smoot, and Latrelle Smoot. Little is known about Dr. John Smoot's first wife. His second wife, Latrelle, was a nurse at Baylor Hospital.

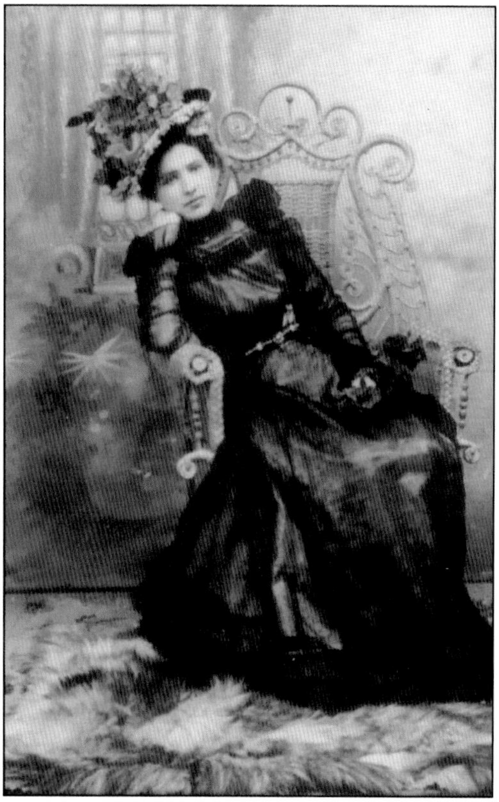

Mattie Blanch Hulse. Granny Smoot took in Mattie Blanch Hulse to rear and educate when her mother died. Mattie was never legally adopted, but she was treated as Granny Smoot's own child throughout her entire life.

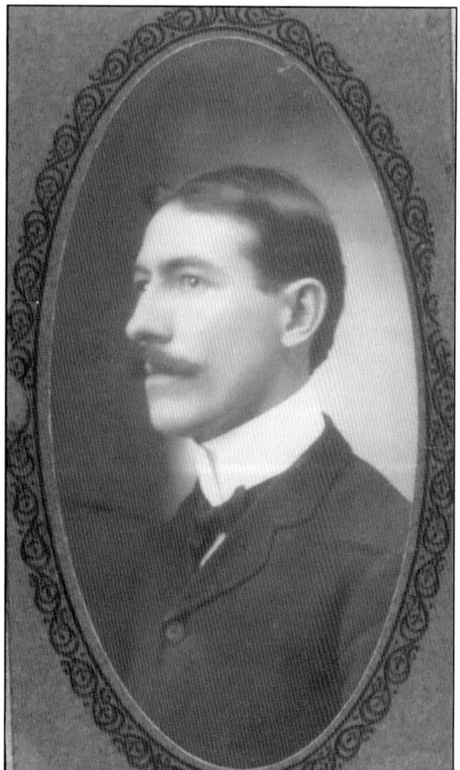

William Muegge. Mattie met William F. Scherff Muegge around 1900. William's father had a feed and grain business in San Antonio where William was a bookkeeper. He was sent to oversee the Plano branch of the business. While there, he met and married Mattie. Granny Smoot wrote of their courtship in her diary. They met around 1900, and it was not until 1908 that Granny Smoot started referring to him by his first name.

Fred Muegge. After Mattie and William married, they lived in this house with Granny Smoot. While living in the house, their son, Fred, was born in 1906. Ms. Saigling, who lived across the street, assisted in the birth.

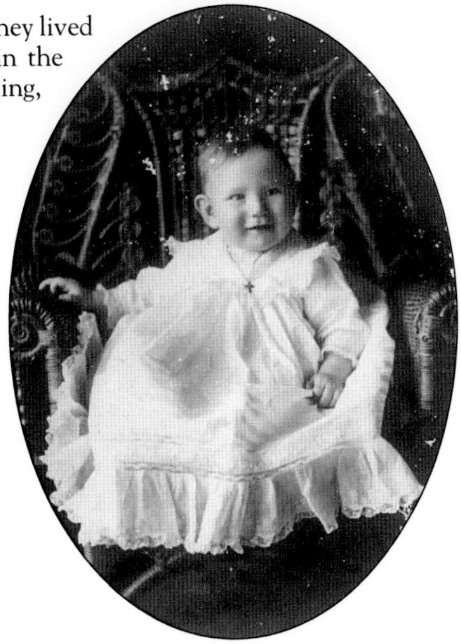

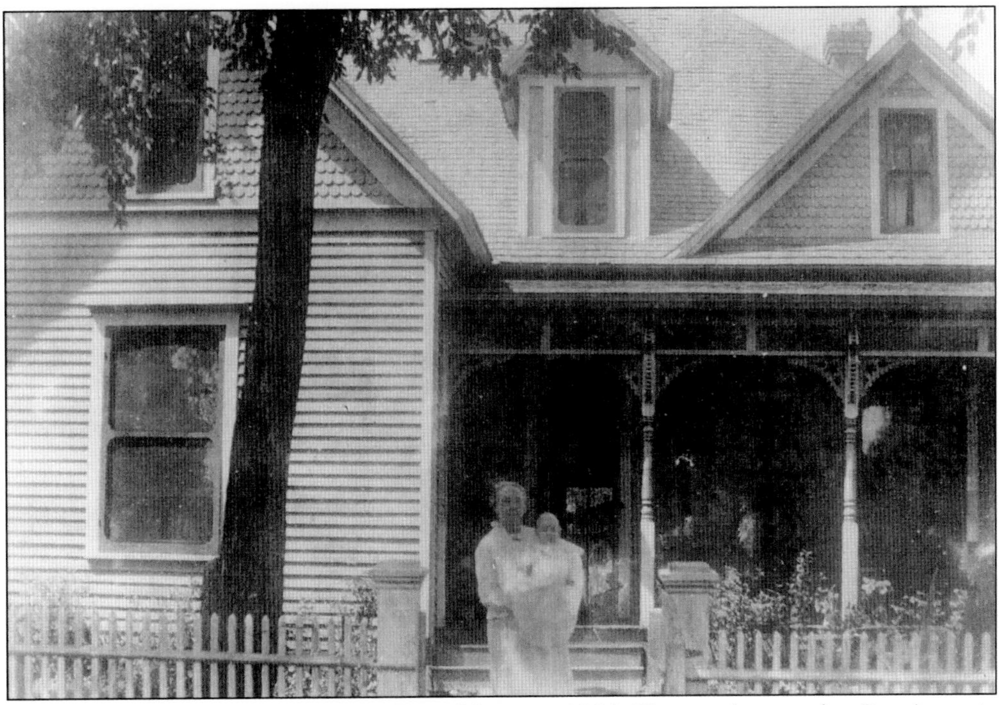

Granny Smoot Holding Newborn Fred Muegge, 1906. The couple moved to San Antonio shortly after Fred was born, and Granny Smoot came to visit often. William Muegge died in 1912, and Mattie was left with three boys to support. The four of them moved back to Plano and lived with Granny Smoot until she died in 1914. Shortly after her death, Mattie and her boys moved to Comfort, Texas.

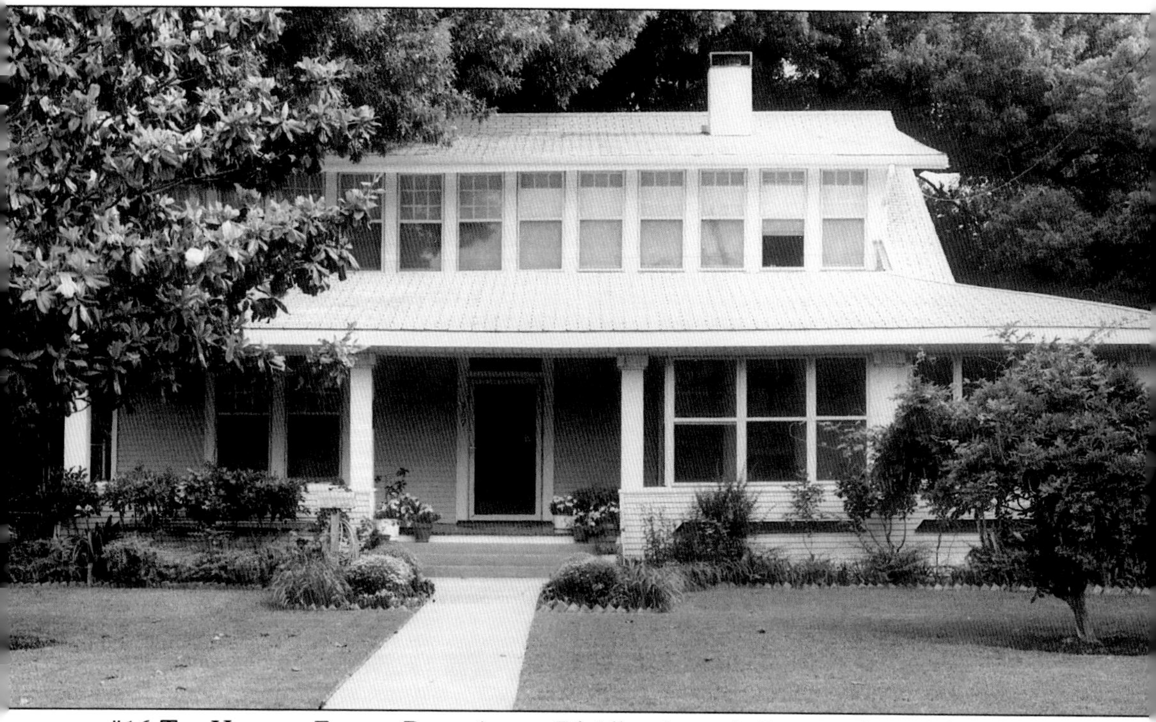

#16 The Home of Ed and Price Allen. Ed Allen, his wife, Price, and son, Edward, lived in this house in the early 1900s. The room on the second story with many windows was built as a playroom for Edward. Ed Allen and his brother, Carl, ran the Allen Drug Store. The brothers purchased the E.A. Carpenter Drug Store and changed the name to the Allen Drug Store.

Fred Meugge, who was born next door in the Elizabeth Smoot house, recounted that one Halloween night, the horse-drawn wagon that advertised the Airdome was dismantled and reassembled on the Allen's front porch as a prank. The Airdome showed "movies under the stars" in downtown Plano in the early 1900s. (Photography by Adam Towber.)

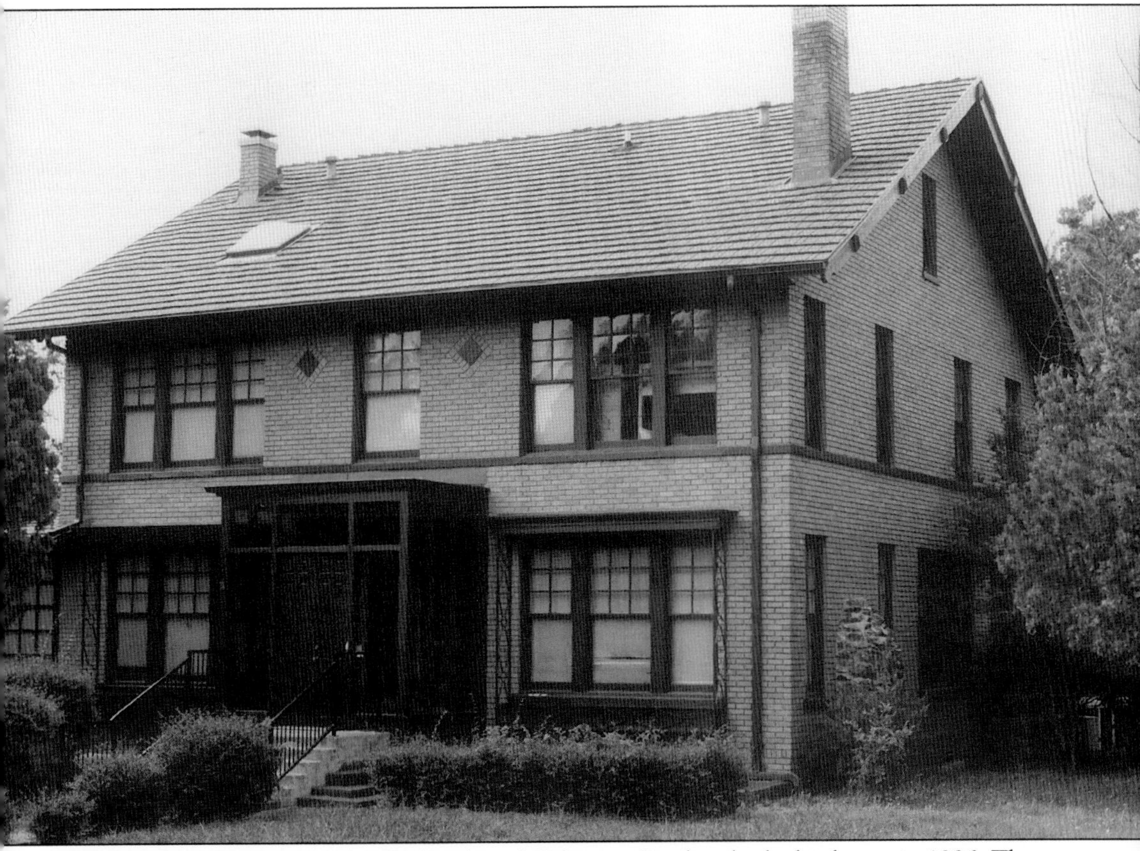

#17 Saigling House. Charles Frederick and Celestine Saigling built this house in 1906. They lived in it until their deaths. Celestine was the last to die in 1933. The house originally had a large porch that wrapped around the sides and started where the front door is now located. It is one of the few old houses in Plano that has a basement. When the Saiglings lived there, they heated the house by burning coal in a large furnace located in the basement.

Jim Bowen was hired to maintain the yard and to act as the couple's chauffeur. Lizzie Drake was hired as their cook. Lizzie spent her free time in the small house in the back of the property. (Photography by Adam Towber.)

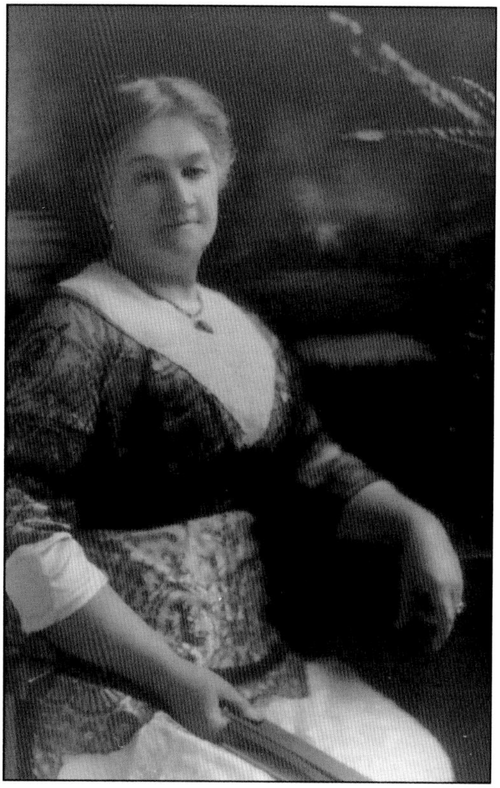

Celestine Saigling. Celestine came from a wealthy French family. Her brother was Eugene Pellot, a famous poet.

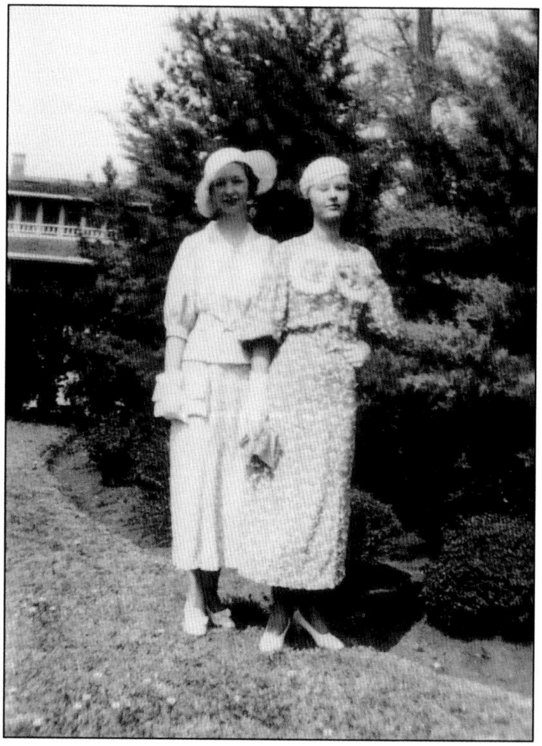

Hazel and Ouida Saigling. Hazel and Ouida, two of the Saigling's granddaughters, are pictured in their grandparents' front yard. The Ed Allen house is visible in the background.

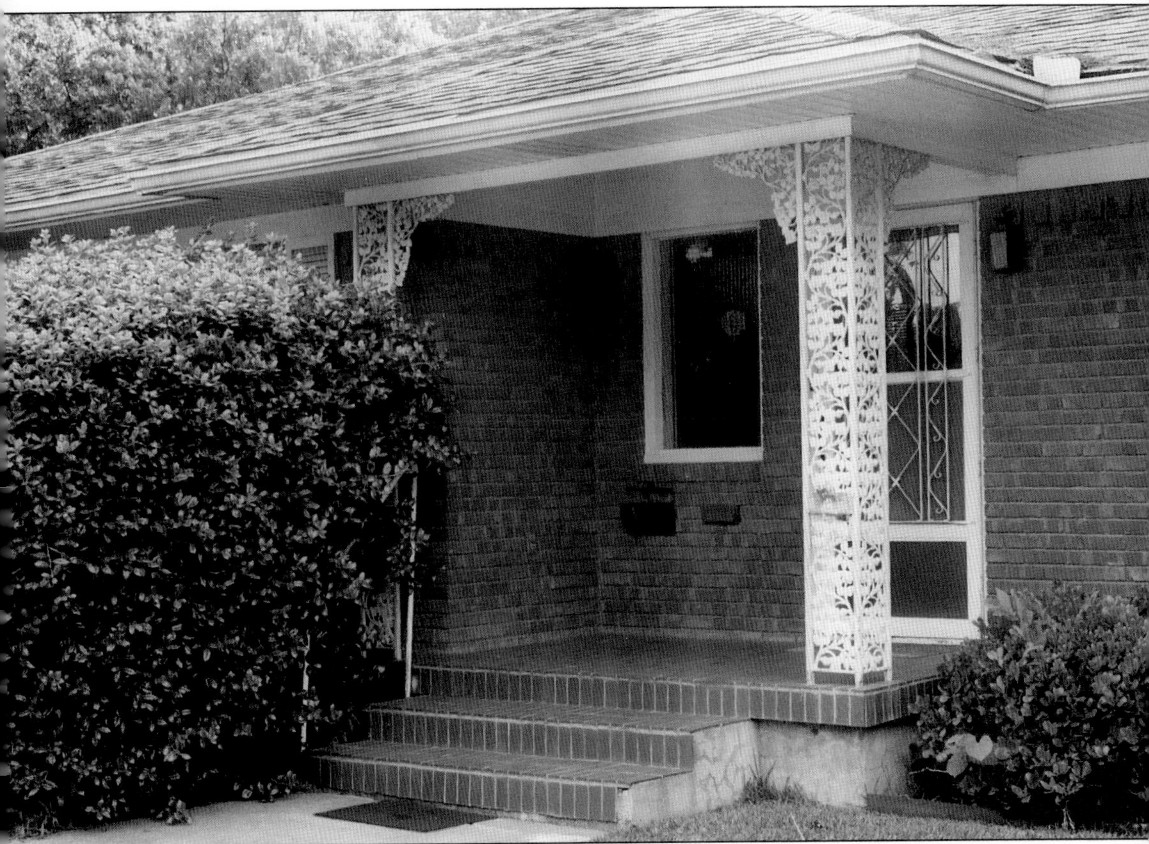

#18 Gladys Harrington House. Gladys Harrington has lived in Plano since she was 16. She had this house built to her specifications around 1955, and she has lived in this house ever since.

Mrs. Harrington was visiting a church in McKinney with her sister one Sunday, and the preacher mentioned that Plano did not have a library. His comment prompted her to enlist the help of some of the members of the Federation of Church Women to help her establish a library in Plano around 1955. (Photography by Adam Towber.)

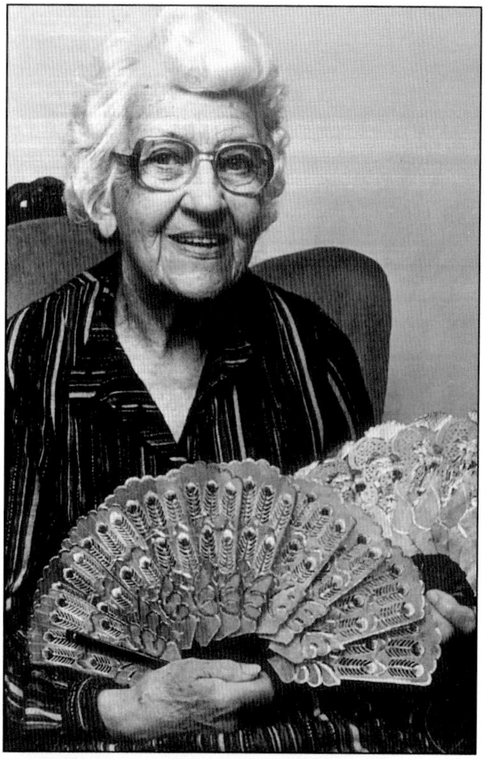

GLADYS HARRINGTON.

GLADYS HARRINGTON LIBRARY. The first library operated in more than one location. The first was in the Plano Community House and was open two hours a week. At its storefront location on 15th Place, it was open six days a week. The city council passed an ordinance to establish a municipal library on May 24, 1965, and citizens approved a bond election on September 9, 1967. The Gladys Harrington Public Library opened on June 2, 1969, on 18th Street.

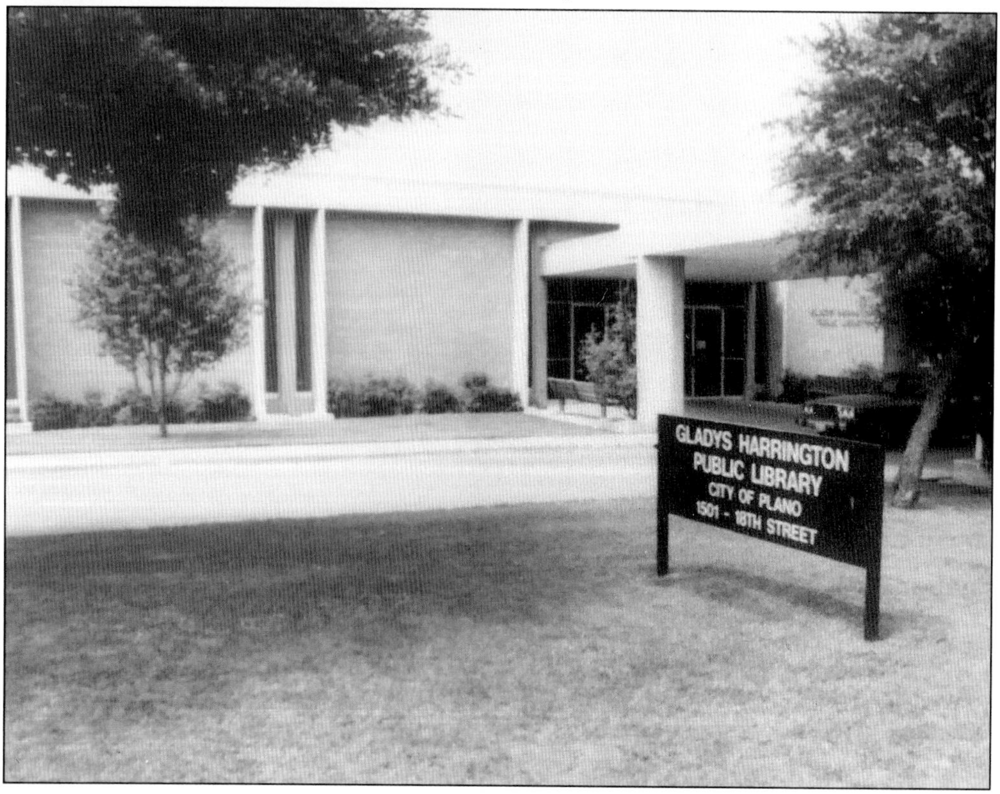

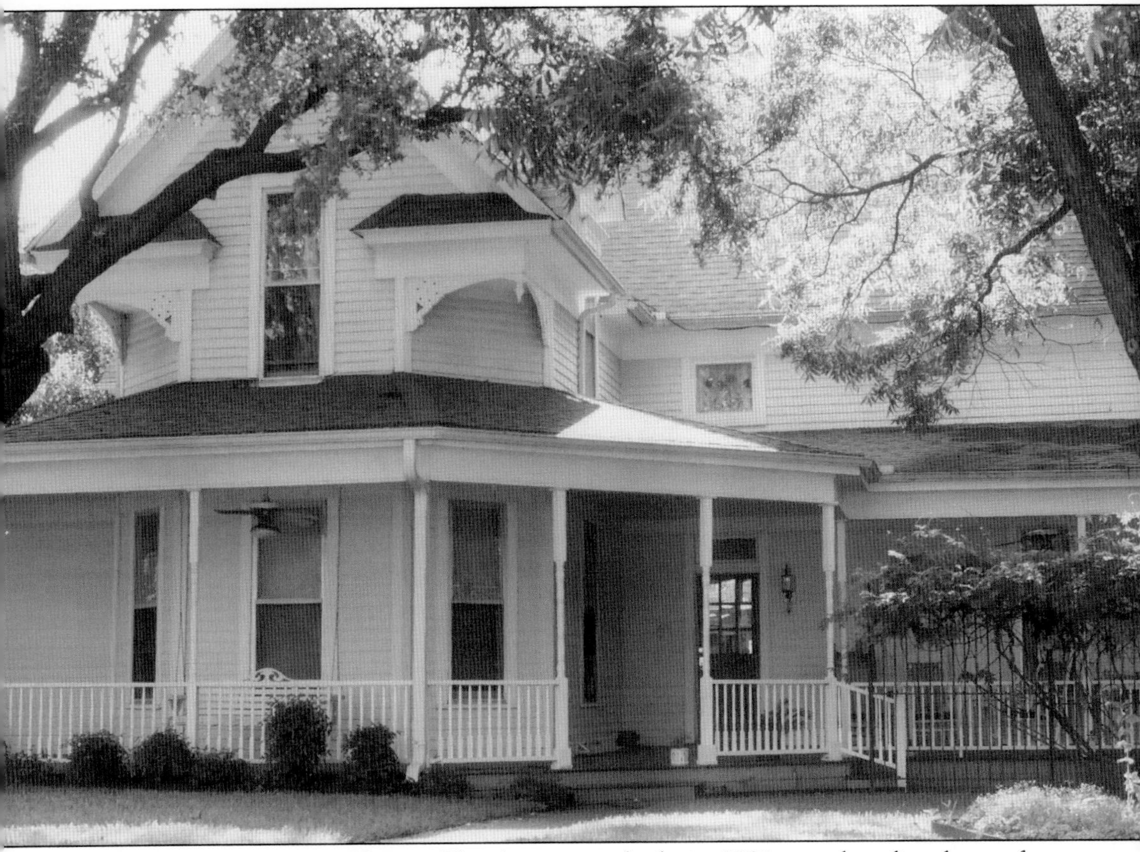

#19 Will Schimelpfenig House. This house was built in 1901 as a boarding house for schoolteachers who taught at the nearby Plano school. Like many houses of its day, it had a porch in the back with a well.

Will Schimelpfenig first lived next door at 907 17th Street in the house in which he was born. Will was Fred Schimelpfenig's nephew. It is believed that Will met his wife, Effie, when she lived in this house as a schoolteacher. After the couple married, they lived next door in Will's childhood home until they purchased this house in 1920. Will passed away first, and Effie remained in the house until she passed away in the 1970s.

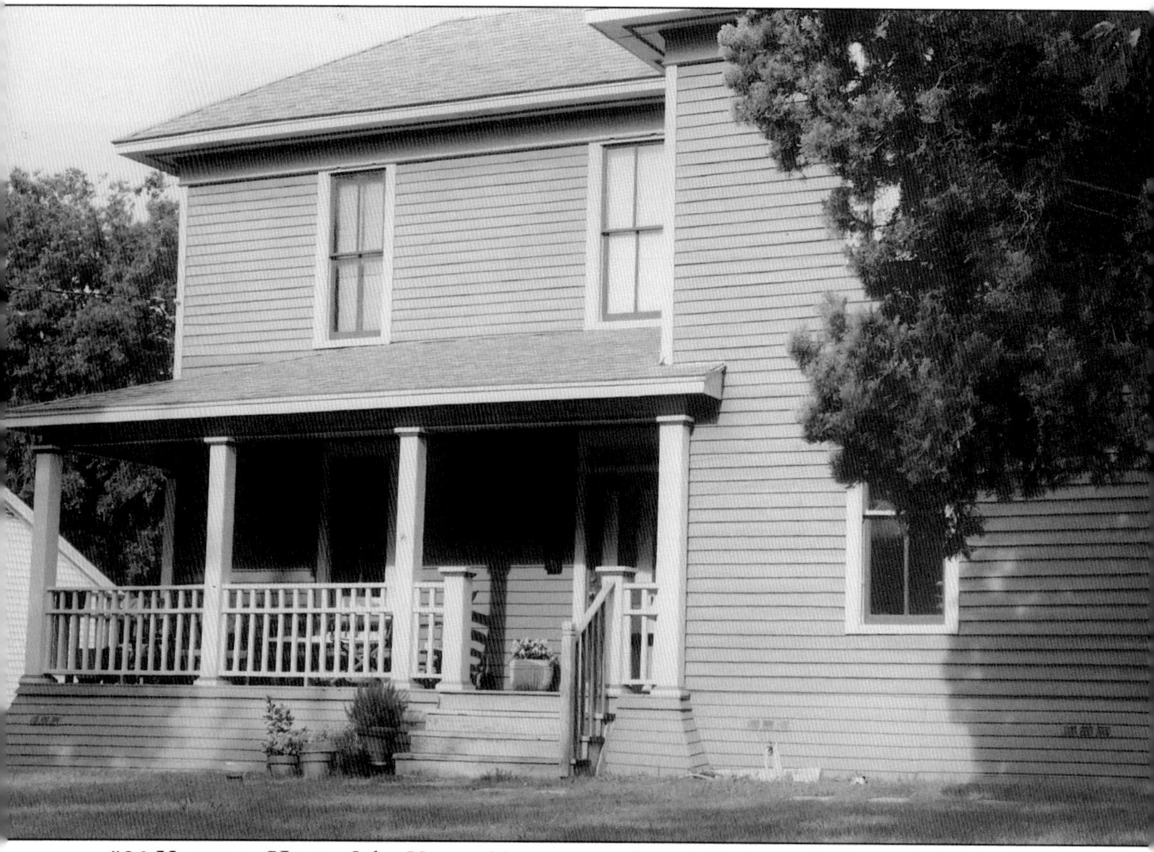

#20 VONTRESS HOUSE. John Harney Vontress purchased this house in the early 1920s. His wife, Berth Ann Rogers Angel, had moved to Plano after her mother, father, husband, and two sisters died from the influenza epidemic of 1918. She lived in a house that needed roofing repairs, and the two met when John Vontress came to give her an estimate on the work.

The house was originally located at 1313 Avenue K. It was painted white with black trim, and it had a dark gray roof. (Photography by Adam Towber.)

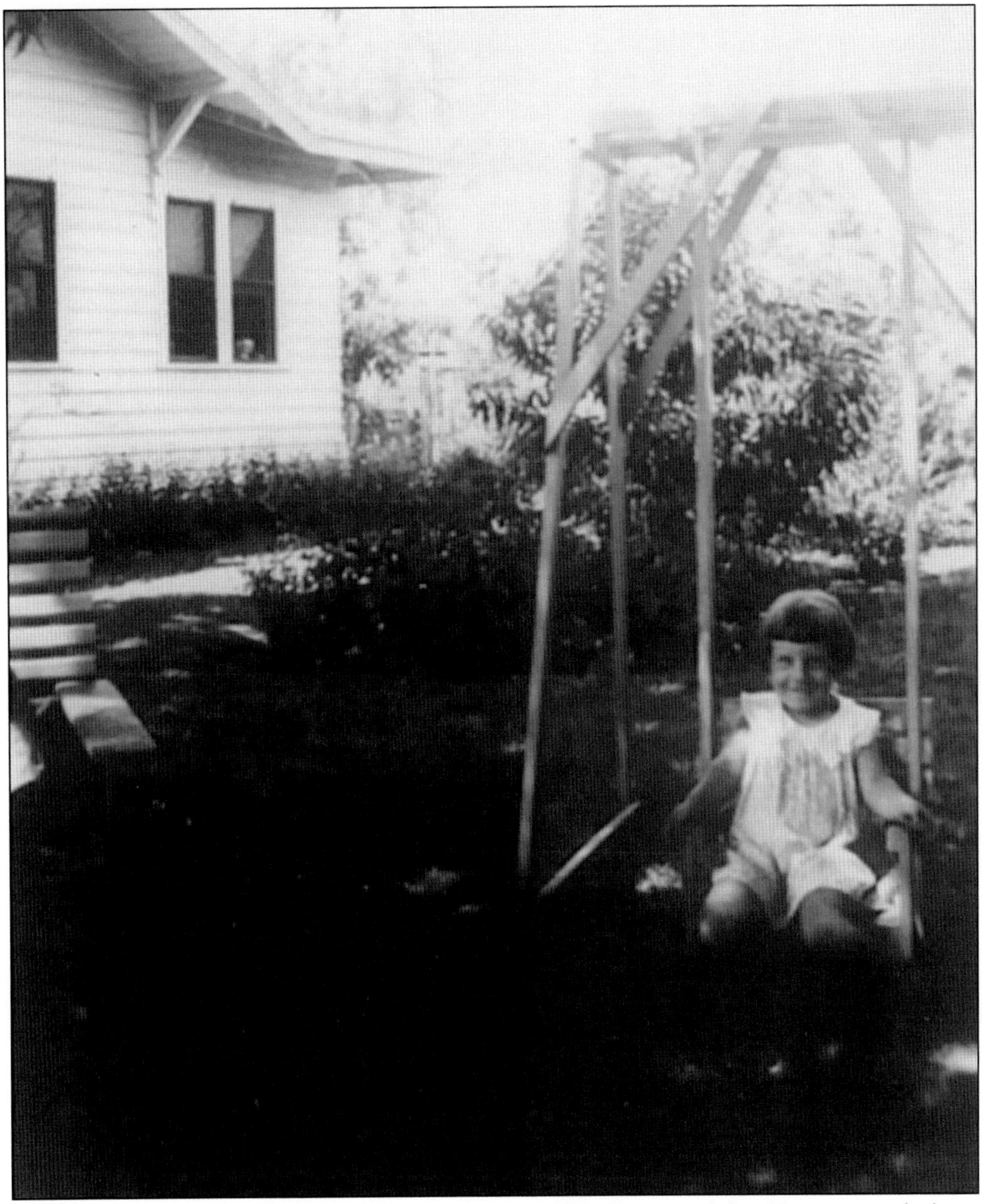

Janelle Vontress in Outdoor Swing Made by Her Father. John Vontress made lawn furniture, playground equipment for the city park, and specialized wagon beds, which were used to haul cotton.

At the original location, the backyard was divided down the center. On one side was a chicken run, and on the other was a garden. Blackberries, dewberries, and raspberries were grown on the fence dividing the yard. Peach, apricot, pear, and plum trees grew in the yard. Bertha would can three to four hundred cans of food harvested from their yard each year.

Also in the backyard was a smokehouse that served as more than just storage for cured meat. The Vontress family grew popcorn and peanuts which were hung by the vine in the smokehouse. There were drawers under the smokehouse where potatoes and onions were stored, and sliced peaches and apricots were left out on the galvanized roof to make dried fruit.

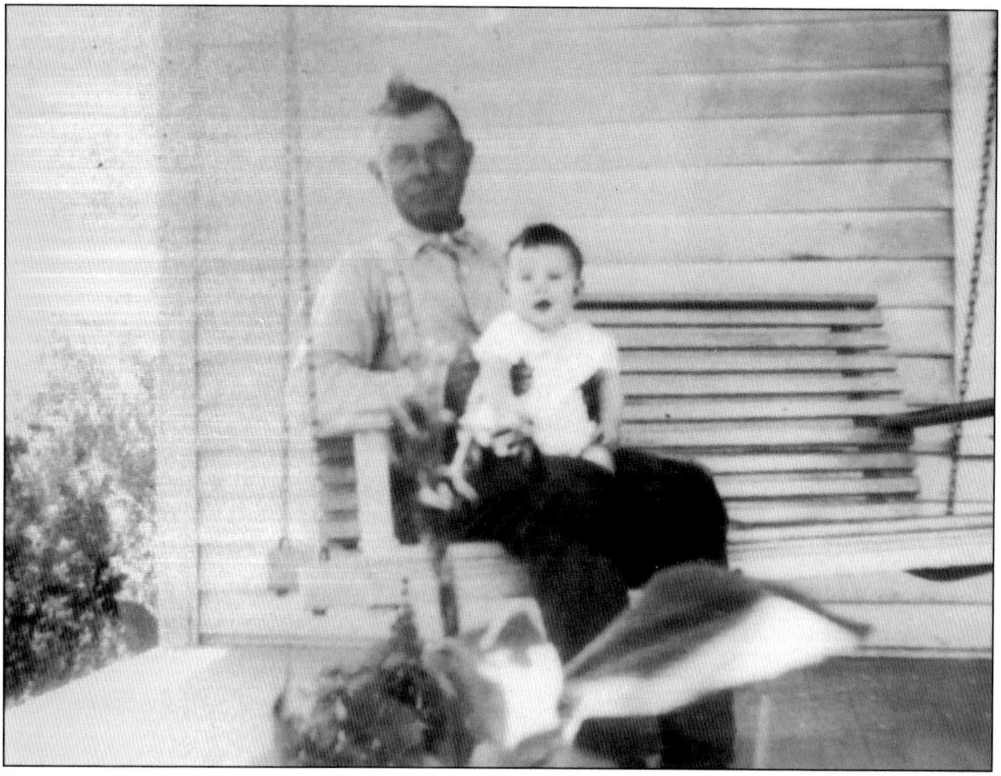

John and Janelle Vontress. This swing was always located on the front porch of the house. John Vontress made this one and others like it for a living.

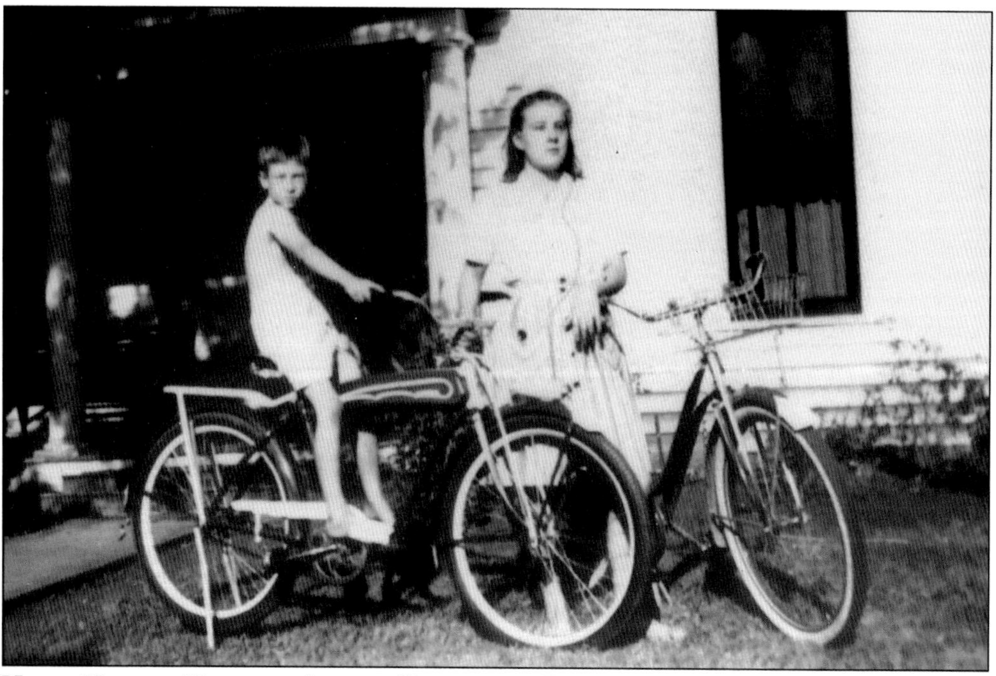

Henry Howard Hayes and Janelle Vontress in Front of the Vontress House.

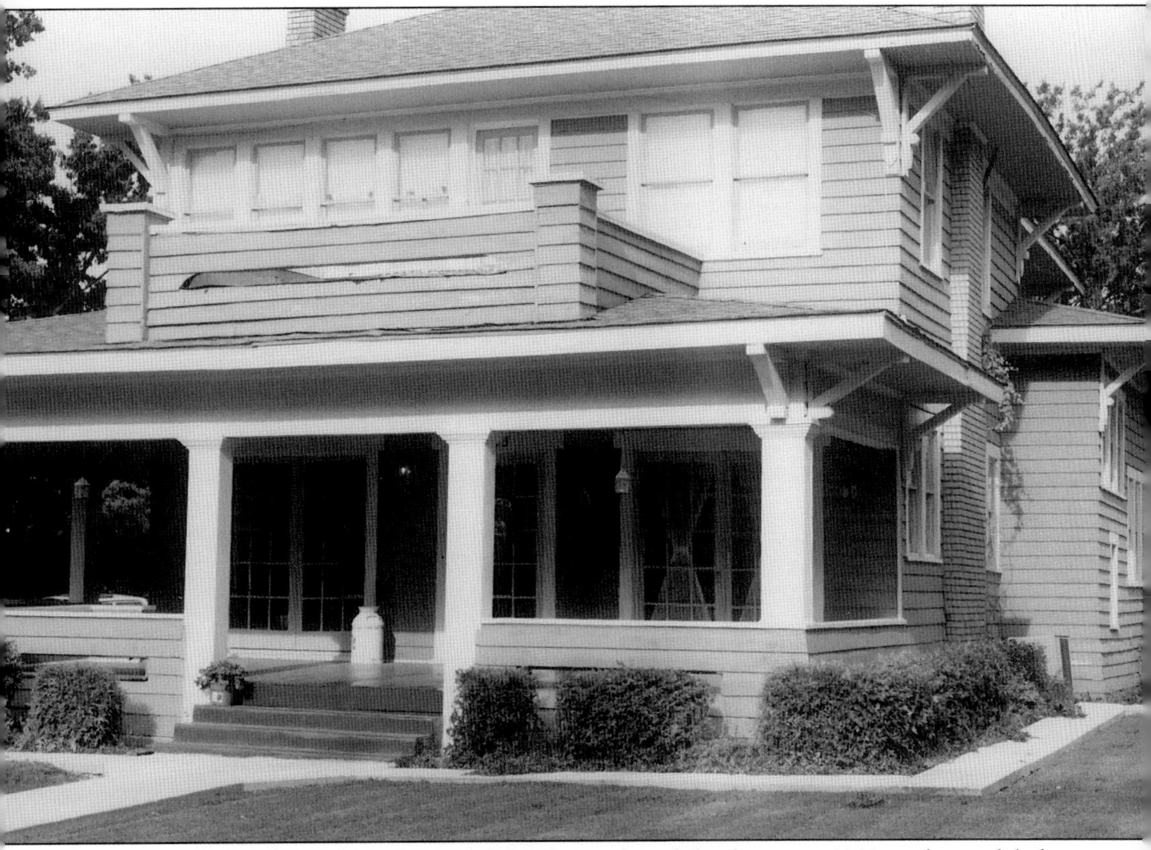

#21 The Aldridge House. The Aldridge family purchased this house in 1910, and remodeled it in 1918. The house had a tennis court in the backyard and became the first house with a refrigerator in Collin County. People from all over the county came to the Aldridge's home to see it. The workings were outside of the house in a wooden box. Mr. Aldridge also purchased one of the first cars in Plano.

Mr. Aldridge was a very forward-thinking man. Some of the first meetings involving the organization and beginnings of Plano took place in this house. The family owned a farm near Central Expressway and Aldridge Road where cotton was grown, and Mr. Aldridge perfected a specialized type of cotton. He also built a nine-hole golf course on the farm. Sometimes he would play the course twice just to get in his 18 holes of golf. (Photography by Adam Towber.)

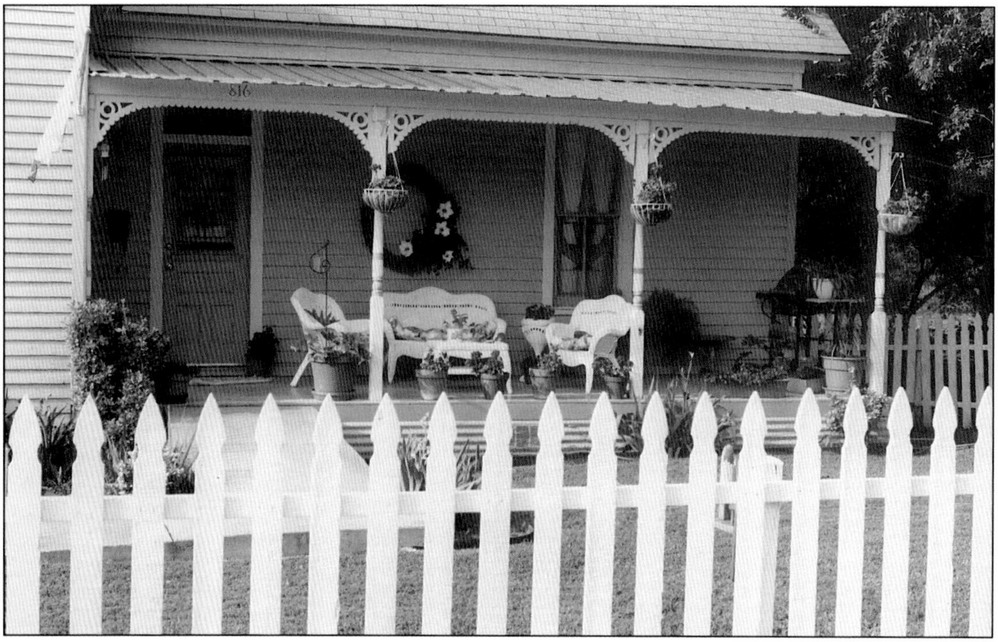

#22 Magnolia House. This house was built in the late 1800s. At its former location at 1206 14th Street, it was the site of an antique shop. Since a large magnolia tree graced the front yard, the antique shop was called the "Magnolia House." The name has stayed with the house to this day.

Today, the Aldridge house shares the same lot with this house. The owner purchased the house for $1 and had it moved to this site in 1993. (Photography by Adam Towber.)

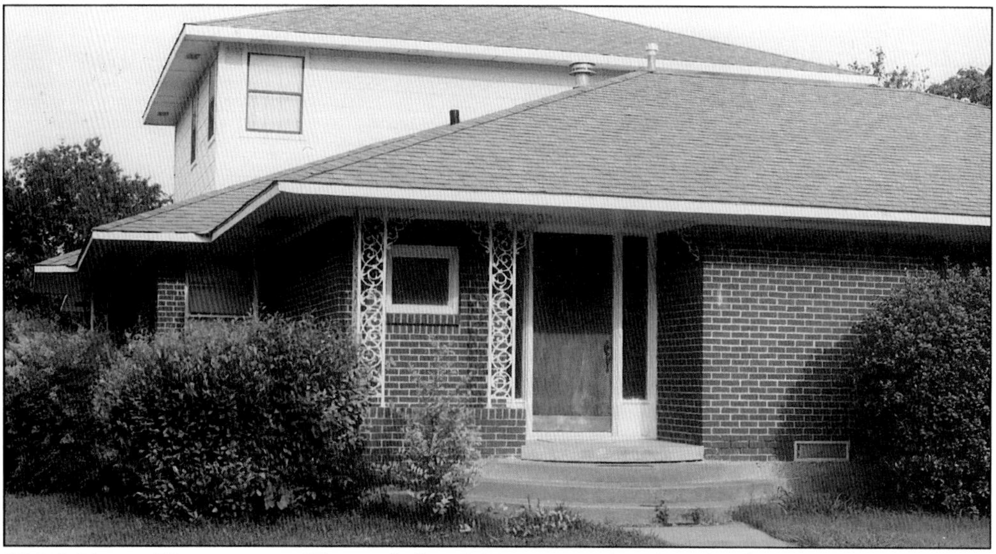

#23 J. Frank Harrington House. J. Frank Harrington lived in this house in the 1950s. He moved here from the prairie-style house located on 16th Street. Frank Harrington served on the state legislature and was the attorney for the Southern Pacific Railroad. He was elected as county judge and moved to McKinney to serve in that capacity. After returning to Plano, he sold his house on 16th Street and moved into this one, where he remained until his death. (Photography by Adam Towber.)

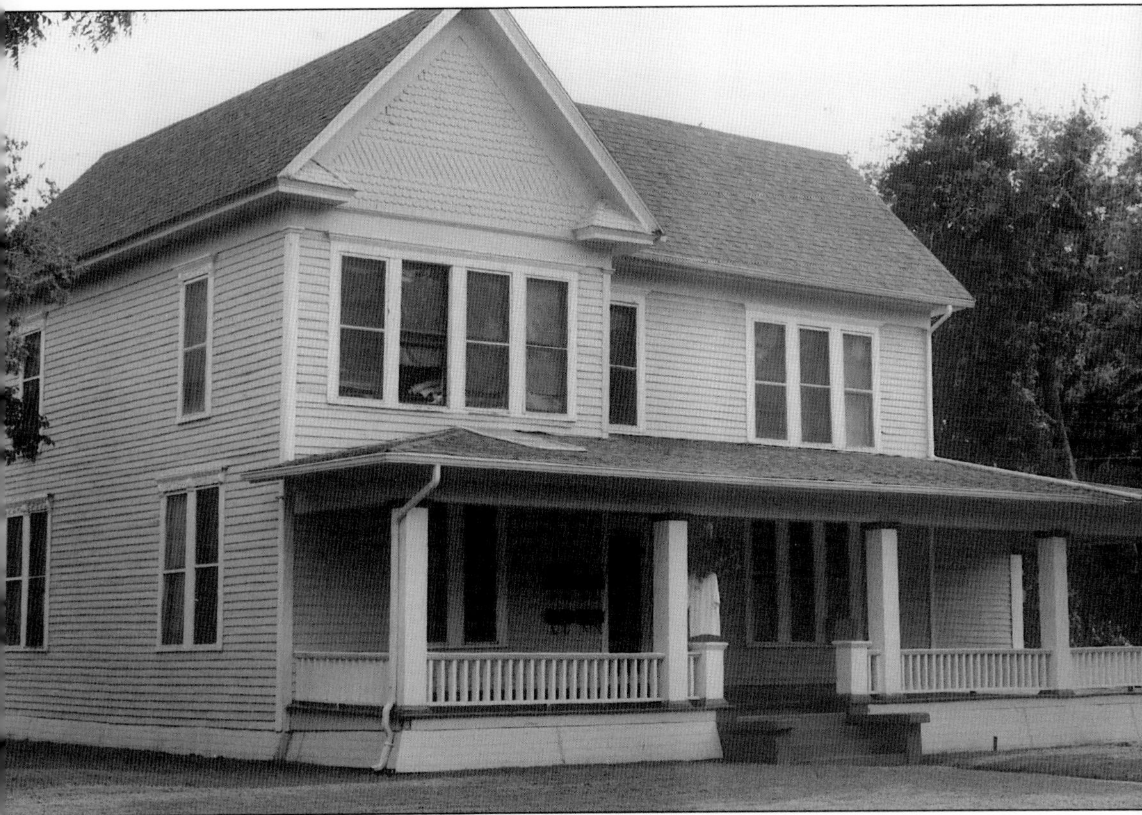

#24 The Mathews House. This house was built around 1888 by J.H. Gulledge. It was sold to S.J. Mathews in 1900. At one time, the house was a more ornate Victorian style with a small front porch. As was the case with many homes in Plano, the large front porch was added to provide more shade from the Texas sun. The addition of the porch and columns altered the style from Victorian to prairie.

S.J. Mathews ran a general store in downtown Plano from 1895 to 1947. Mathews's wife, Nancy, worked as a milliner and made hats to be sold in her husband's store. (Photography by Adam Towber.)

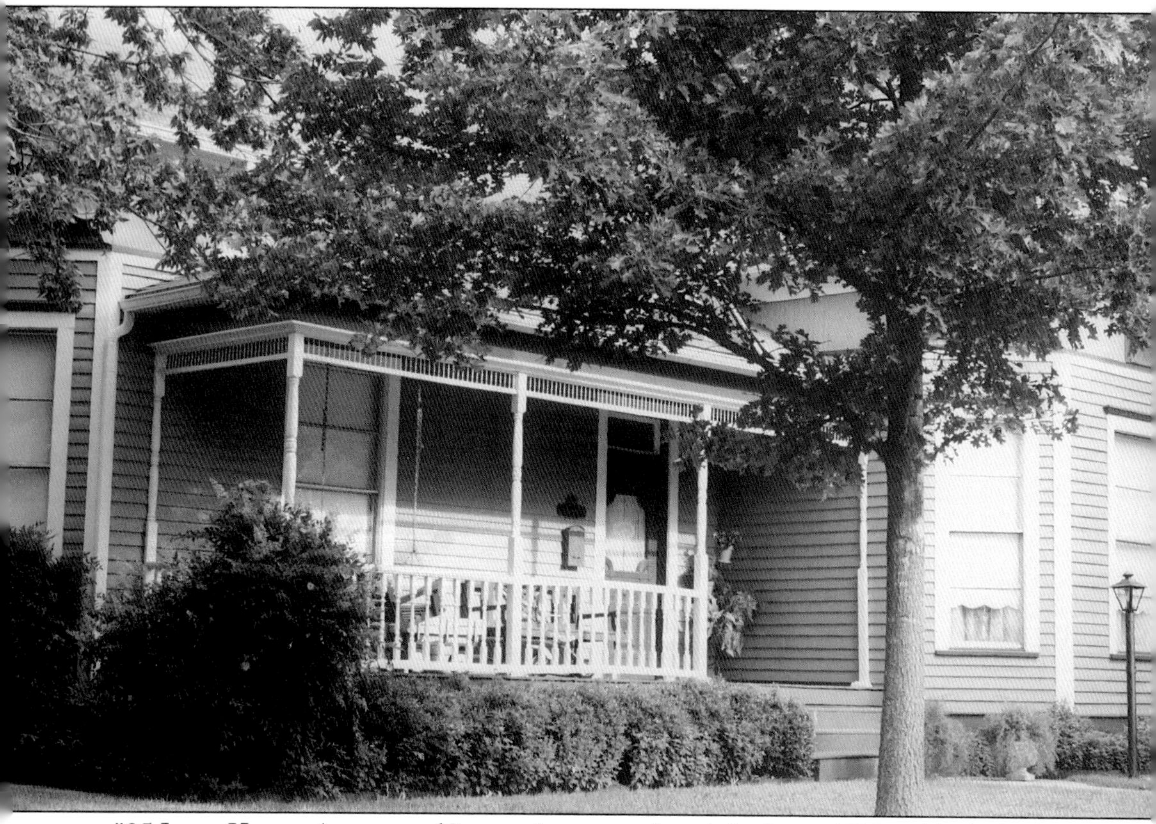

#25 Lamm House. Auguste and Leonne Lamm purchased this lot in 1893 and built this house. The couple had two sons, Virgin and Gilbert. Auguste served as the public weigher for the Plano precinct from 1879 to 1880. In 1881, Auguste became the day clerk for the H&TC Railway Company. In 1921, he became railroad agent for the Southern Pacific, which had taken over the H&TC, and worked in this capacity for the remainder of his career. He also served as the telegraph operator for 40 years beginning in 1880, and as the Wells Fargo Express Agent until 1910.

After the Lamm family lived in the house, Frances and Henry Schimelpfenig lived in it with Brother Thurman, a Methodist minister. (Photography by Adam Towber.)

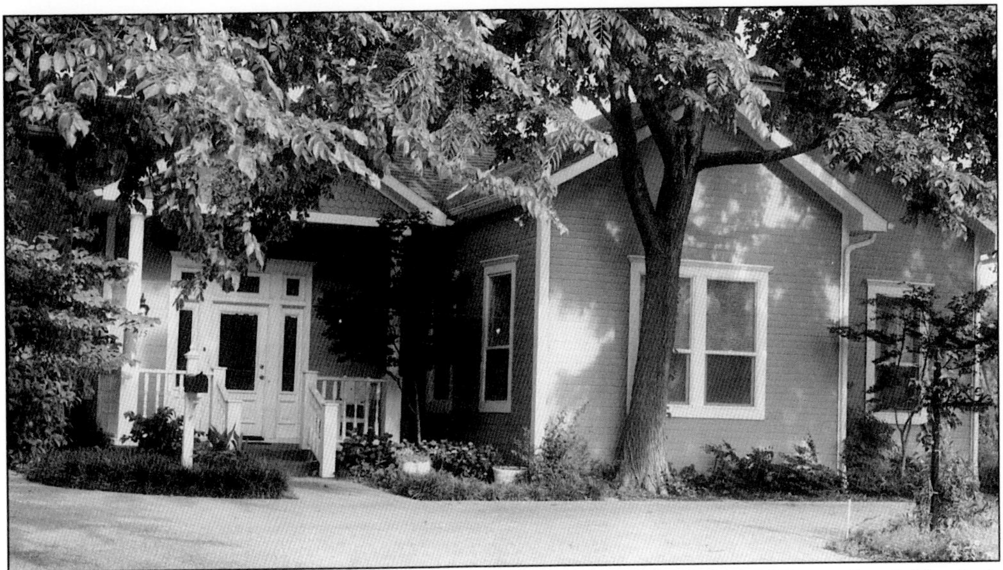

#26 Dr. Apple House. Around 1953, Dr. George William Apple and his wife, Addie Bob Apple, purchased this house and lived here with their four children, Ginny, Penny, Nancy, and George William III. Dr. Apple's first office was located on Avenue K, at approximately the current site of the Municipal Building. One of the current owners grew up in Plano and remembers coming to this house for visits to Dr. Apple as a girl.

It is believed that this house first belonged to the Strain family and then the Thomas Harmer family, prior to the purchase of this house by Dr. Apple. (Photography by Adam Towber.)

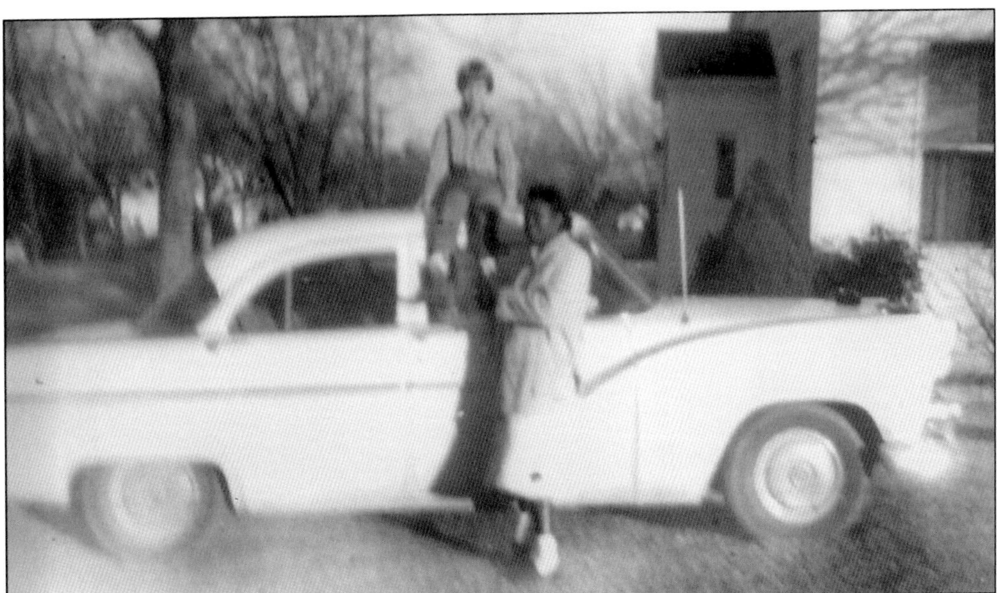

Hallie Thomas Standing and Ginny Apple Sitting on the Car, 1958. Hallie Thomas helped to care for the Apple children.

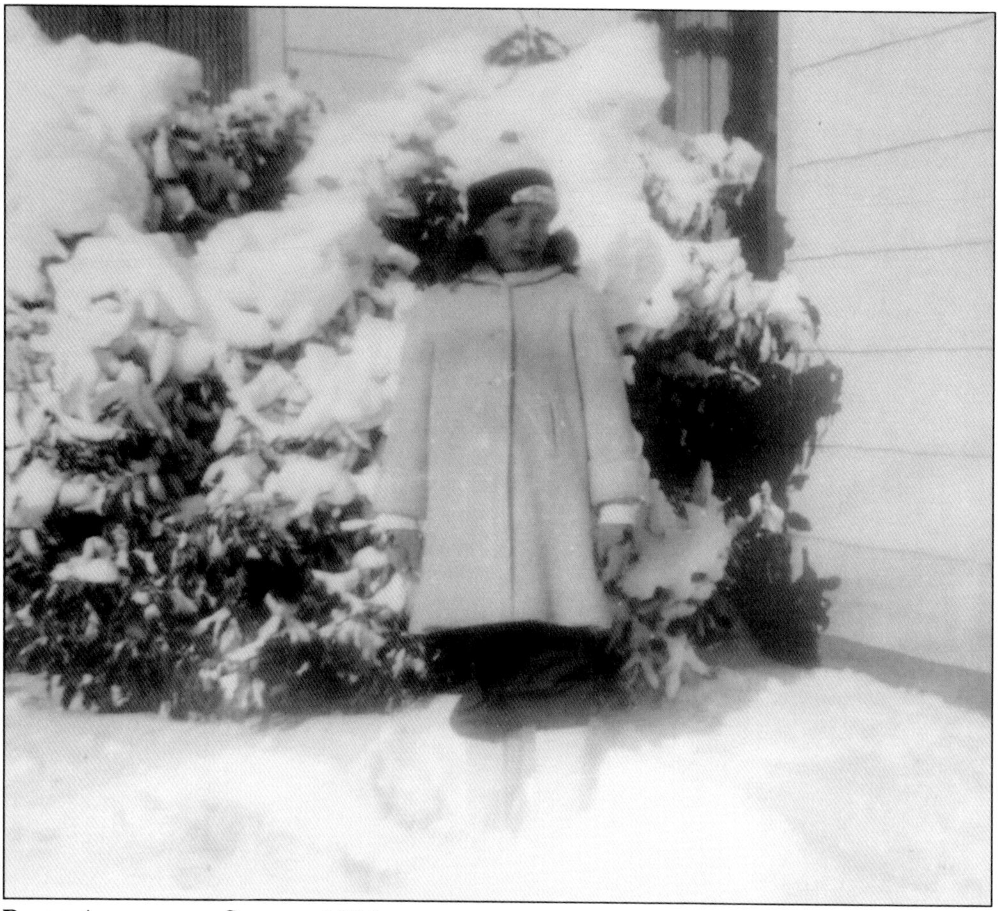

PENNY APPLE IN THE SNOW IN 1956.

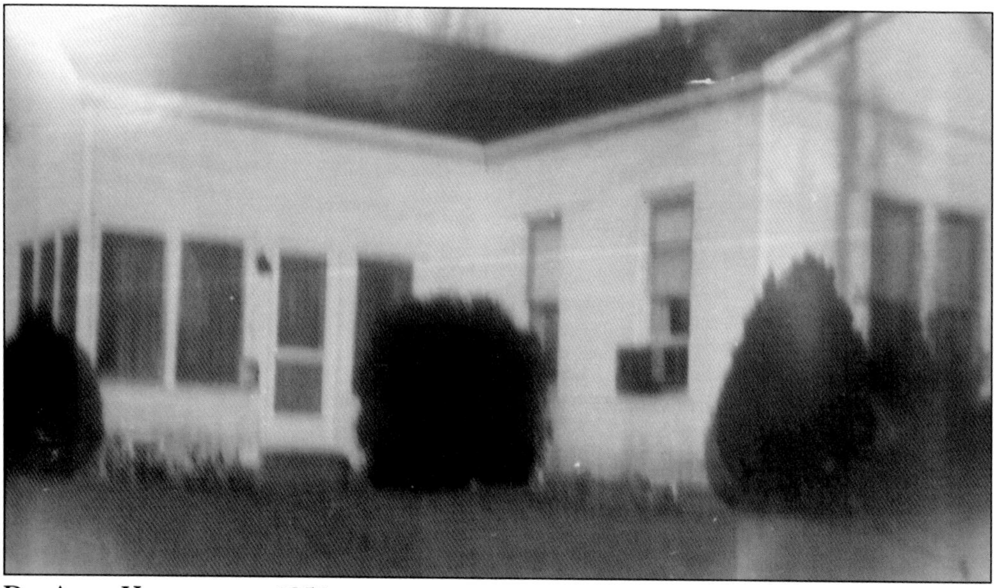

DR. APPLE HOUSE IN THE 1950S.

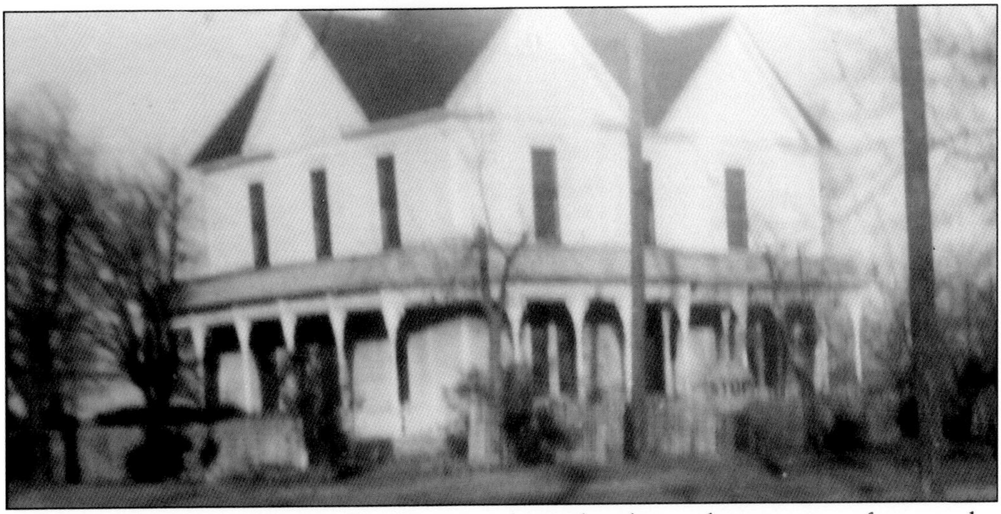

#27 Barnett Sisters' House. This house was located at the northwest corner of present-day Avenue G and 18th Street. Donna Barnett Carpenter and Captola "Cappie" Barnett lived in the house. Donna passed away first, and Cappie lived there until she passed away. The house has since been torn down.

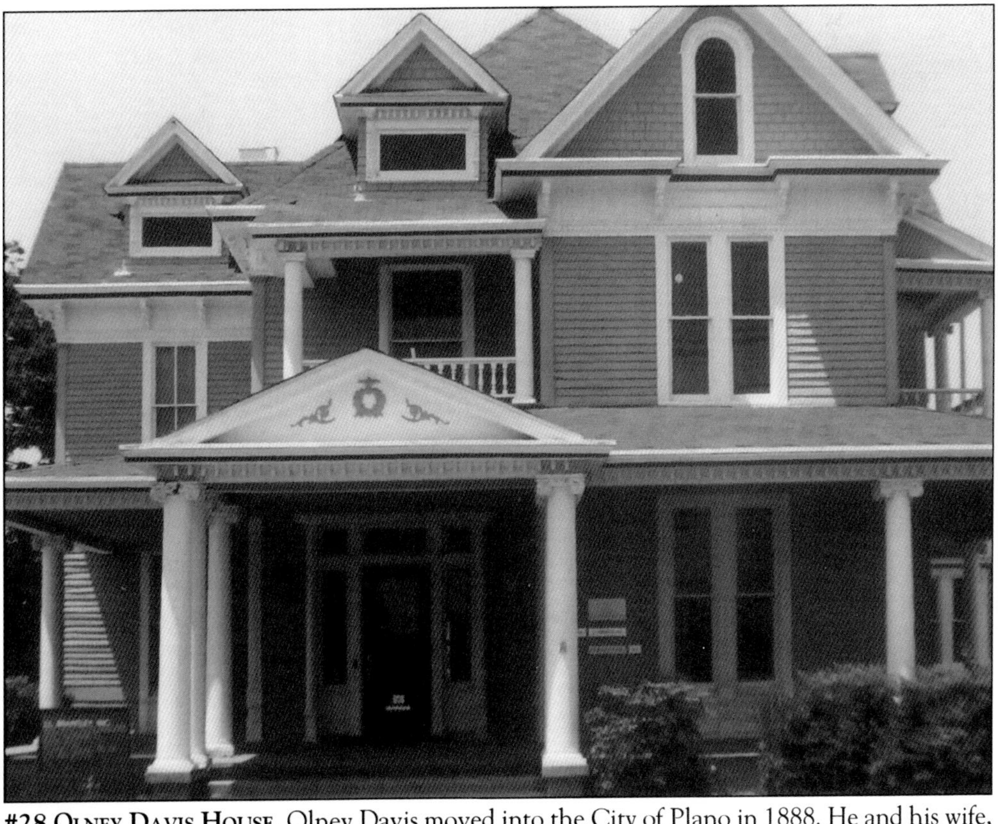

#28 Olney Davis House. Olney Davis moved into the City of Plano in 1888. He and his wife, Effie Susan, lived with their six children in this house. When the family lived in the house, they maintained the lot next door to the east of the house as their garden. (Courtesy of the Harrington Library.)

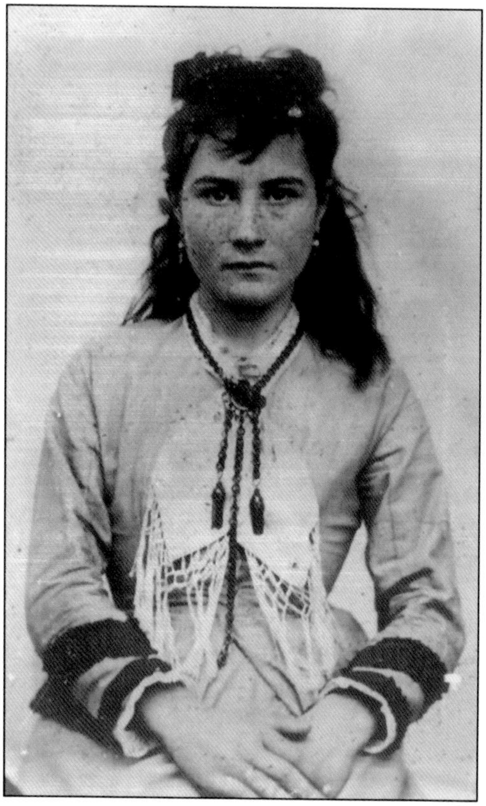

Effie Susan Mathews Davis. (Courtesy of the Frances Wells Collection.)

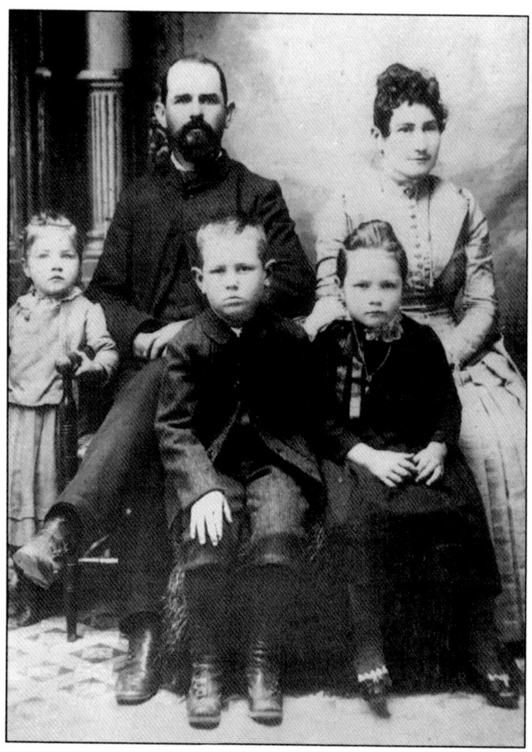

The Olney Davis Family. (Courtesy of the Frances Wells Collection.)

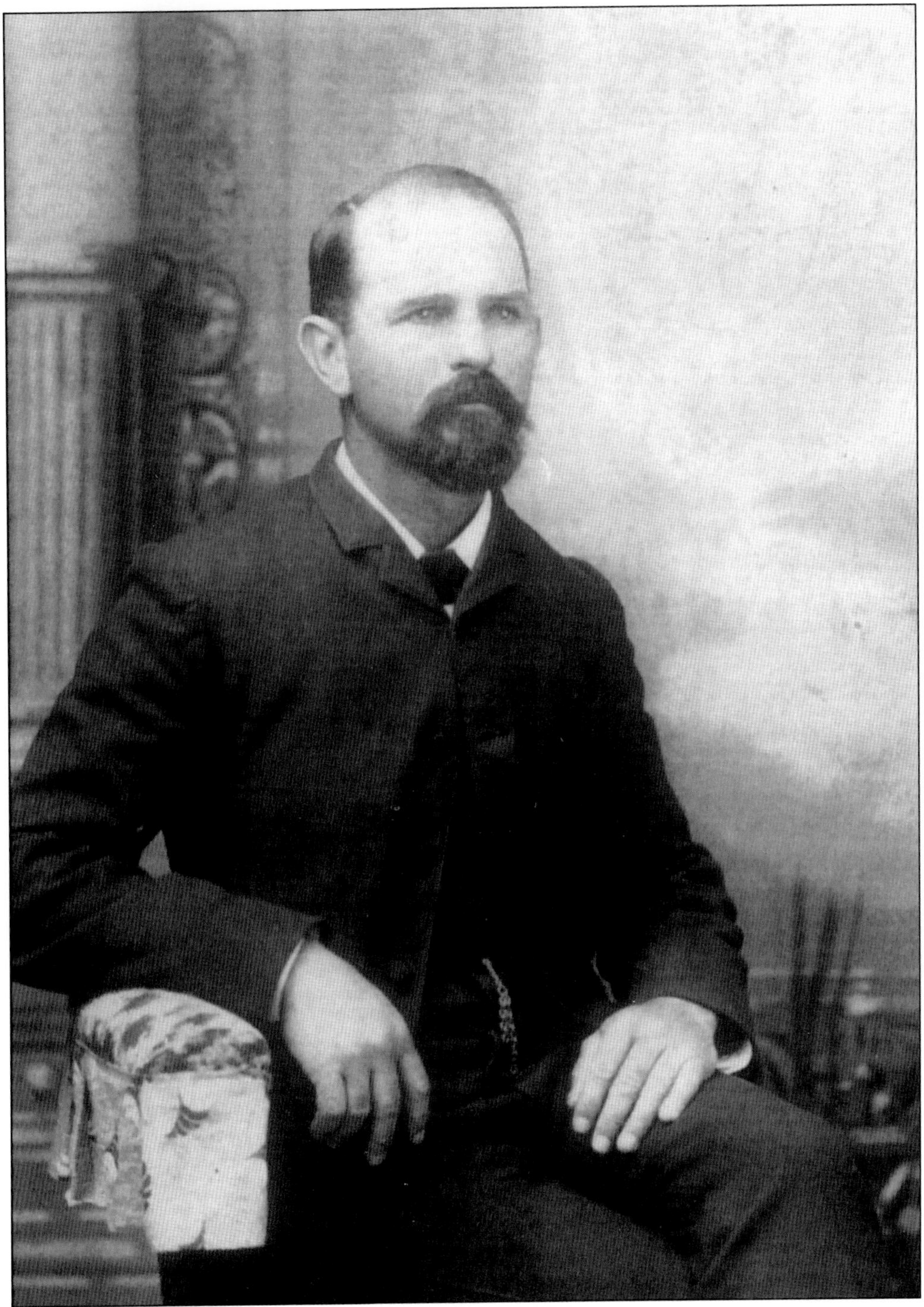

Olney Davis. Olney Davis served as vice president of Plano National Bank for several years. In 1900, he helped to organize the Farmers and Merchants National Bank of Plano and served as its president until his death in 1922. He also was a part owner and president of both the Farmers Gin Company and the Plano Lumber Company. The first Plano School Board of Education elected him as president.

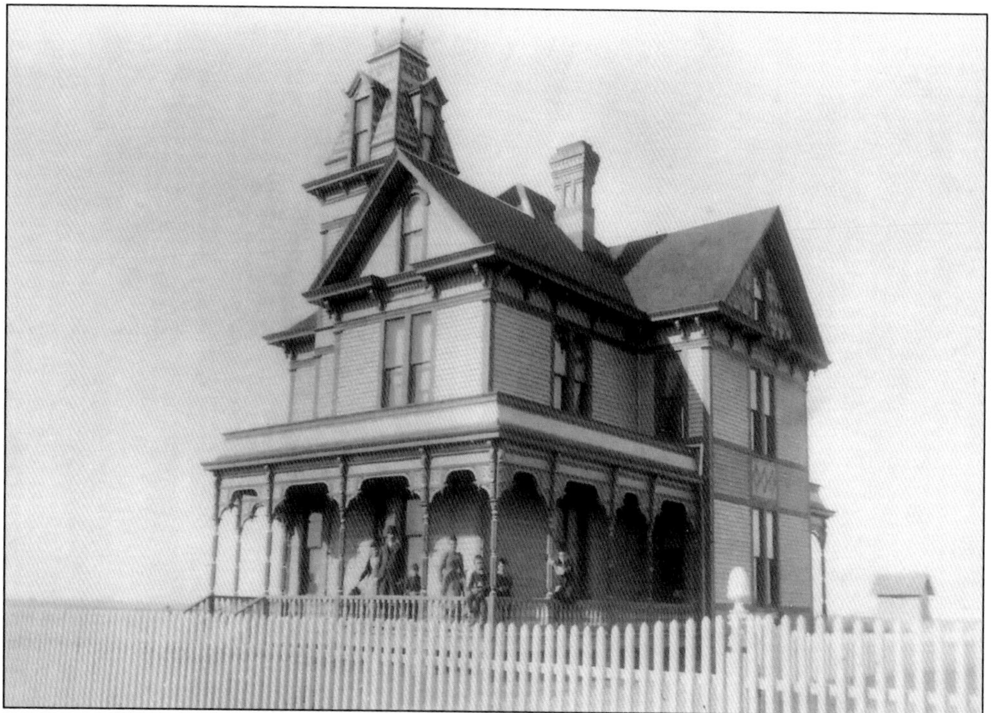

THE OLNEY DAVIS HOUSE BUILT IN 1890. The original appearance of the house was quite different than it is today. The house underwent remodeling sometime after this picture was taken. (Courtesy of the Frances Wells Collection.)

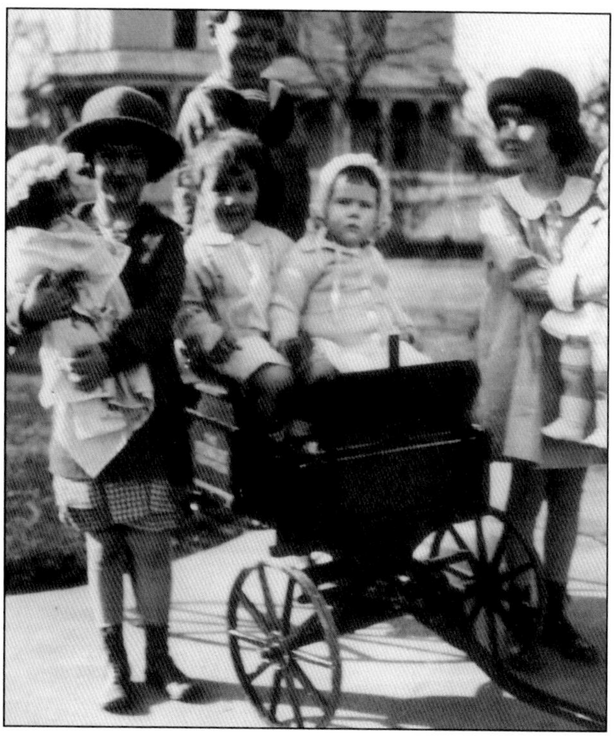

FROM LEFT TO RIGHT: HELEN MARGARET DAVIS, SUSAN BECKHAM, DAVIS THOMPSON (STANDING), DOROTHY DAVIS, AND MARY SUE THOMPSON IN FRONT OF THEIR GRANDPARENTS' HOUSE. When the Davis children grew up, three of them—Robert, Pauline, and Helen—lived on the same street. Some of the Davis grandchildren grew up living on the same street with each other and their grandparents.

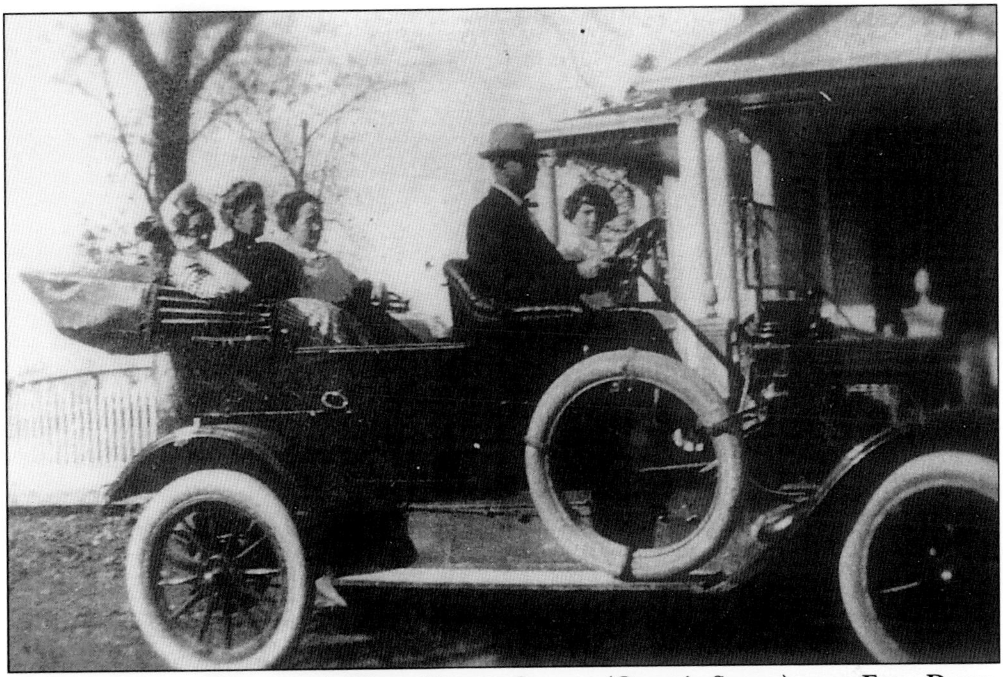

LEFT TO RIGHT: (BACK SEAT) HELEN DAVIS, QUINCY (OLNEY'S SISTER), AND EFFIE DAVIS; (FRONT SEAT) OLNEY DAVIS AND PAULINE DAVIS IN THEIR STANLEY STEAMER, 1910.

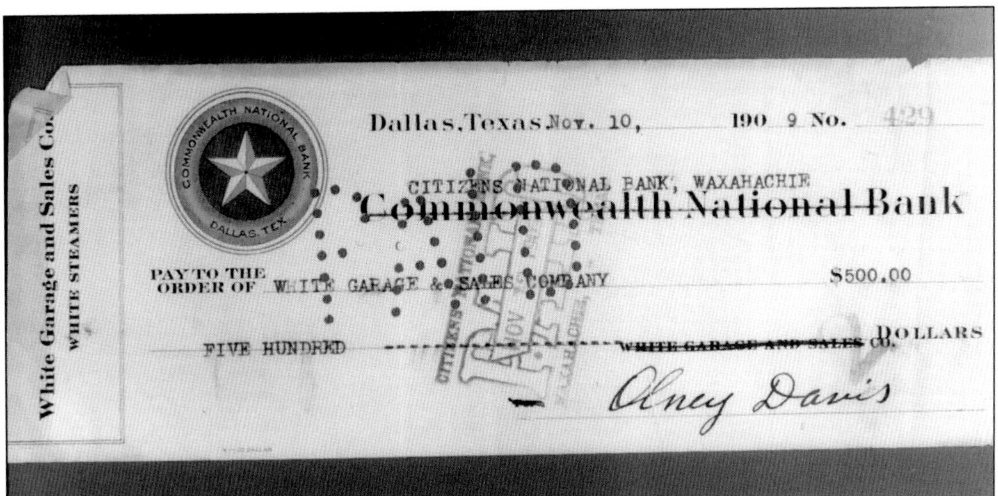

THE CHECK OLNEY DAVIS USED TO PURCHASE HIS STANLEY STEAMER. Olney Davis purchased his Stanley Steamer from the White Garage and Sales Company in 1909 for $500. This was one of the first cars in Plano.

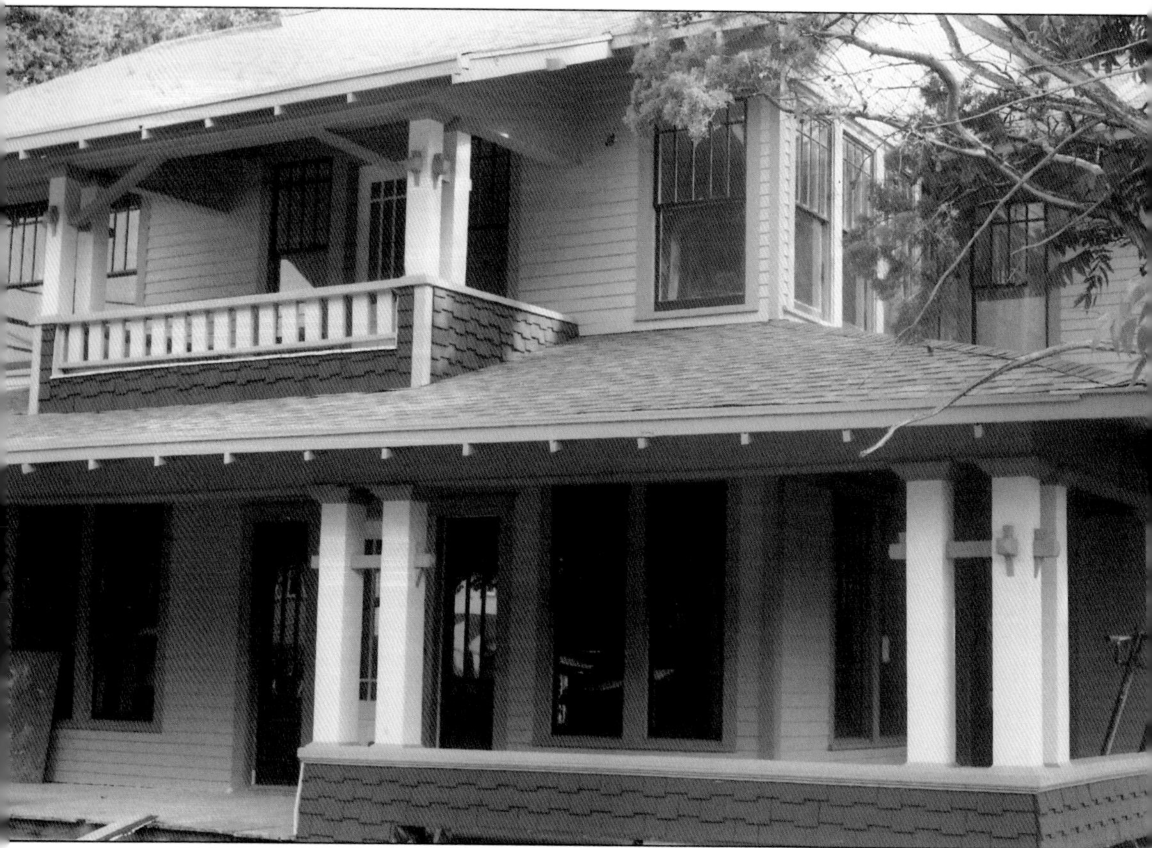

#29 Hughston House. Fred Schimelpfenig built this house around 1890 as rental property. Later, the house was purchased by Arch Hughston, and he lived there with his wife, Emma, and their six children. The original house style was Victorian. When the front section and porch were added, the front style became prairie, and the back section remained Victorian.

Around 1912, Emma Hughston and her baby were involved in one of early Plano's worst accidents. The family approached the train tracks a short distance to the east of their house in their touring car. The train did not sound its alert whistle, and Emma and the baby were thrown out of the car. The baby was killed instantly. Emma was thrown against the train and was dragged from 18th Street past the Interurban Station.

Arch Hughston was left alone to care for the remaining five children. At a cousin's suggestion, he contacted Emma's sister, Ollie, who was divorced and caring for her two children alone. The two married and lived in this house with their children. (Photography by Adam Towber.)

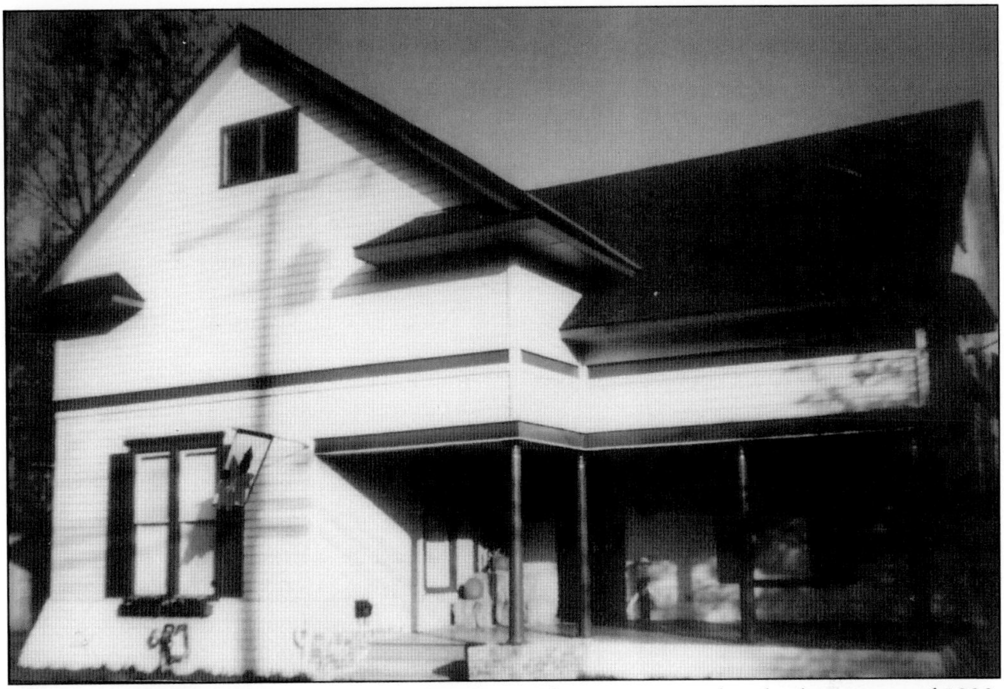

#30 Thompson House. Francis and Pauline Davis Thompson moved to this house around 1920. They had lived across the street before moving here. Pauline's father, Olney Davis, bought this house for the couple. At one time, her brother, Robert, and sister, Helen, also lived on the street. Pauline was the valedictorian of the Plano Class of 1914.

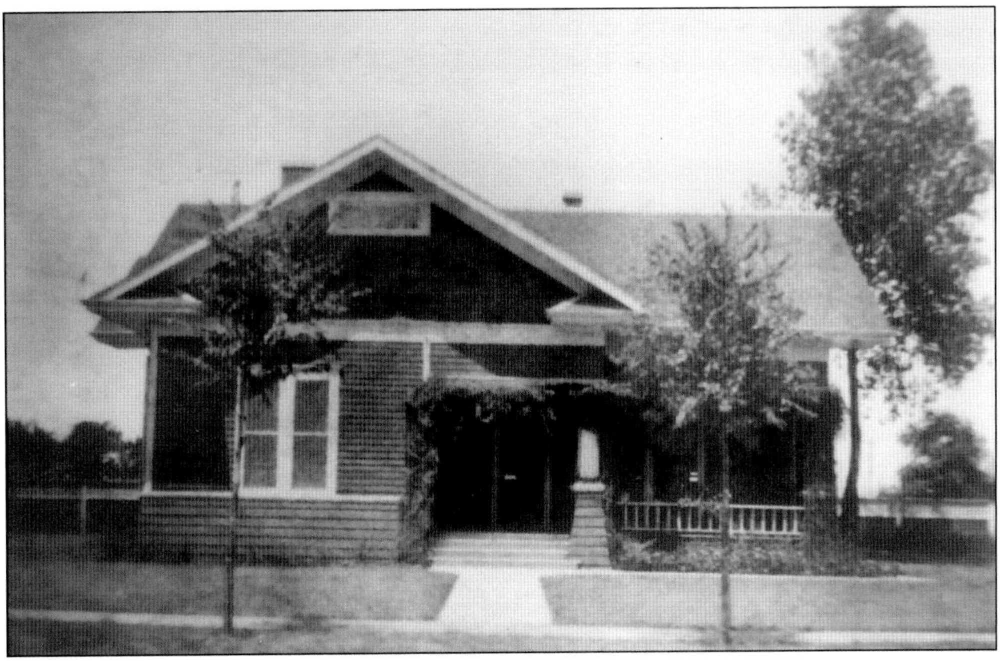

Thompson House, c. 1920.

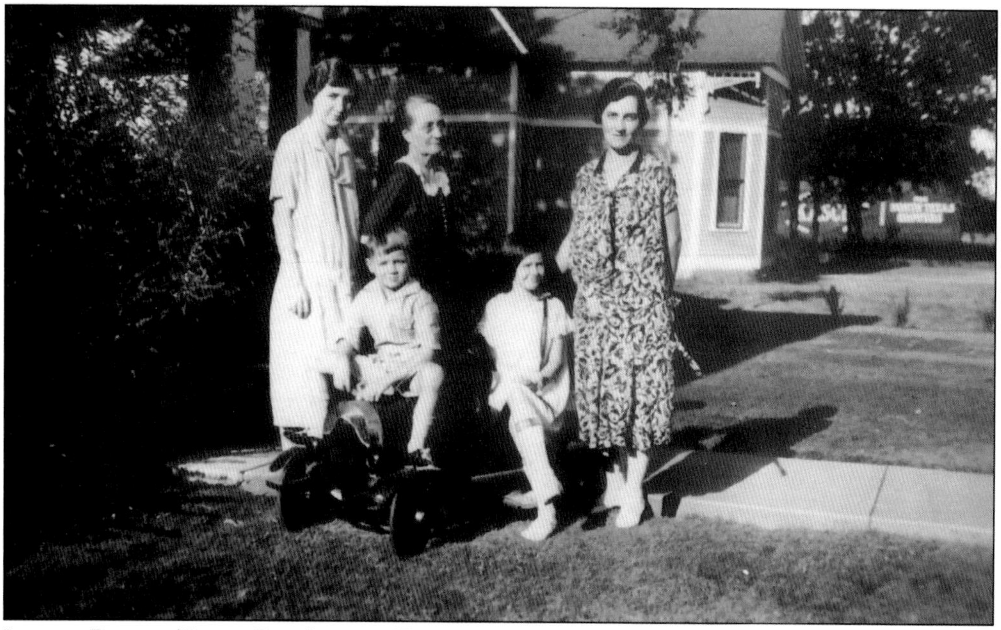

LEFT TO RIGHT: (FRONT ROW) DAVIS THOMPSON, MARY SUE THOMPSON; (BACK ROW) PAULINE DAVIS THOMPSON, EFFIE DAVIS, AND EDNA DAVIS HOUSTON. Helen's (Pauline's sister) house next door is visible in the background of this photograph.

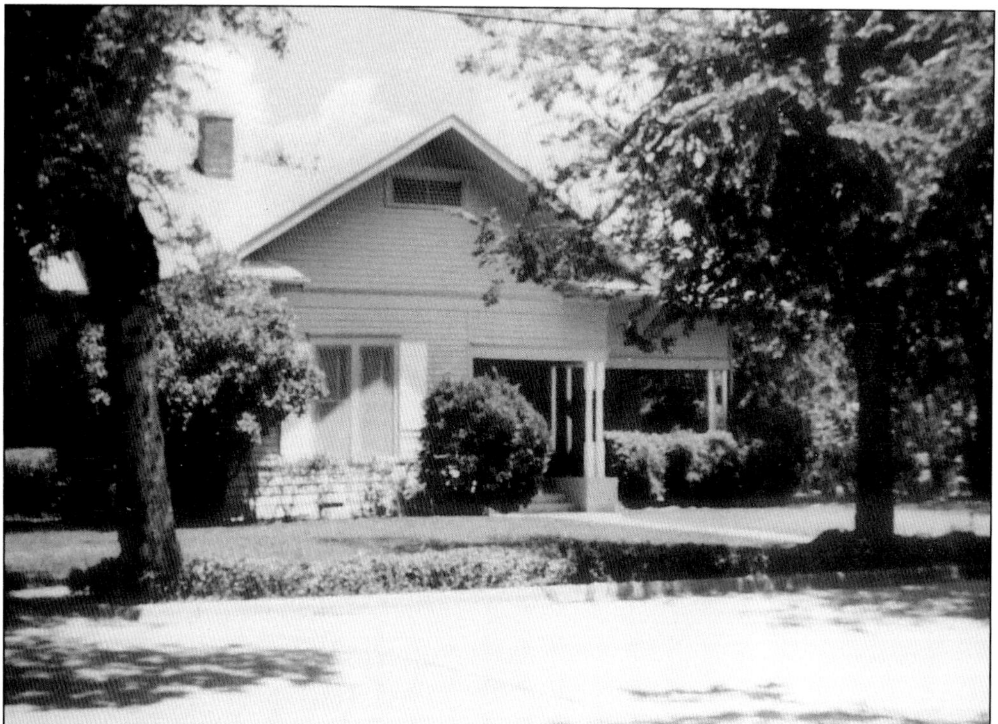

THE THOMPSON HOUSE, YEAR UNKNOWN. Fred Schimelpfenig built this house and three other houses on the block as rental property in the 1890s. Records indicate that Fred Schimelpfenig's unmarried daughter, Lydia Mary, was the owner at one time.

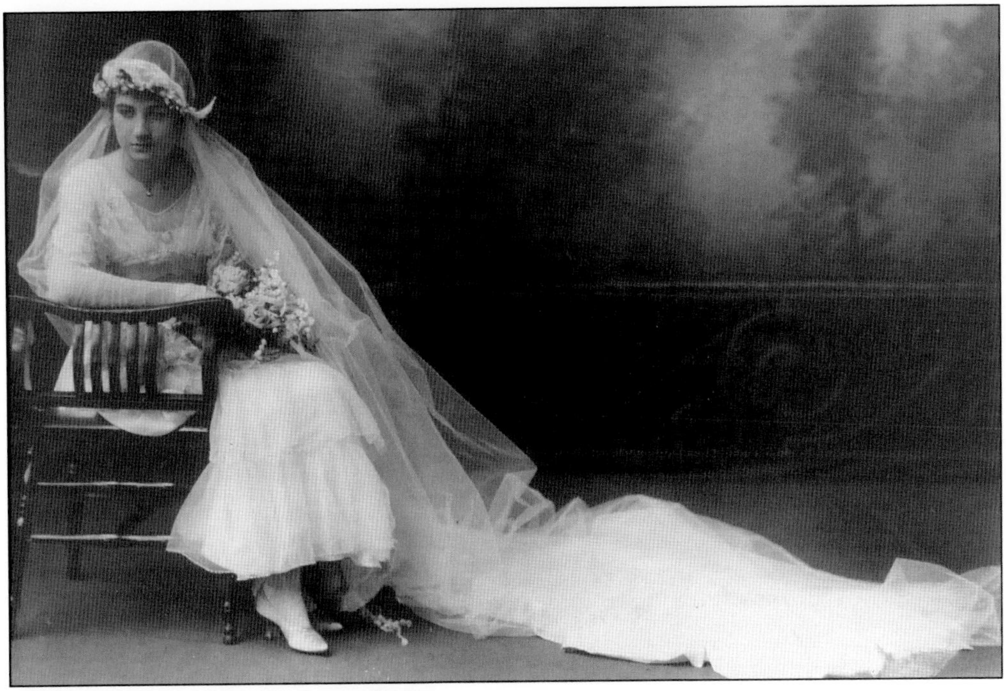

PAULINE DAVIS IN HER WEDDING GOWN.

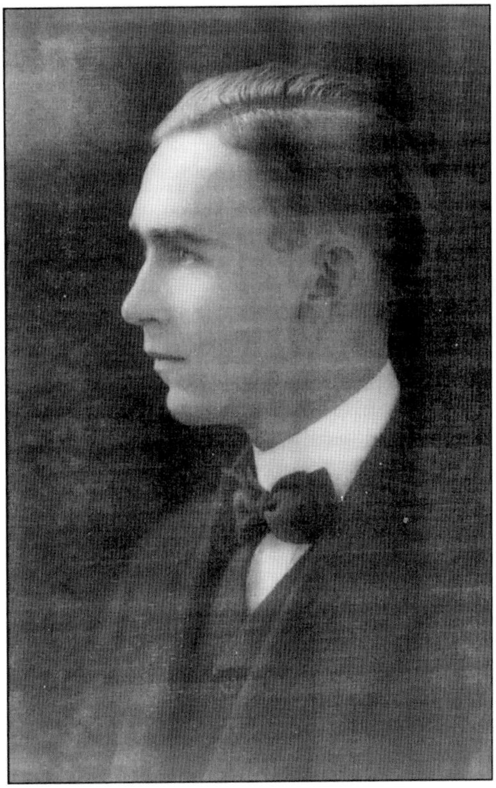

FRANCIS THOMPSON.

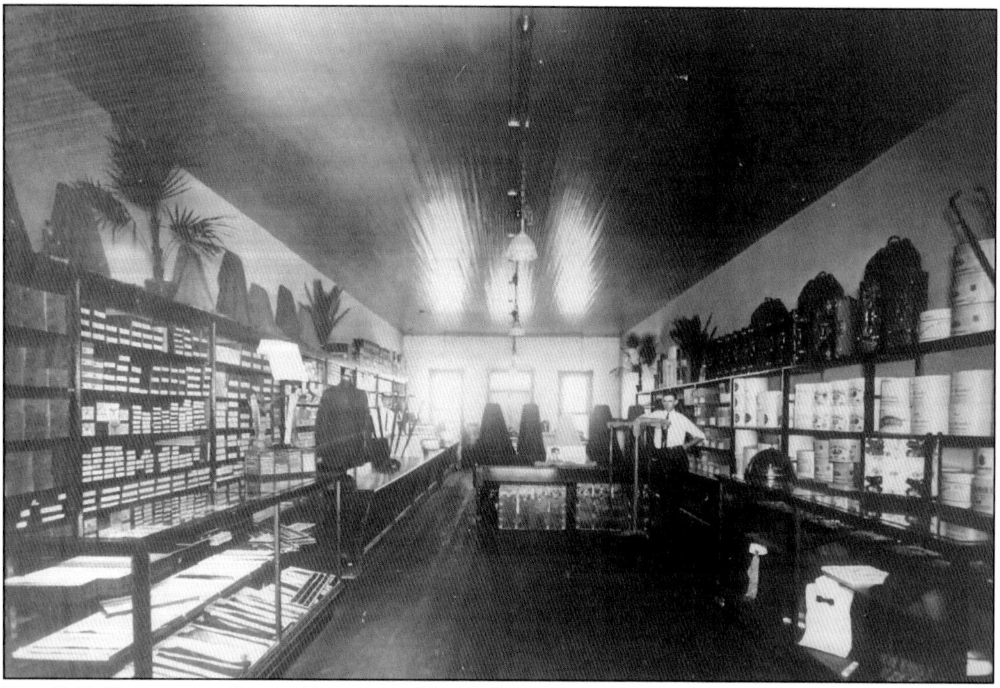

The J.G. Thompson Store. Francis and his father, J.G. Thompson, ran the family store. Their slogan was "value first." The store was known for the gentlemen's clothing sold there.

The couple had three children, Mary Sue, Davis, and F.H. ("Jimmy") Thompson.

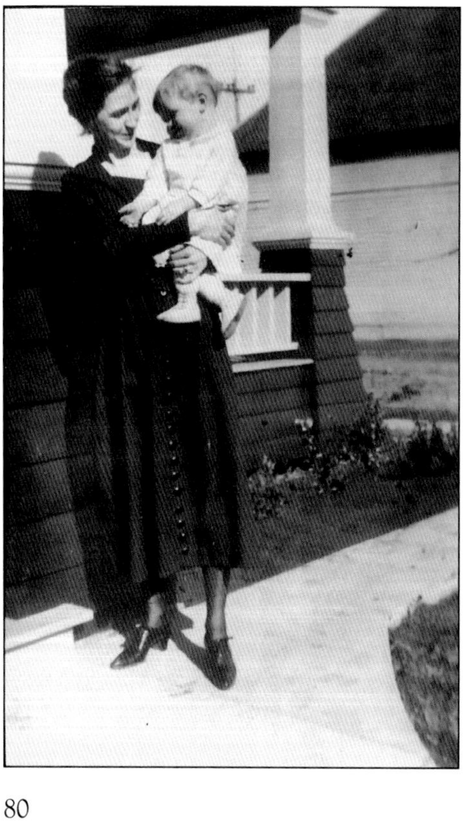

Pauline and Davis Thompson.

Mary Sue Thompson. Mary Sue was the couple's oldest child. Her Aunt Helen lived next door to the east of the Thompson's house. In this picture of Mary Sue, her Aunt Helen's house can be seen in the background.

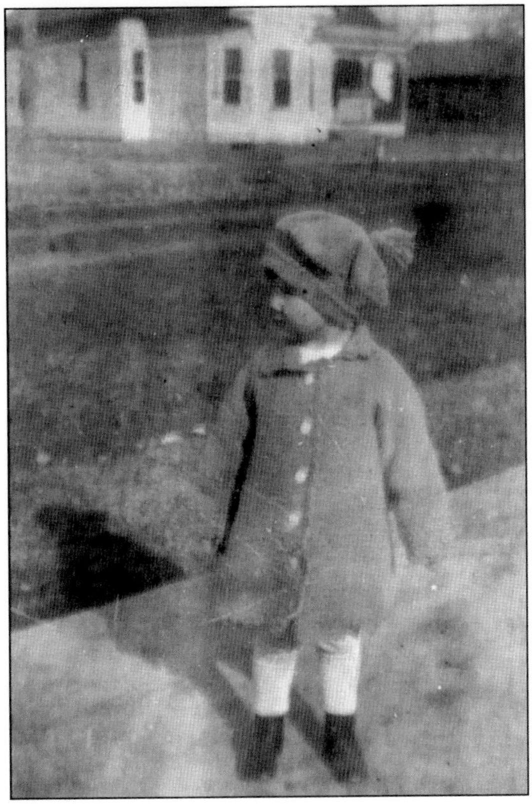

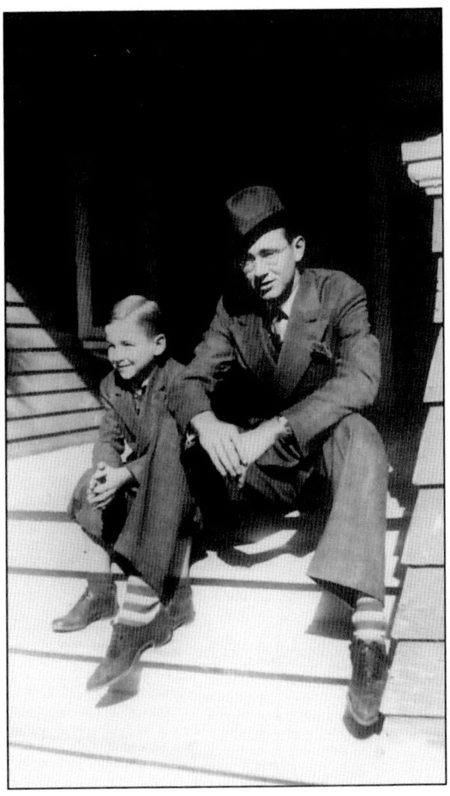

Jimmy With His Older Brother, Davis Thompson, on the Front Porch of the House.

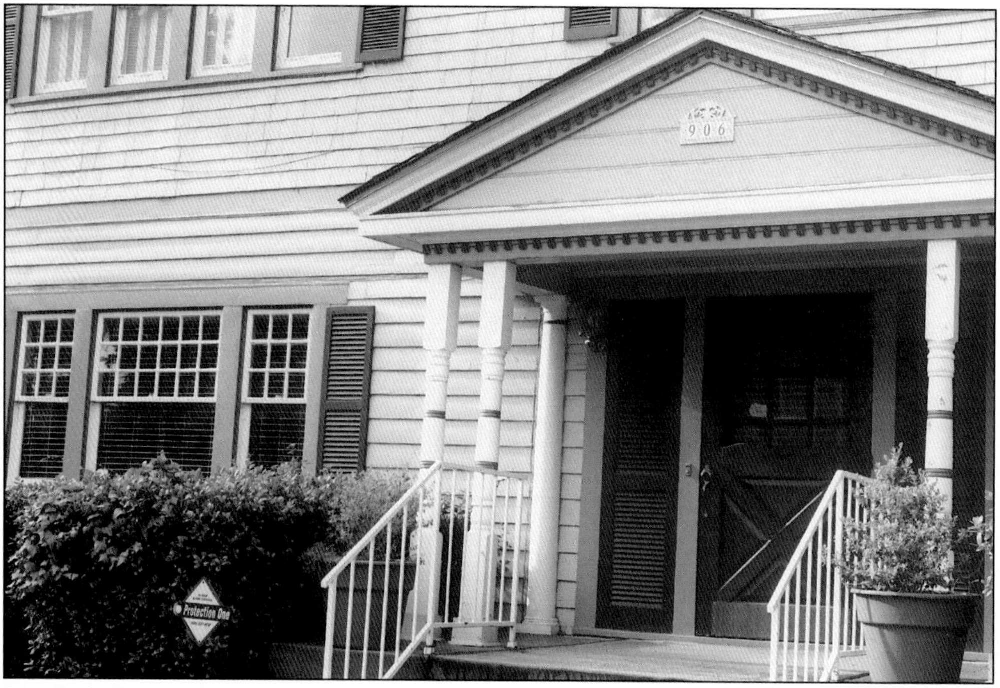

#31 R.A. DAVIS HOUSE. Robert A. Davis and his family lived in this house. Robert's parents, Olney and Effie Davis, lived across the street. (Photography by Adam Towber.)

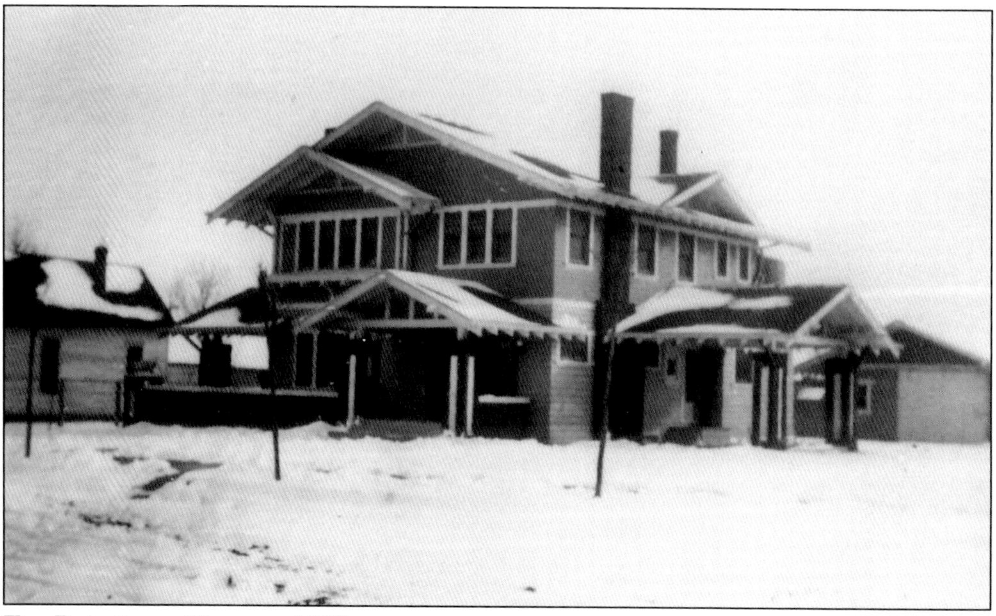

THE R.A. DAVIS HOUSE IN 1917.

R.A. Davis While a Student at Texas A&M University. Robert A. Davis attended Texas A&M University and then went to work as cashier at the Farmers State Bank where his father was president. When his father passed away, Robert became president of the bank.

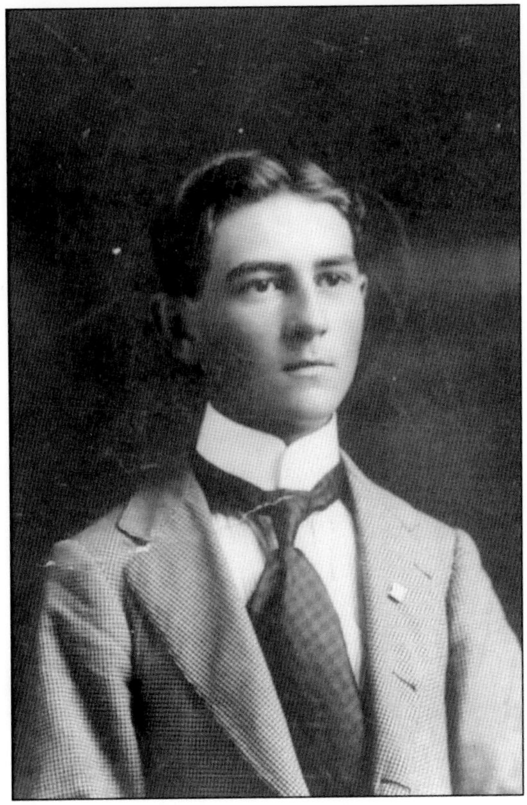

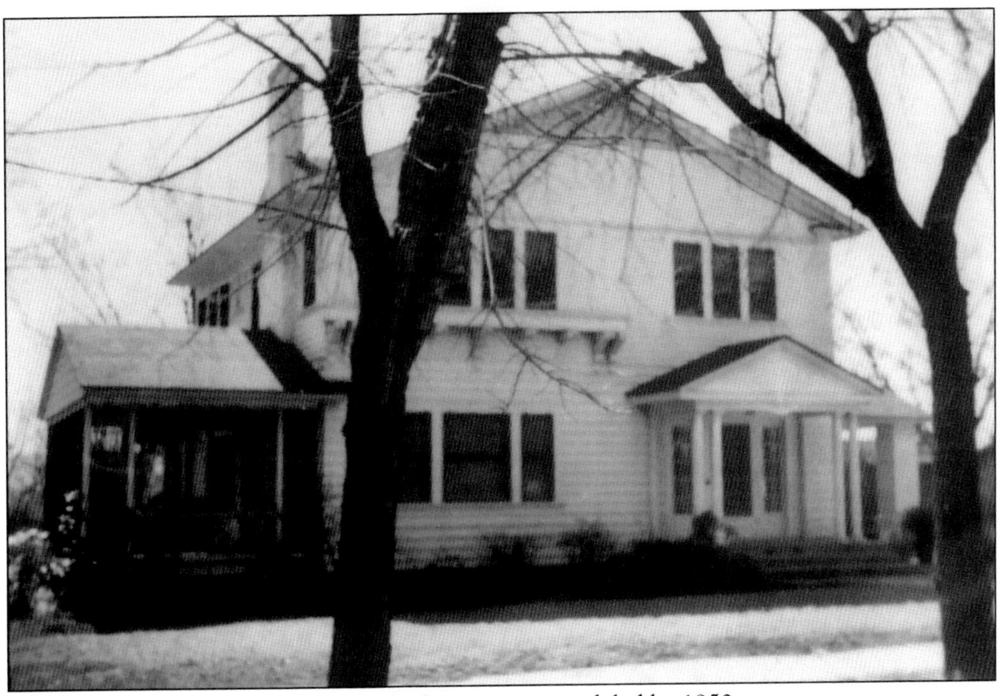

The R.A. Davis House in 1950. The house was remodeled by 1950.

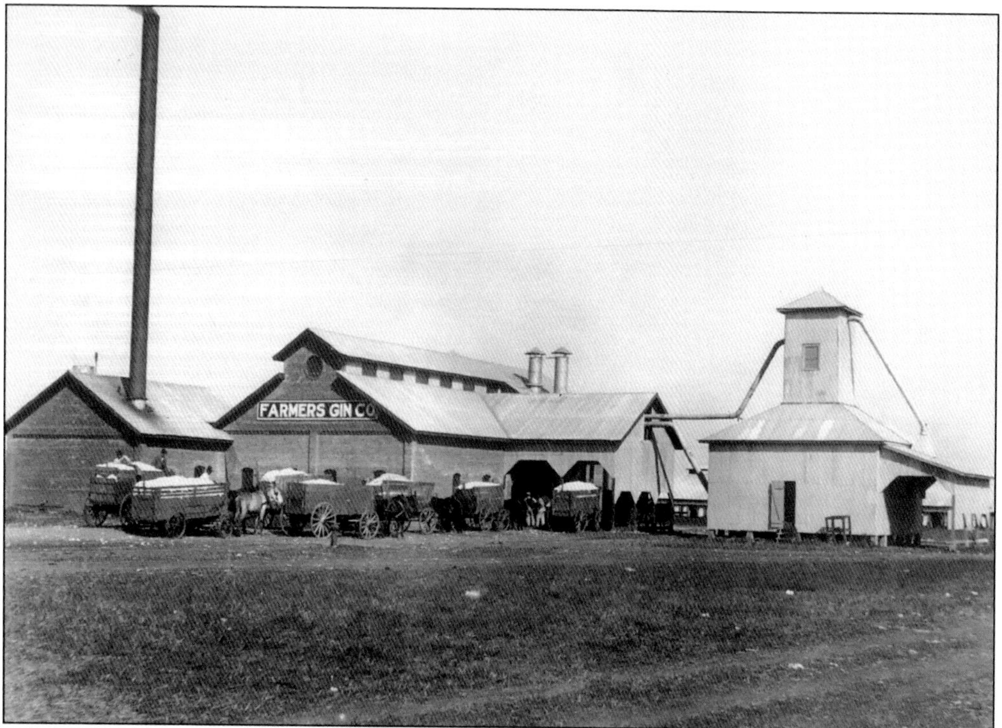

The Farmers Gin Company. Robert A. Davis, his father, Olney Davis, and others were part owners of the Farmers Gin Company.

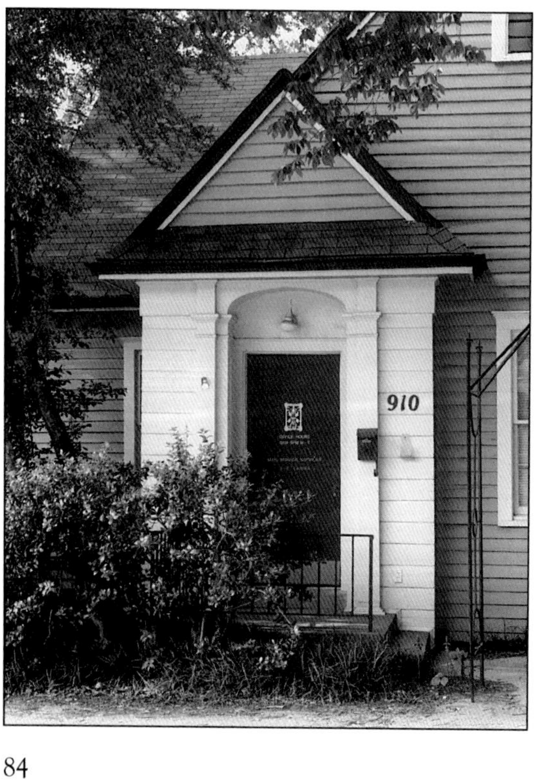

#32 Oliver Hughston House. Oliver Hughston was the son of Arch Hughston, who lived across the street. Oliver operated a grain business with his father. (Photography by Adam Towber.)

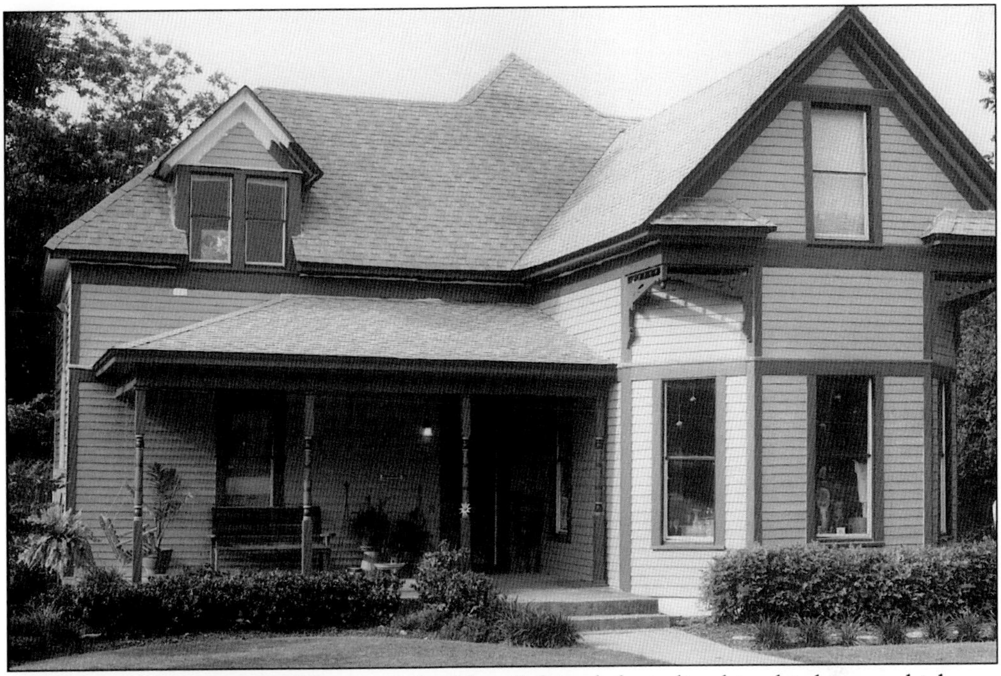

#33 Mary Schimelpfenig House. Lydia Mary Schimelpfenig lived in this house, which was next door to her father, Fred, for a short time. She passed away in her thirties after suffering from a skin affliction. (Photography by Adam Towber.)

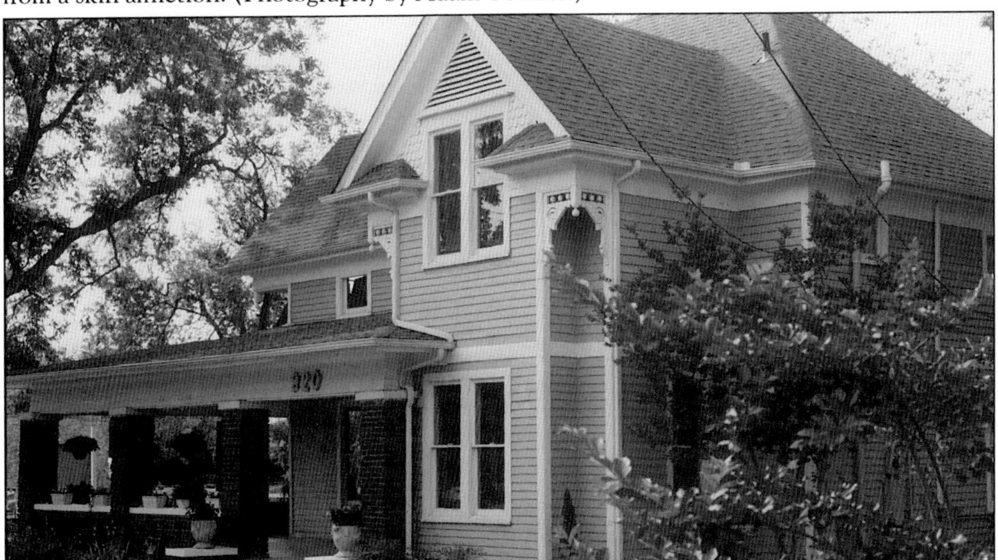

#34 Fred Schimelpfenig House. Fred Schimelpfenig moved to this house after his wife, L.E.R., passed away. He owned several rental properties on this street and around town. He was the manager of the G.W. Owens Lumber Company for 18 years and went on to become manager of the J.T. Elliott Lumber Company. He served as mayor from 1902 to 1908, and played a large role in the construction of water mains in the city. (Photography by Adam Towber.)

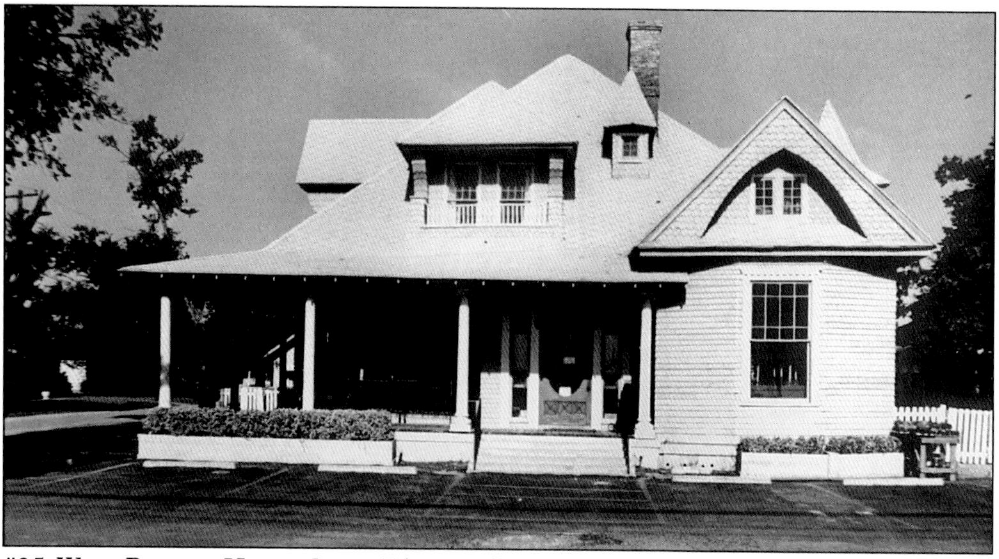

#35 Wall-Robbins House. James Edgar Wall built this house in 1898. The Jellison family owned the home from November 1907 until December 1908. Cattle dealer Jeff Robbins bought the house in 1908, and the house remained in the Robbins family until the 1960s. While the Robbins owned the house, part of the upper story was used as a room for one of the hired hands. (Courtesy of the Gladys Harrington Library.)

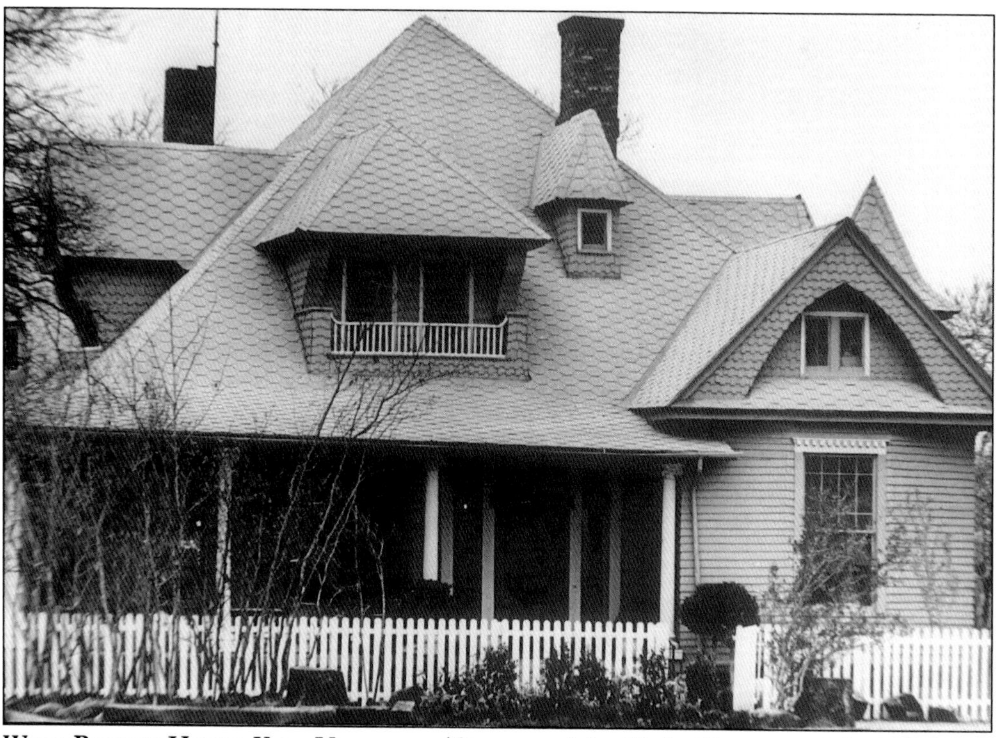

Wall-Robbins House, Year Unknown. (Courtesy of the Gladys Harrington Library.)

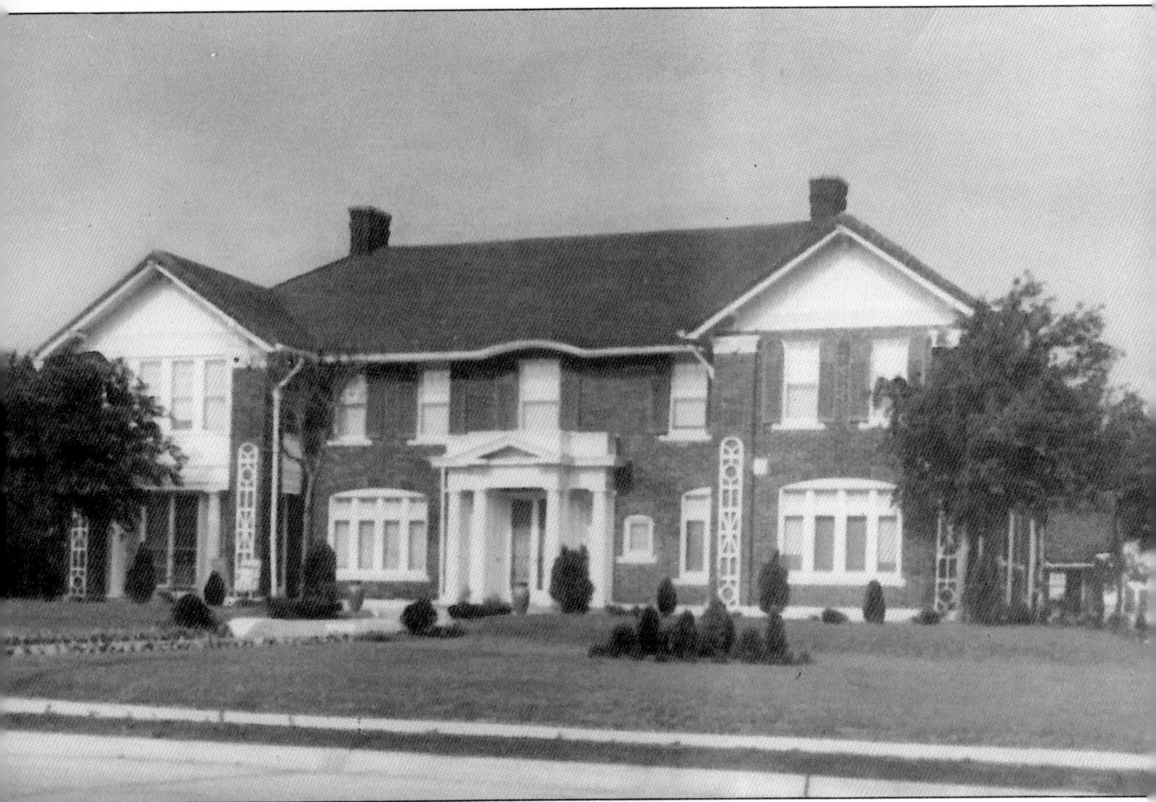

#36 Sandifer-Wyatt House in the 1930s. R.W. Sandifer built this house around 1913. It is located on present-day Avenue K at the corner of 18th Street. Sandifer, along with several partners, owned R.W. Sandifer Dry Goods. The Sandifers lived in the house until 1935, when Sandifer and his wife, Paralee, worked out a house trade with Dr. S.B. Wyatt. The trade included the Wyatt's house located on present-day 16th Street and the Wyatt Hatchery.

When the Wyatts purchased the house, it contained beautiful Canadian Mahogany paneling, a basement, and a rare three-car garage to which the family added servants' quarters. The Wyatt's daughter, Peggy, used the servants' quarters as a dollhouse. The green shutters contrasted beautifully against the red brick, and the Wyatts took great pride in the landscaping. The roof shingles were layered to give a unique thatched look.

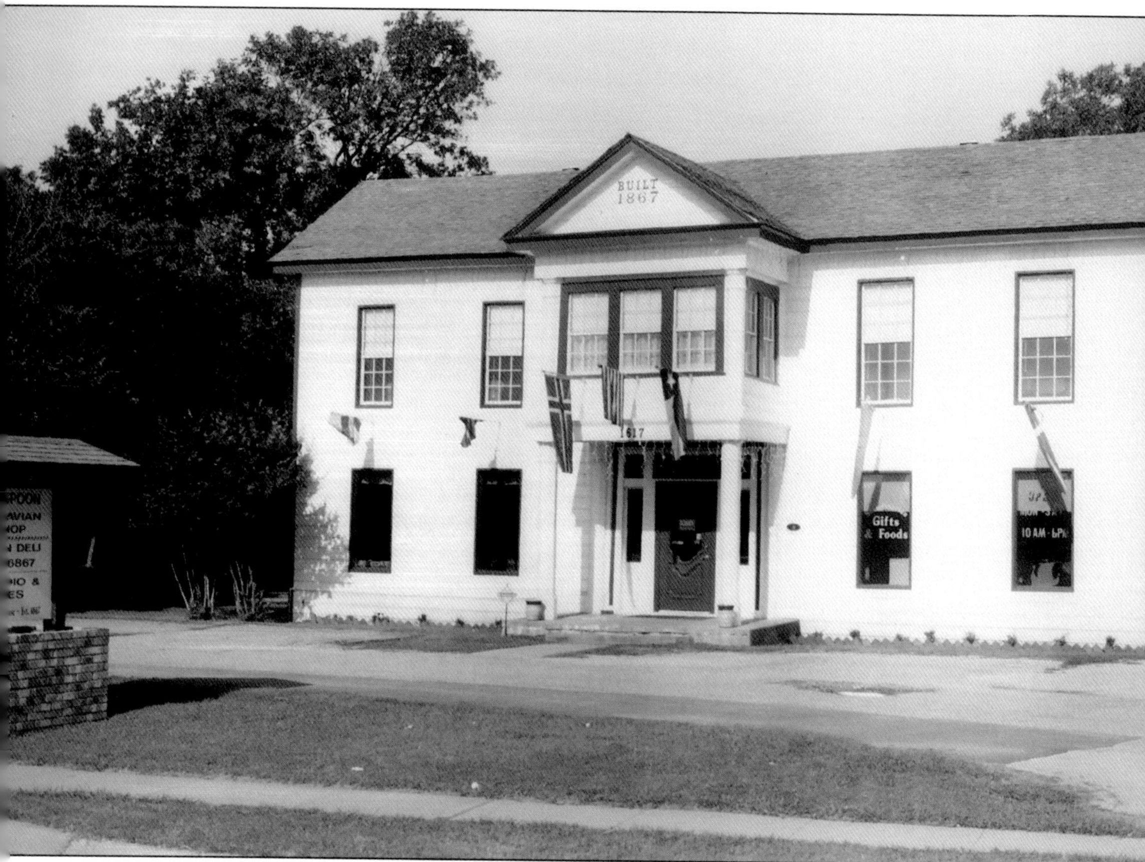

#37 Forman House. In 1867, Joe Forman and his wife, Elizabeth, built this house on the 2,000 acres they owned. It is believed that the original house faced south and consisted of a 20 by 20 two-story wood-framed house. Apparently, the first addition to the house was a 20 by 20 addition to the south end of the house. A small porch was added to the north end of the house as an entrance to the kitchen. There were two buildings behind the main house—a barn to the west and a milk house to the north on what is now 18th Street.

Along with farming, the Formans also built a distillery, a cooperage, a sawmill, and a gristmill, which were located on a small stream near the present-day Plano Mutual Cemetery. They dammed up the stream to provide water for the mills and cooperage. The Forman family changed the economy of Plano from a barter system to a cash system with their businesses.

JOE FORMAN. In 1851, Joseph Forman applied for permission to establish an official post office in this home. He served as Plano's first postmaster. It was during this process that Mr. Forman, with the help of Dr. Henry Dye, named the city Plano.

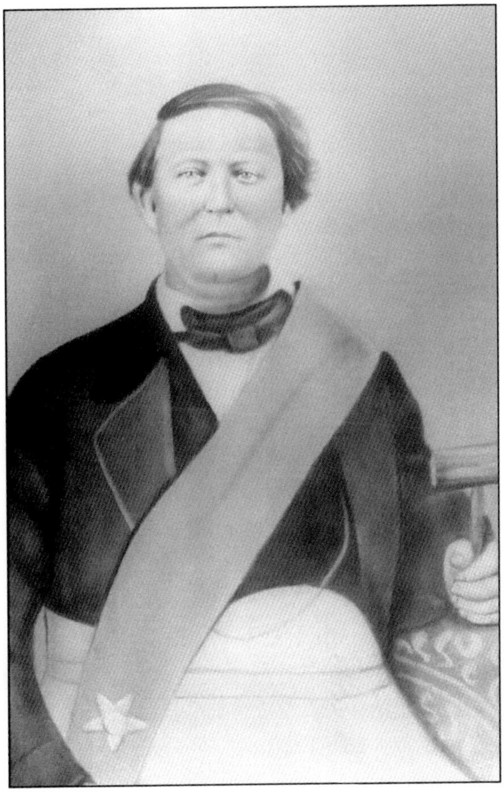

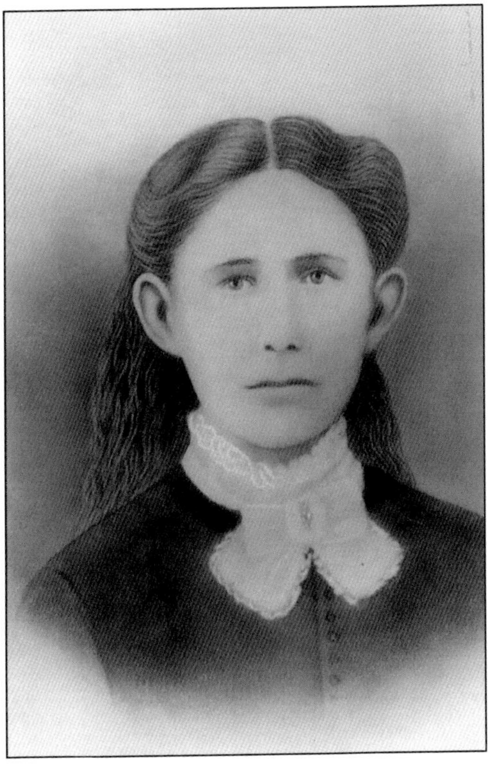

ELIZABETH FORMAN. These pictures of Joe and Elizabeth Forman were found hanging inside of a wall when some remodeling was done by recent owners of the house.

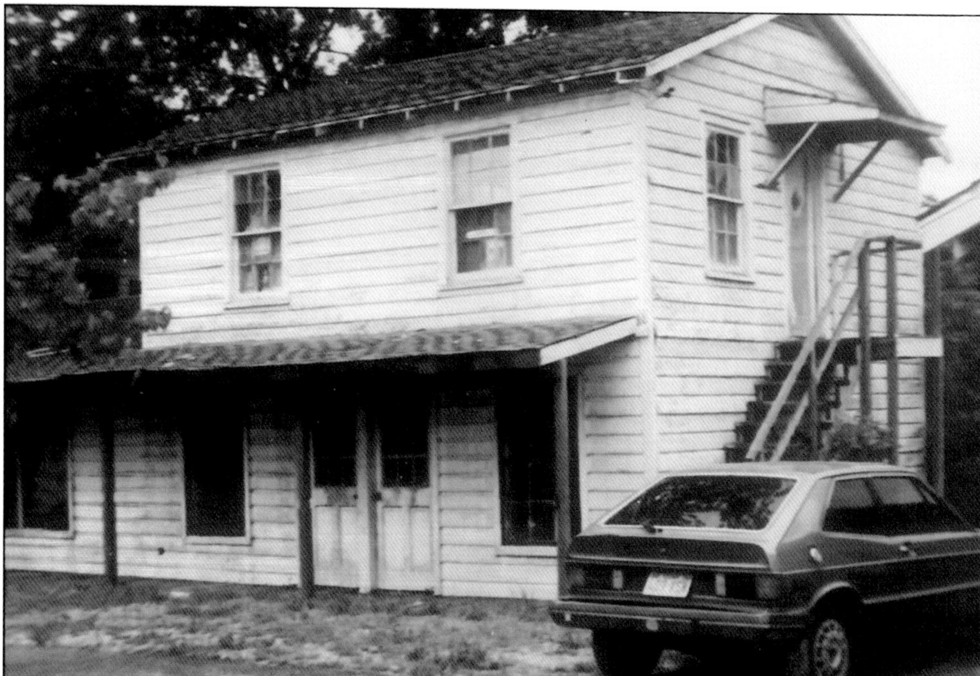

Building Behind the House. In the 1940s, the building behind the house replaced the original large barn. Additions were later made to each end of this building.

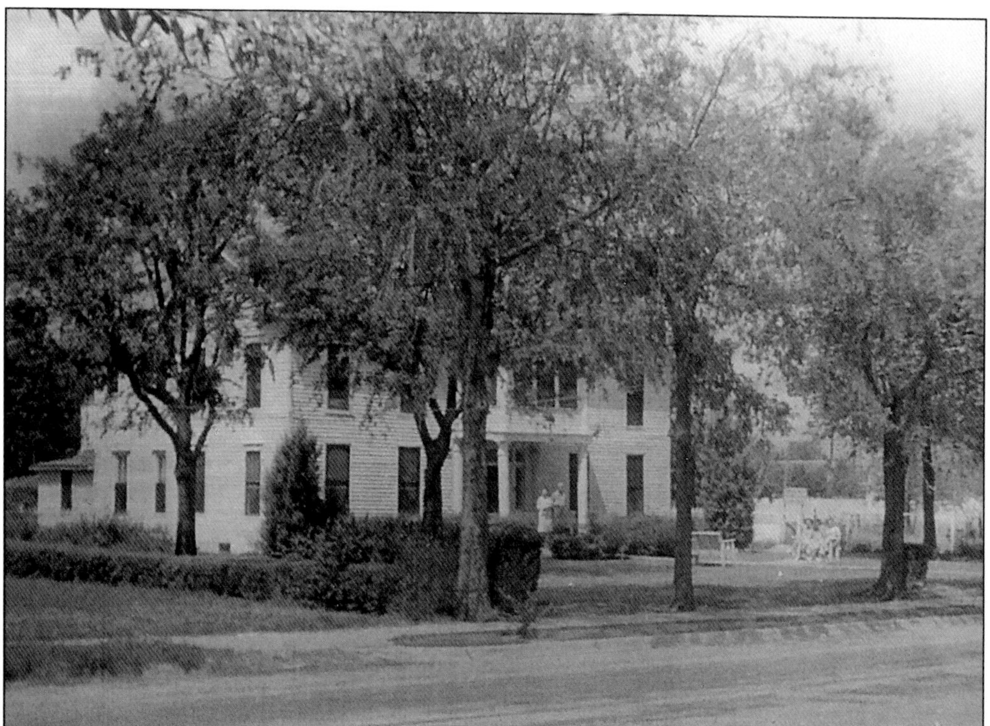

The Forman House in 1930s.

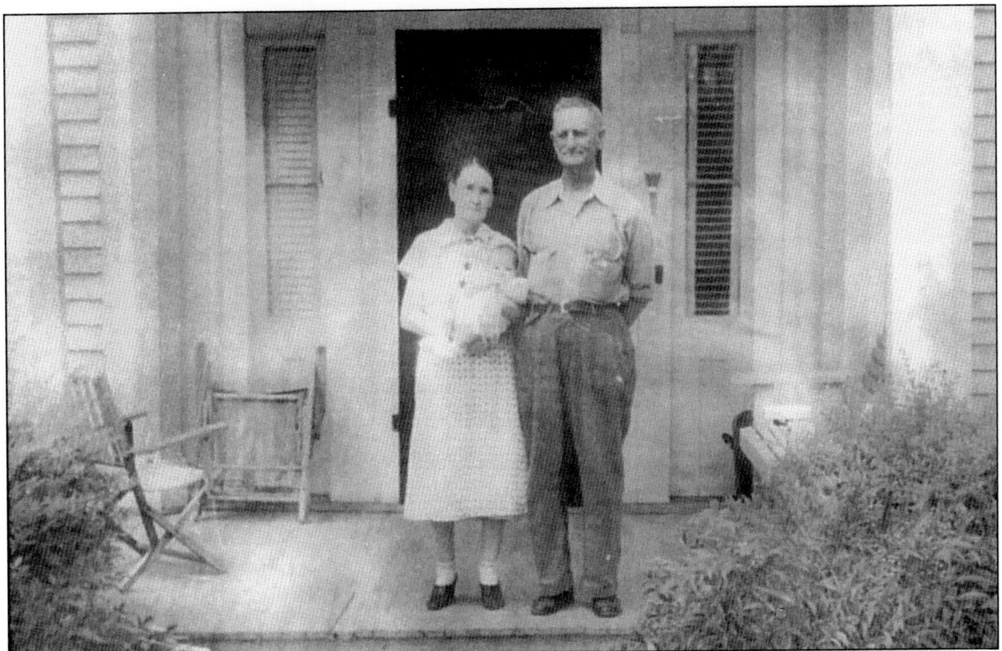

LEFT TO RIGHT: GENOA FORMAN AND MERONEY FORMAN, 1930s. In the 1950s, the house and the building behind it were turned into the Forman Apartment House. It was Plano's only apartment complex at the time, and it was the place where couples who married and did not own a home would live. The house stayed in the Forman family until 1971. It is currently a Scandinavian Shop and Cultural Center owned and renovated by Gwen and Jim Workman.

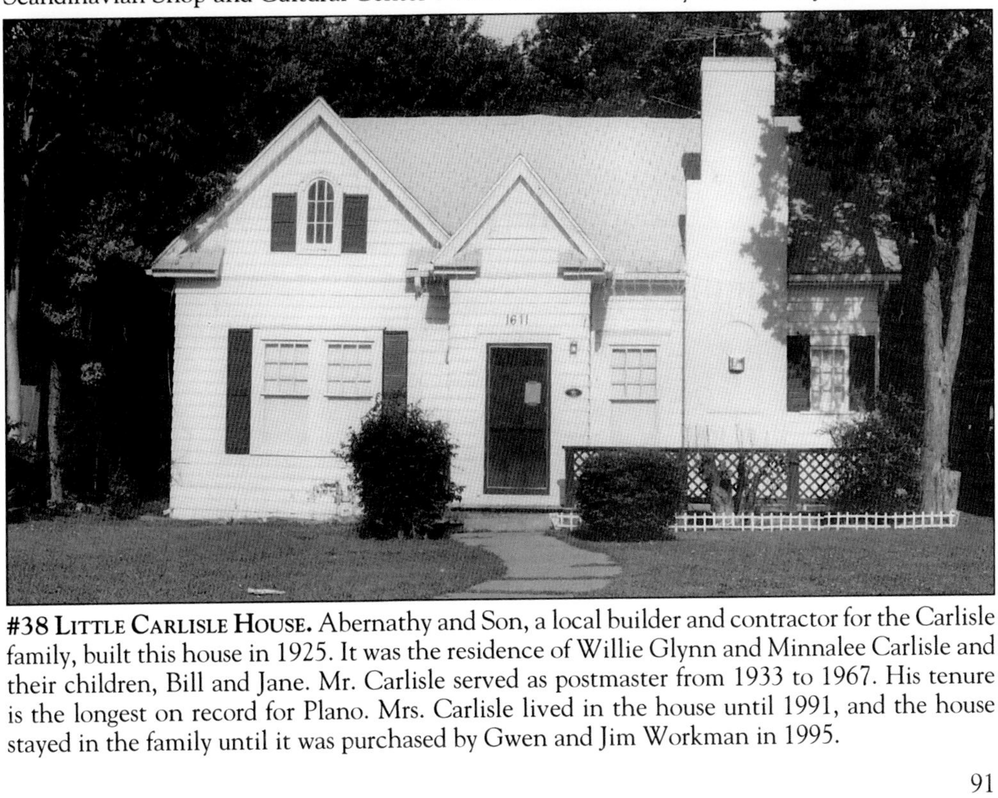

#38 LITTLE CARLISLE HOUSE. Abernathy and Son, a local builder and contractor for the Carlisle family, built this house in 1925. It was the residence of Willie Glynn and Minnalee Carlisle and their children, Bill and Jane. Mr. Carlisle served as postmaster from 1933 to 1967. His tenure is the longest on record for Plano. Mrs. Carlisle lived in the house until 1991, and the house stayed in the family until it was purchased by Gwen and Jim Workman in 1995.

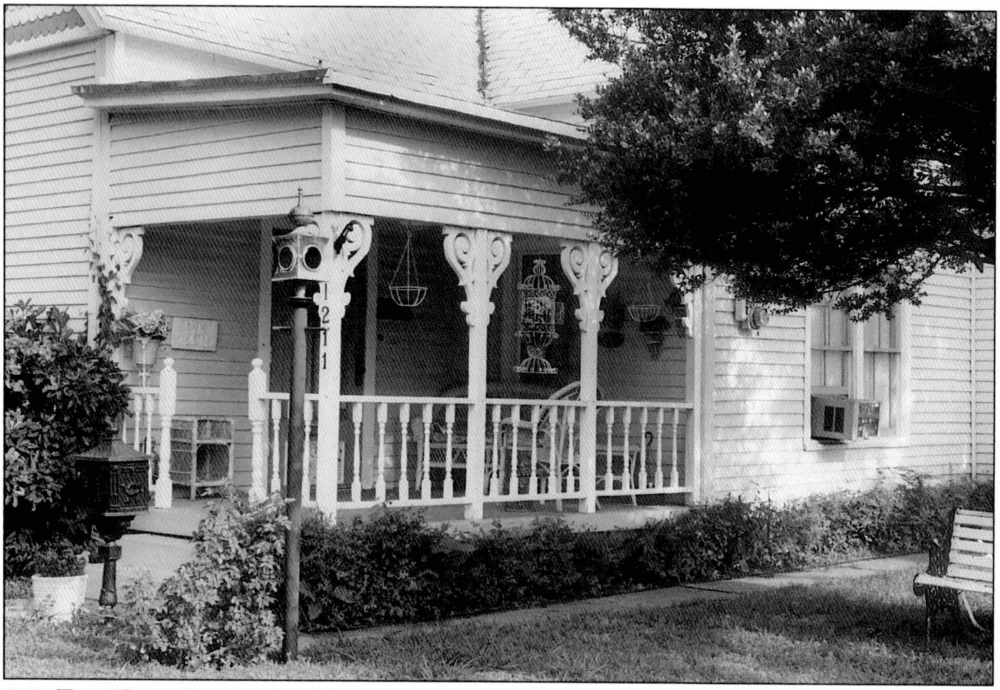

#39 THE HOOD HOUSE. Dr. Thomas L. Hood built this house for his mother, Martha Ann. Members of the Hood family have lived in the house throughout the years. (Photography by Adam Towber.)

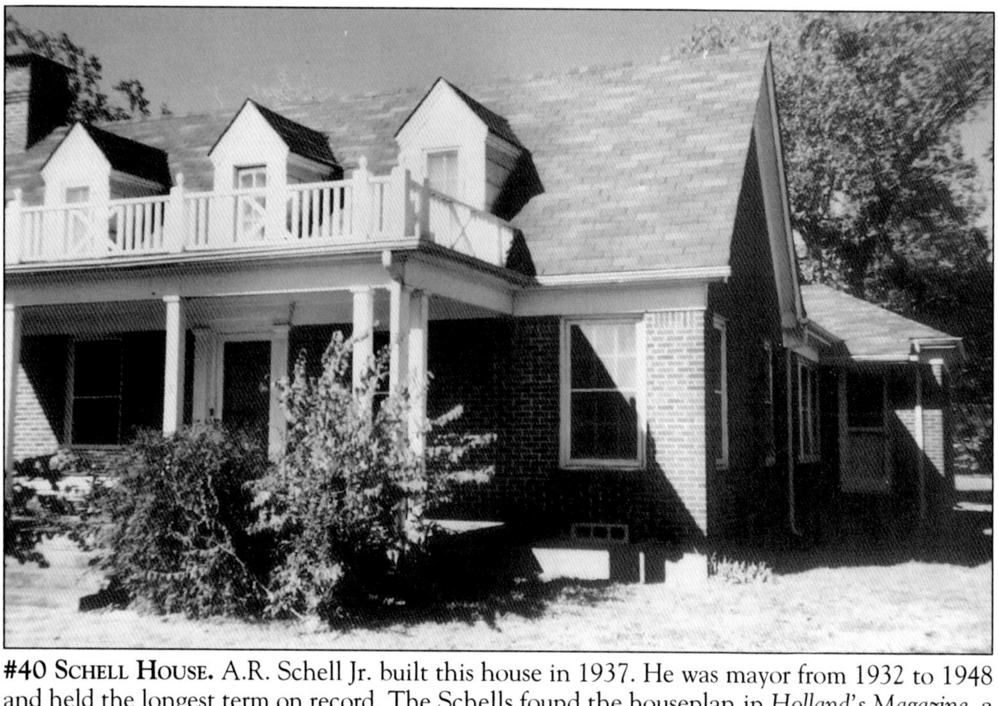

#40 SCHELL HOUSE. A.R. Schell Jr. built this house in 1937. He was mayor from 1932 to 1948 and held the longest term on record. The Schells found the houseplan in *Holland's Magazine*, a fashionable Dallas magazine of the day. The structure was originally located on 14th Street and was moved to this site in 1999.

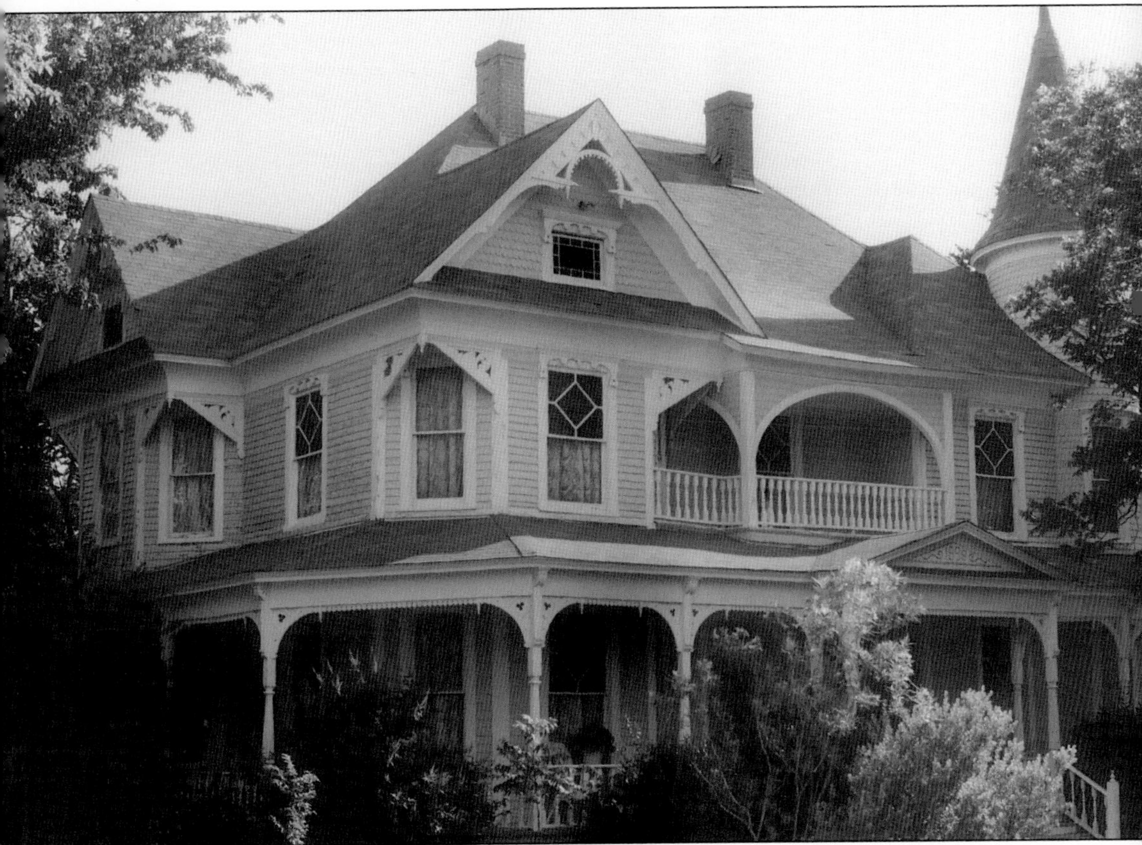

#41 Carpenter House. Henry Overaker commissioned Robert Abernathy to build this home in 1898. At the time, it was located in the middle of a cotton field. Overaker was Plano's eighth postmaster. His wife used to play the piano in the front room of this house, and passersby would sit on the front porch and listen to her play. Overaker died in 1919. Gipson E. Carpenter, son of two of Plano's earliest settlers, later purchased the property.

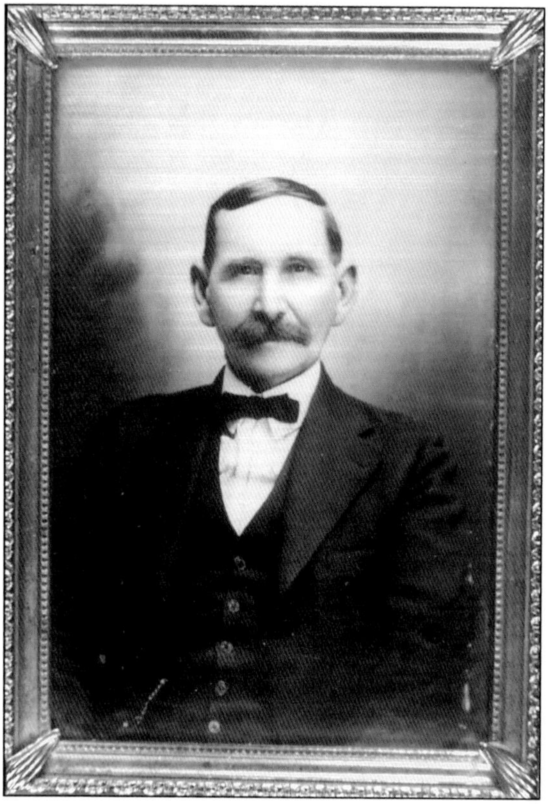

Gibson Carpenter. G.E. Carpenter graduated from Add-Ran College in 1878, and married Lula Bush in the same year. In 1880, he was asked to return to Add-Ran, where he taught Latin for four years.

After teaching, he returned to Collin County where he farmed, taught school, and read law. In 1891, he was admitted to the Bar.

Mr. Carpenter served Plano as city attorney, member of the city council, and as mayor.

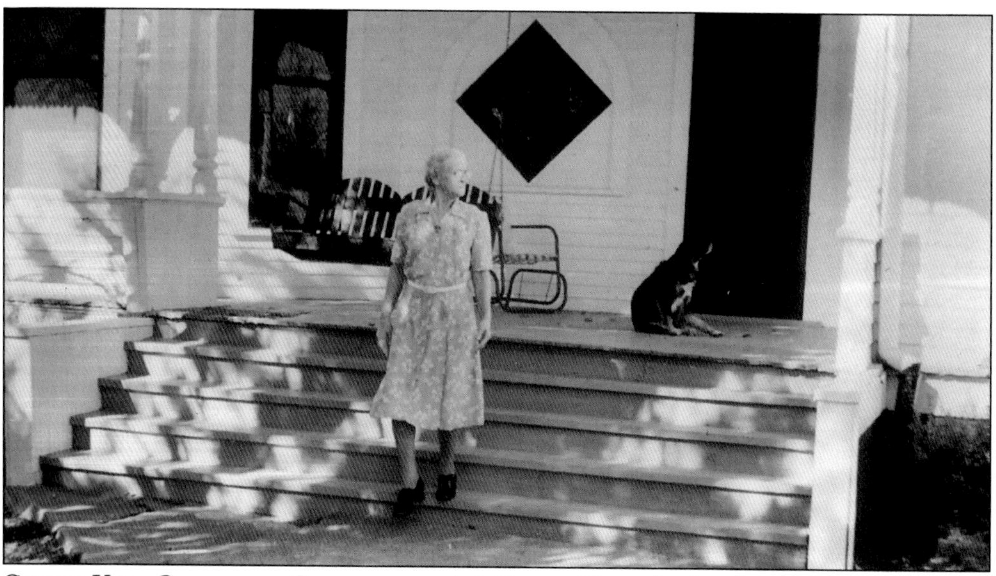

Cyrene King Carpenter. Carpenter married Cyrene King after his first wife passed away in 1895. Here she is seen in her later years on the front porch.

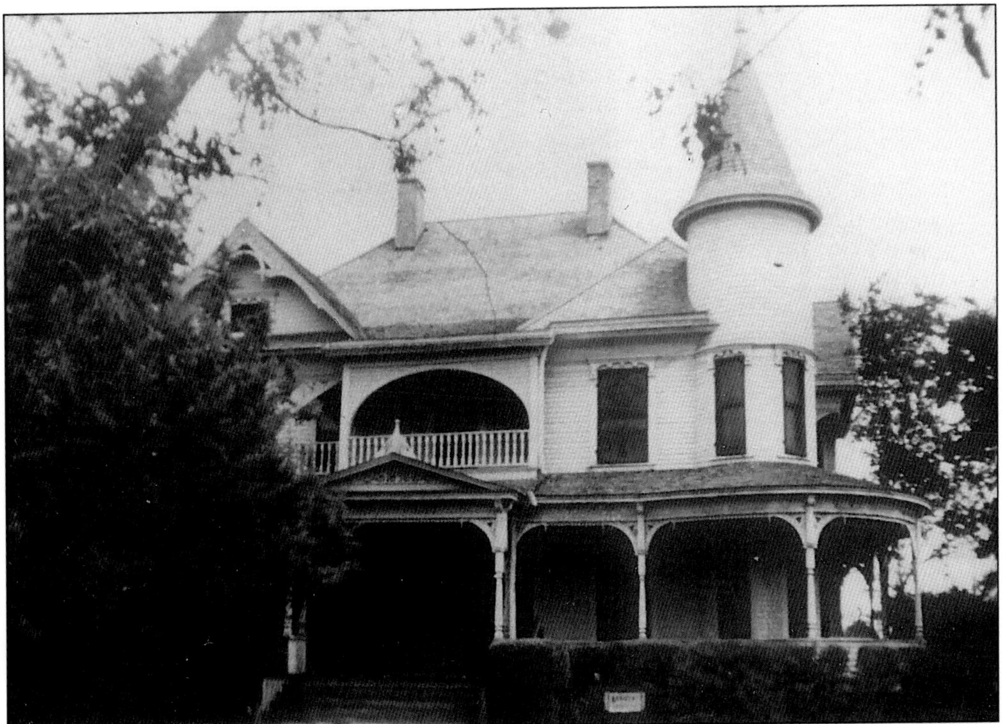

The Carpenter House, 1940. The home stayed in the Carpenter family for more than 40 years. In 1976, Plano Mayor James Edwards purchased the house. He was responsible for many of the renovations.

The house is a Queen Anne Victorian and contains about 5,600 square feet of living space.

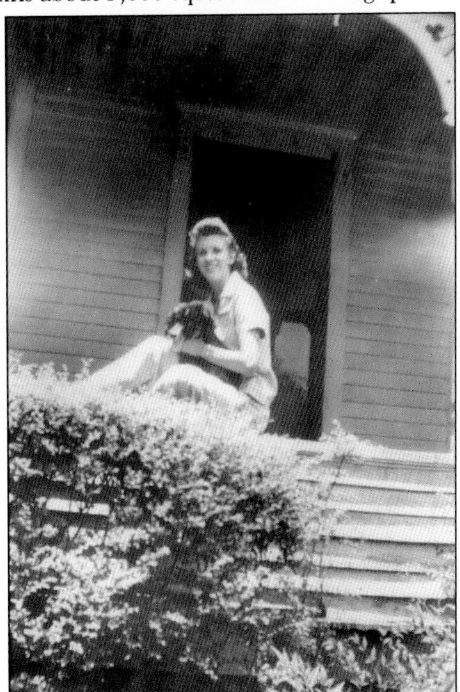

Doris Ann Graves Thompson on the Front Porch. Doris Ann was the Carpenter's granddaughter.

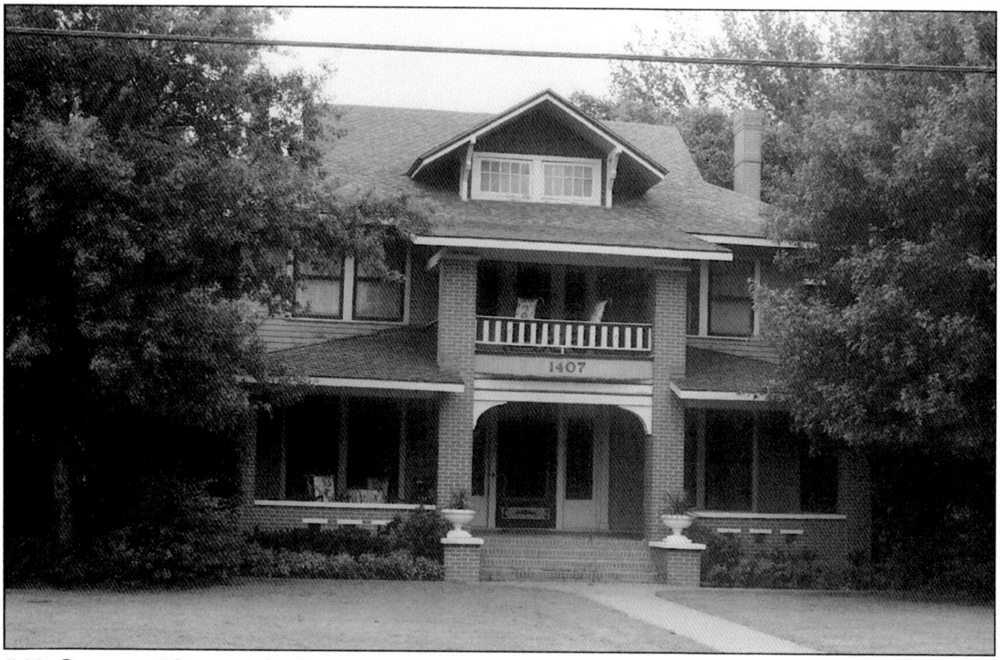

#42 CARLISLE HOUSE. The house was built in the tradition of Frank Lloyd Wright by Roger Abernathy in 1912, and sold to Henry Bascomb Carlisle in 1915.

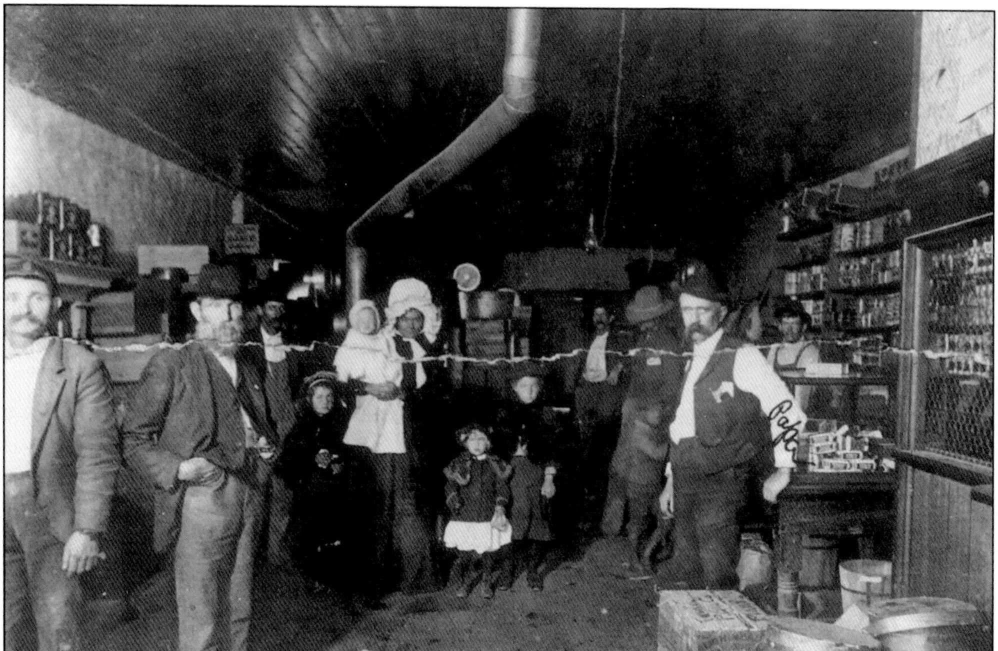

CARLISLE GROCERY STORE. Carlisle ran a grocery store on 15th Street which became the official headquarters for politicians such as the former Speaker of the House, Sam Rayburn. According to legend, Rayburn held one of his first political meetings in the house before he ran for office. (Courtesy of the Frances Wells Collection.)

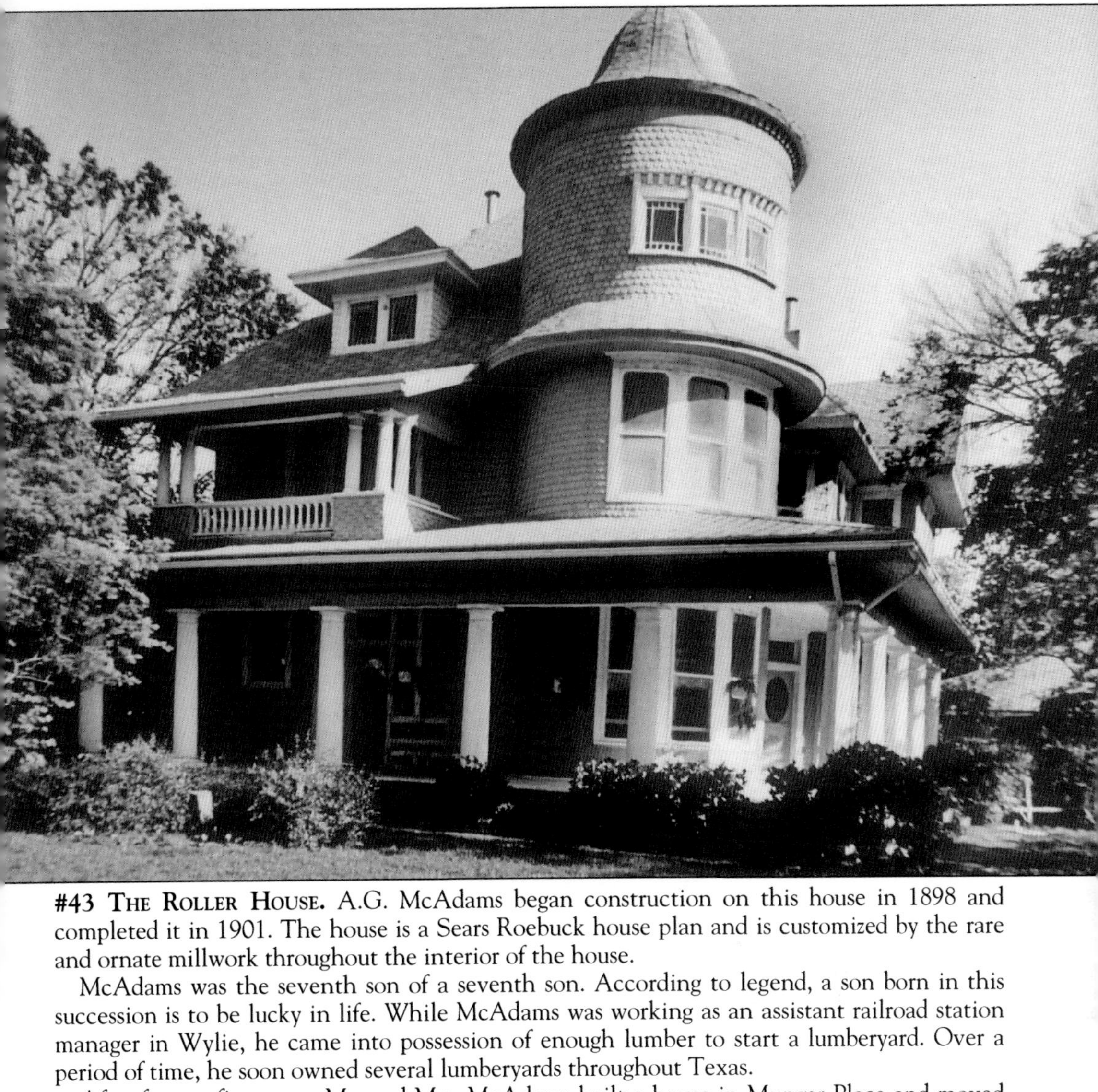

#43 THE ROLLER HOUSE. A.G. McAdams began construction on this house in 1898 and completed it in 1901. The house is a Sears Roebuck house plan and is customized by the rare and ornate millwork throughout the interior of the house.

McAdams was the seventh son of a seventh son. According to legend, a son born in this succession is to be lucky in life. While McAdams was working as an assistant railroad station manager in Wylie, he came into possession of enough lumber to start a lumberyard. Over a period of time, he soon owned several lumberyards throughout Texas.

After four or five years, Mr. and Mrs. McAdams built a house in Munger Place and moved to Dallas.

The house was owned by a couple of other families and was later purchased by the Roller family in 1909. The family came to Plano from Kentucky. They added the large pillars to the front porch. Their daughter, Thelma, was married in the house, and the family lived there until the 1940s. (Courtesy of the Gladys Harrington Library.)

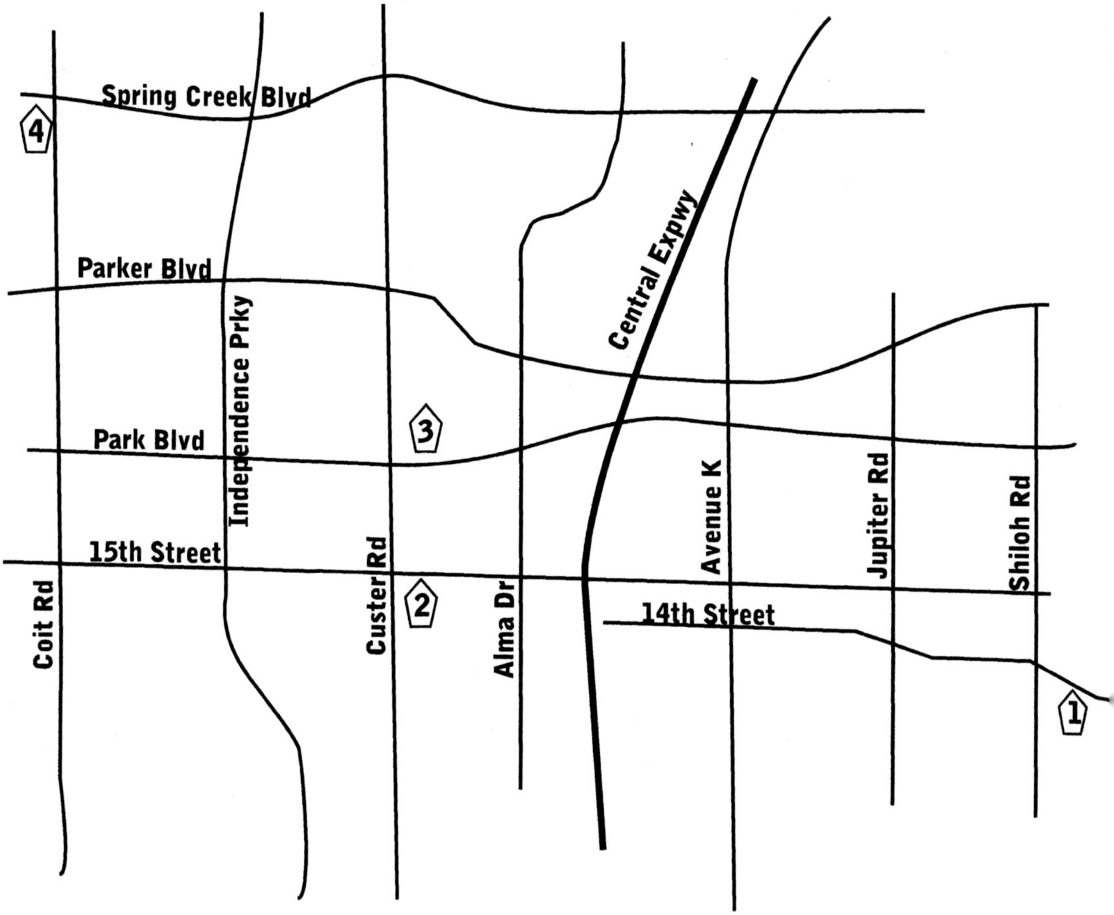
Spring Creek Blvd
Parker Blvd
Park Blvd
15th Street
14th Street
Central Expwy
Independence Prky
Coit Rd
Custer Rd
Alma Dr
Avenue K
Jupiter Rd
Shiloh Rd
1
2
3
4

Two

Out and Around the City

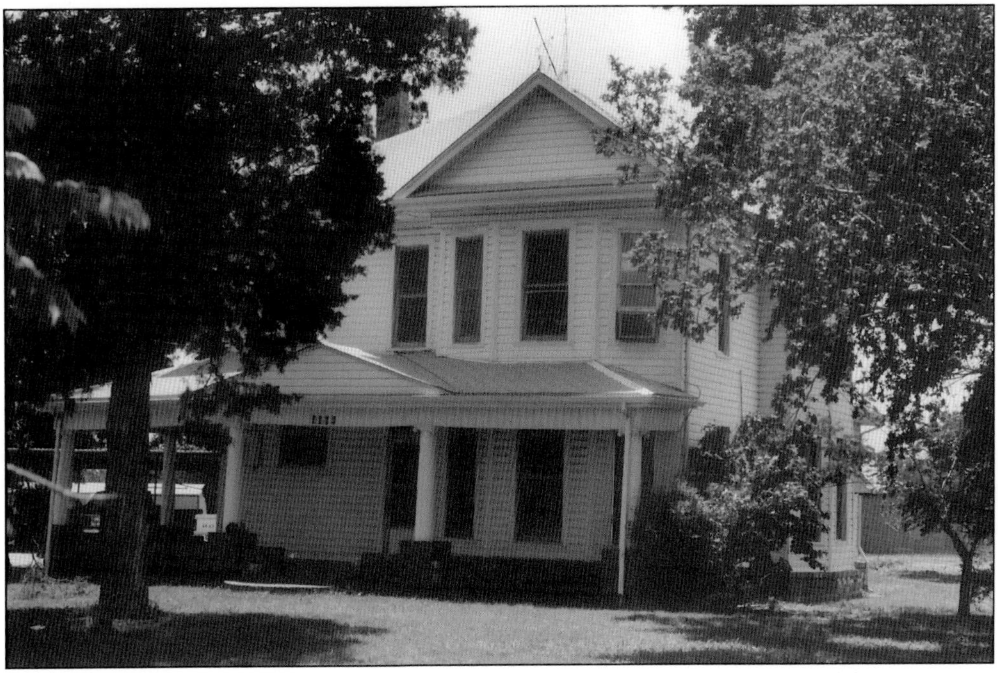

#1 **Boggess House.** Jeremiah and Rebecca Boggess lived on a plantation in Alabama. During the Civil War, Jeremiah served in the Confederacy as an engineer. While he was off at war, Rebecca heard that the Union Army was approaching their home. With the help of their slaves, she buried the silver and meat under some peach trees and hid the cattle in the cane growing on their land. When the Union Army came, they looted and burned the house. Rebecca was left to care for her 13 children alone until the war ended and her husband returned.

After the war, the family moved to Texas and eventually settled east of Plano on Rowlett Creek where they built a large log cabin. It consisted of four rooms, two on each side of a central hallway. Each room was about 20 by 20. The door was outlined with colored glass squares for decoration. Jeremiah died in 1888. In 1905, the log cabin burned, and Rebecca built this house, which is located near the site of the original log cabin.

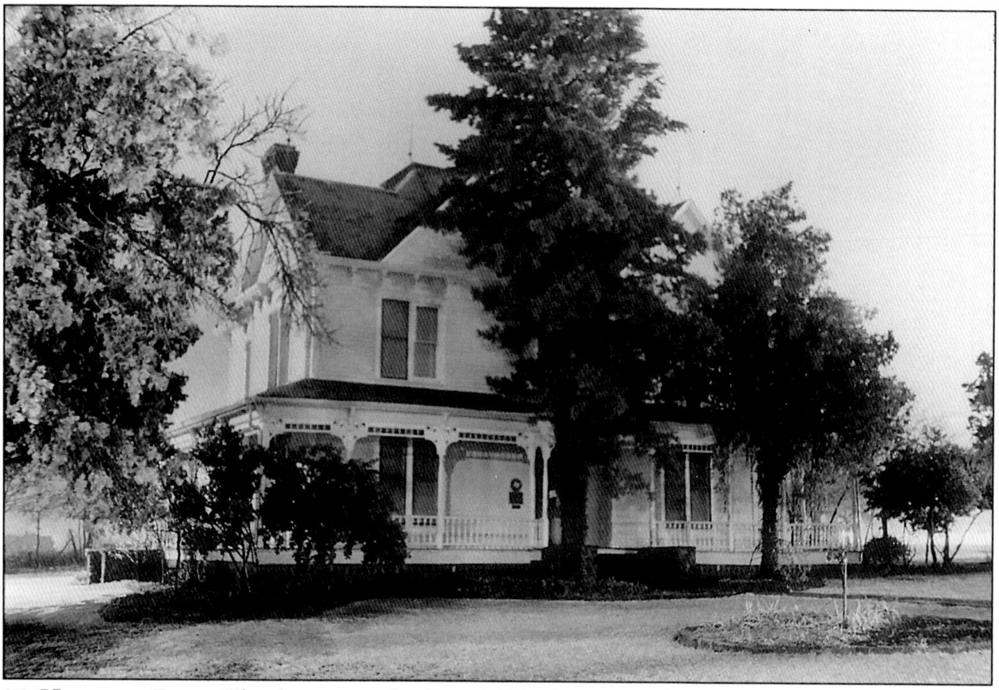

#2 Heritage Farm. This house was built in 1888. Ammie Wilson first married W.W. Lynch and later married Dudley Wilson. Ammie was known for the prize-winning sheep that she raised on the farm. Dudley Wilson was a contractor and later helped Ammie raise sheep. Ammie was known to sleep in the barn with the sheep while they were lambing. (Courtesy of the Gladys Harrington Library.)

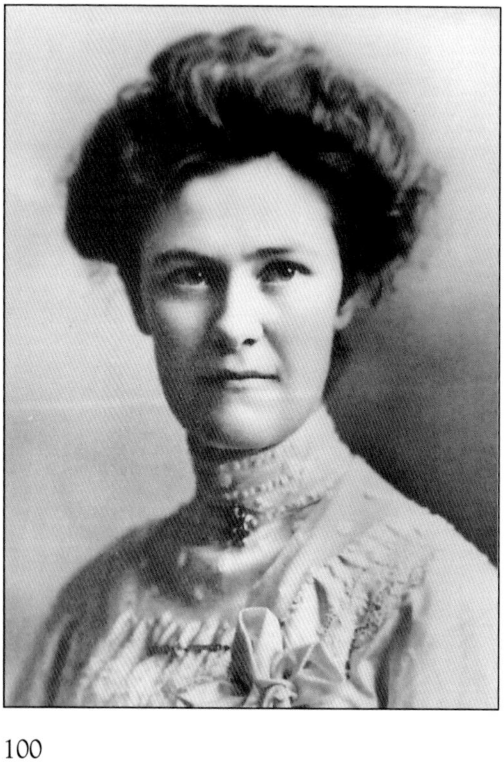

Ammie Wilson. (Courtesy of the Frances Wells Collection.)

Ammie With Her Prize-Winning Sheep. (Courtesy of the Frances Wells Collection.)

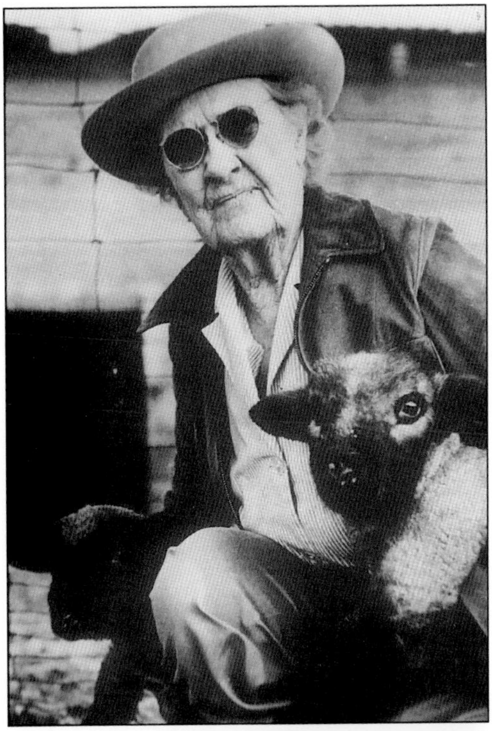

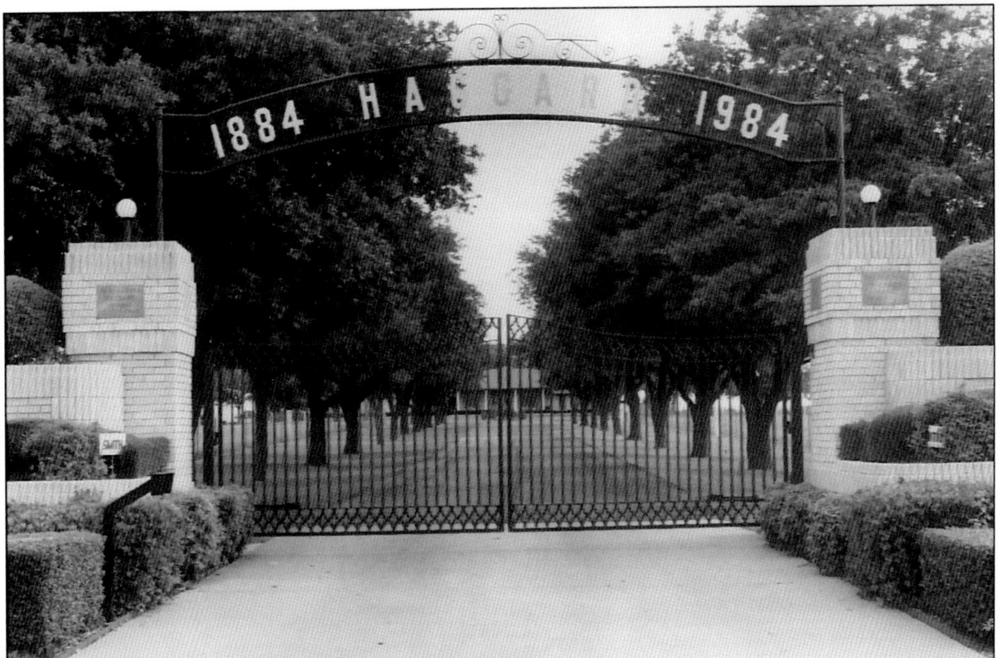

#3 Haggard Farm. The gate to the Haggard Ranch was built in 1984 and was dedicated to C.S. and Nannie Kate Haggard who moved to this site in 1884. C.S. and Nannie Kate built the first of three houses to occupy the site. Nannie Kate named the farm Fairview.

C.S. Haggard was among others in Plano who loaned money to help establish Add-Ran College, which is now known as Texas Christian University. (Photography by Adam Towber.)

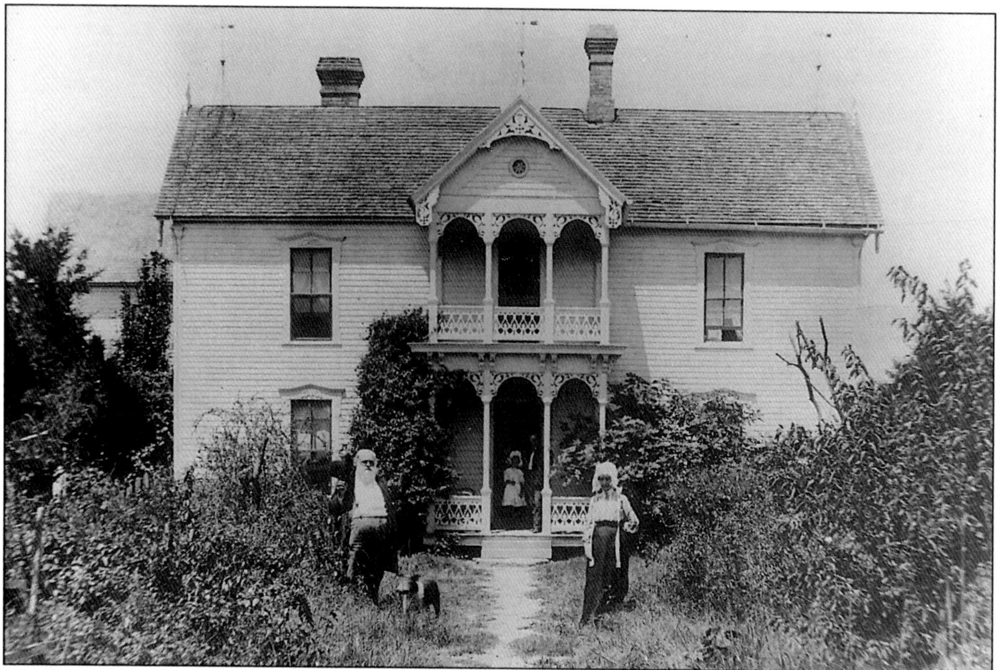

The First Haggard House. The first house was built on this site in 1884. (Courtesy of the Frances Wells Collection.)

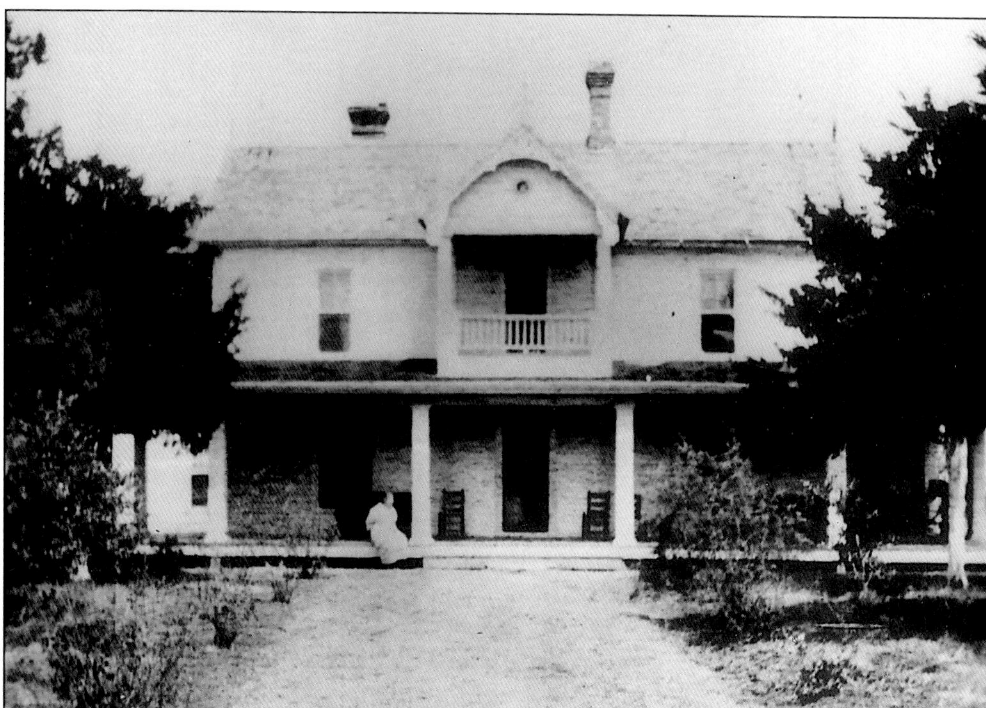

Haggard House in 1906. The house was remodeled in 1906, and among the changes was the enlargement of the front porch. (Courtesy of the Frances Wells Collection.)

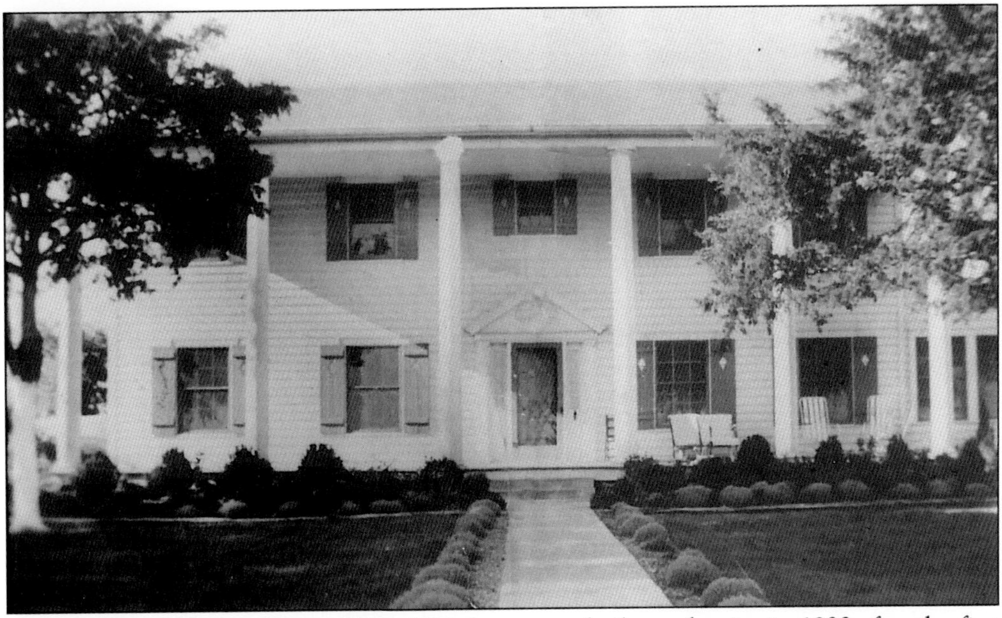

The Haggard House, Built 1933. This house was built on the site in 1933 after the first house was torn down. In 1967, this colonial house was torn down, and the current house was constructed. (Courtesy of the Frances Wells Collection.)

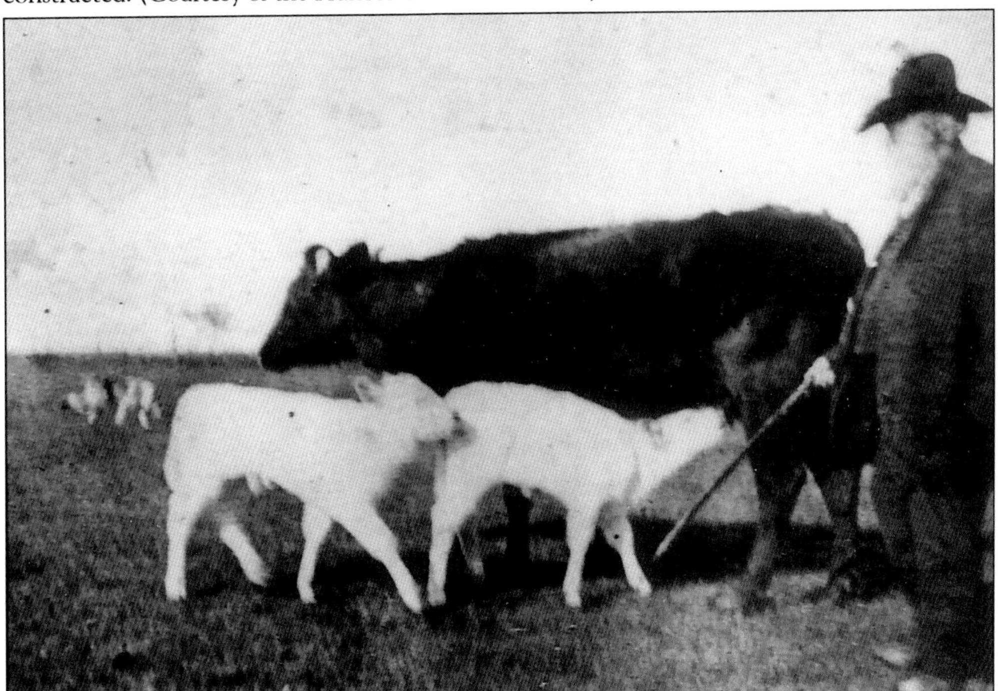

C.S. Haggard With Twin Calves. C.S. raised livestock and sold horses and mules to farmers. Demand for mules dwindled with the invention of the tractor. As a result, his son, W.O. Haggard Jr., converted to growing cotton. When the cotton gin in the area closed, cotton farming ceased. The ranch has remained in the family since 1884. (Courtesy of the Frances Wells Collection.)

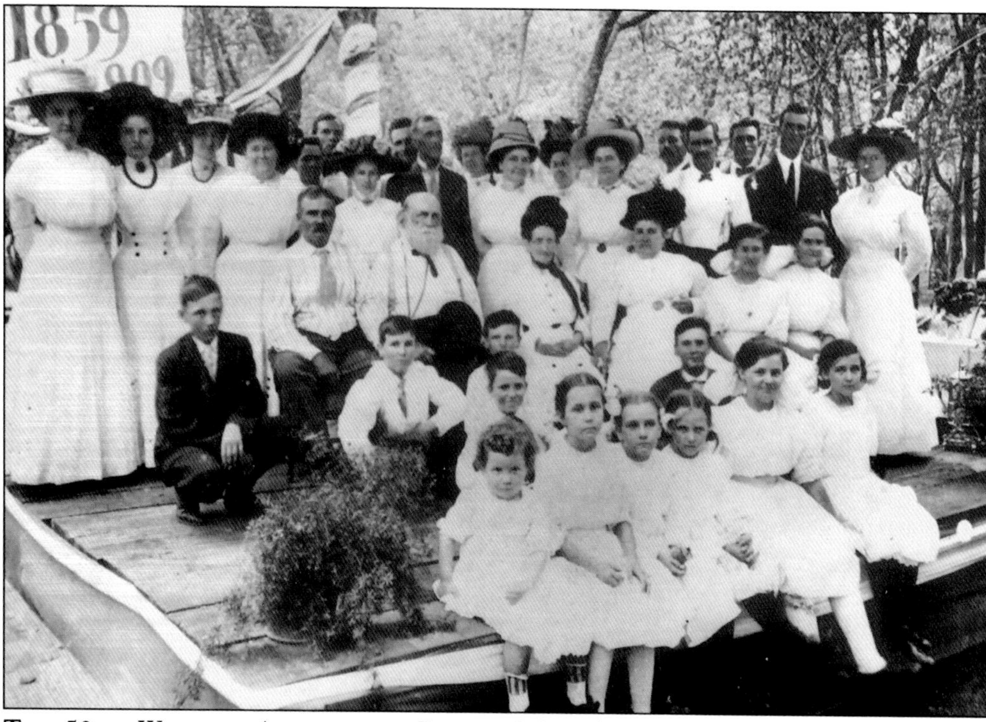

THE 50TH WEDDING ANNIVERSARY PARTY. C.S and Nannie Kate Haggard celebrated their 50th wedding anniversary on the front yard of the property. (Courtesy of the Frances Wells Collection.)

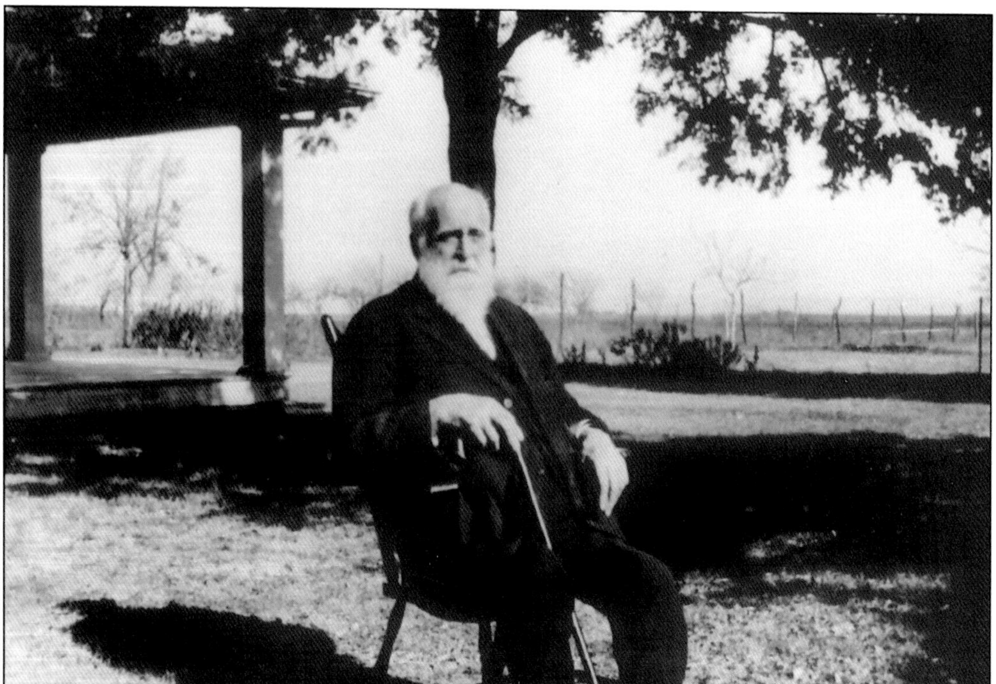

C.S. HAGGARD IN THE FRONT YARD. (Courtesy of the Frances Wells Collection.)

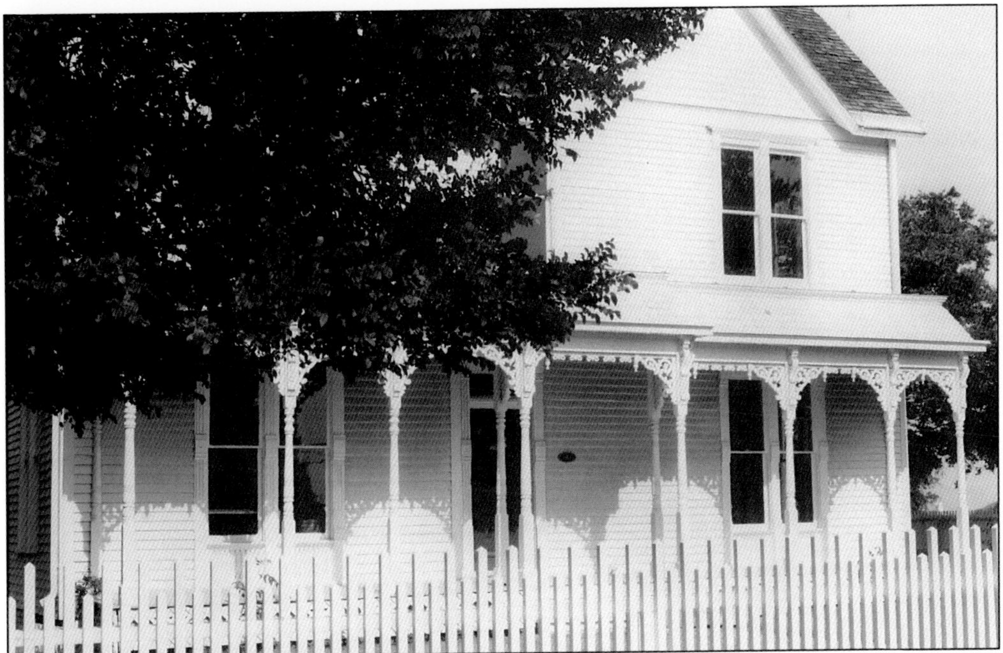

#4 Wells Farm. William H.L. Wells saved his money while working in Virginia, and he then came to Texas. He built this house in 1893 at a cost of $1,500. Mr. Wells was very particular about the lumber that was used to construct the house. If there were any boards that were not the best of quality, he hauled them back to the lumberyard. The cypress siding was hauled by ox cart from Marshall, Texas.

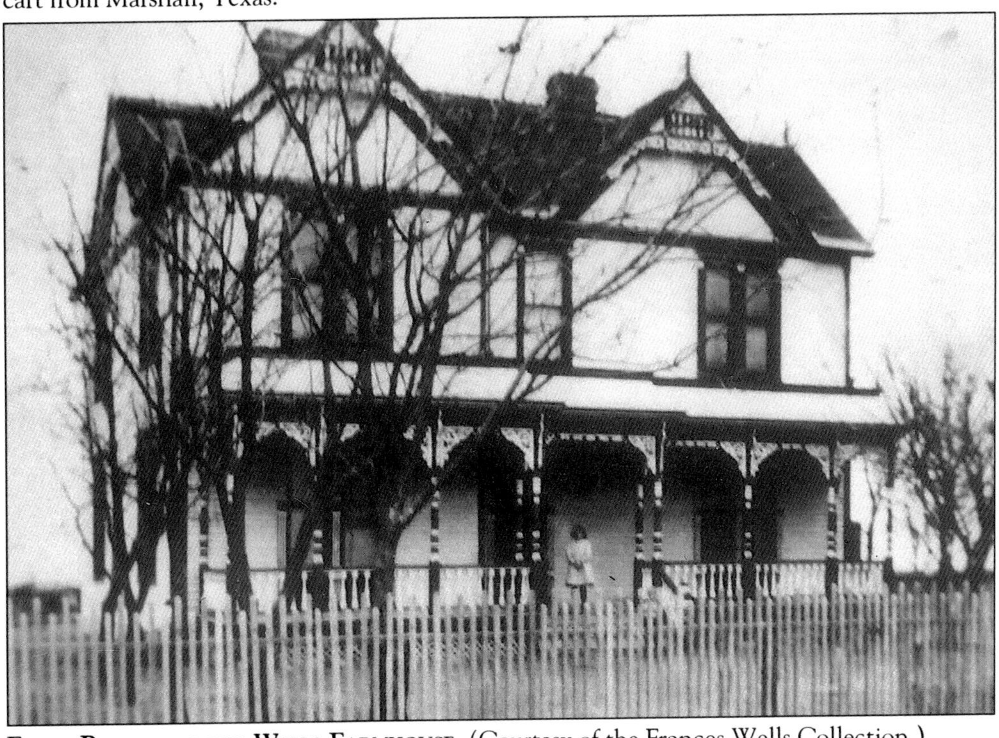

Early Picture of the Wells Farmhouse. (Courtesy of the Frances Wells Collection.)

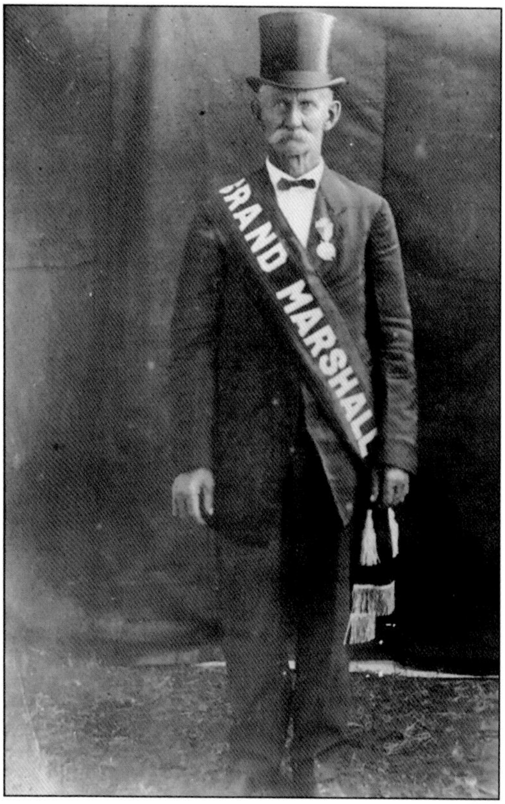

W.H.L. Wells. (Courtesy of the Frances Wells Collection.)

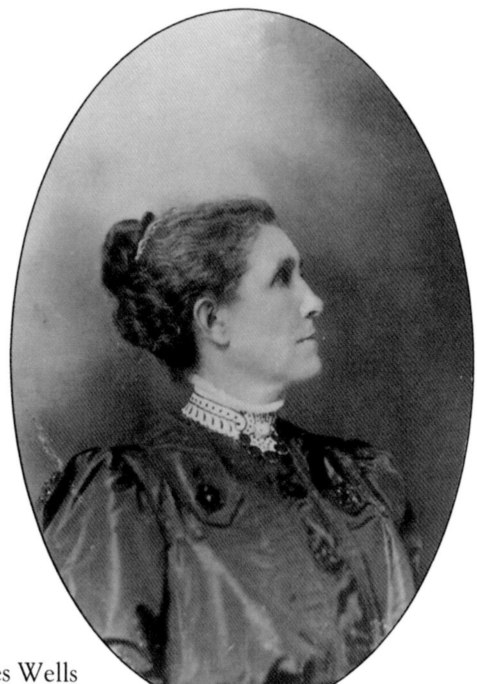

Sarah McClary Wells. (Courtesy of the Frances Wells Collection.)

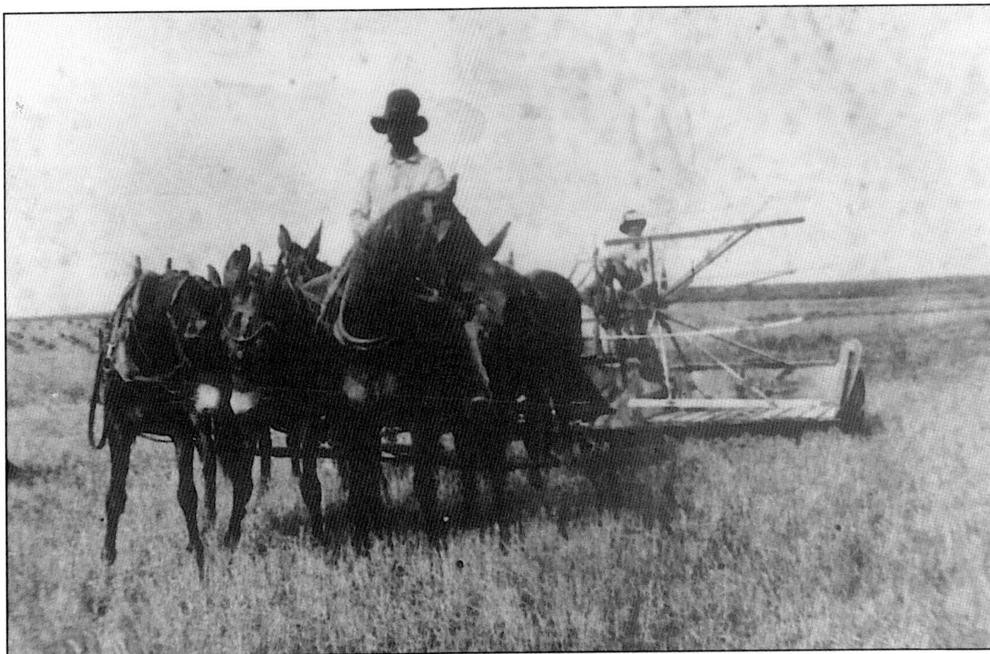

HARVESTING ON THE WELLS FARM. The original farm consisted of about 258 acres stretching between the current streets of Spring Creek and Parker Road. Corn, wheat, oats, and cotton were among the crops farmed. (Courtesy of the Frances Wells Collection.)

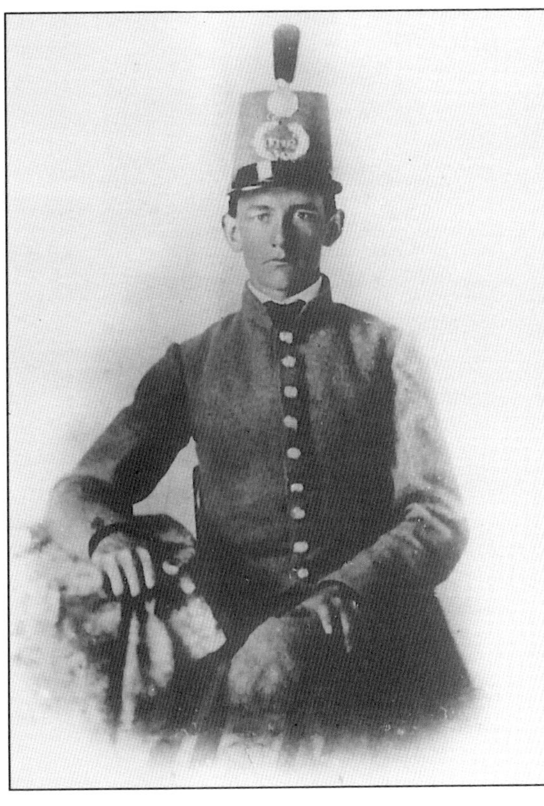

W.H.L. WELLS. Mr. Wells fought for the Confederacy during the Civil War. A picture of Robert E. Lee hung over one of the mantels in the house. Each time Mr. Wells walked by it, he would salute the picture of General Lee. (Courtesy of the Frances Wells Collection)

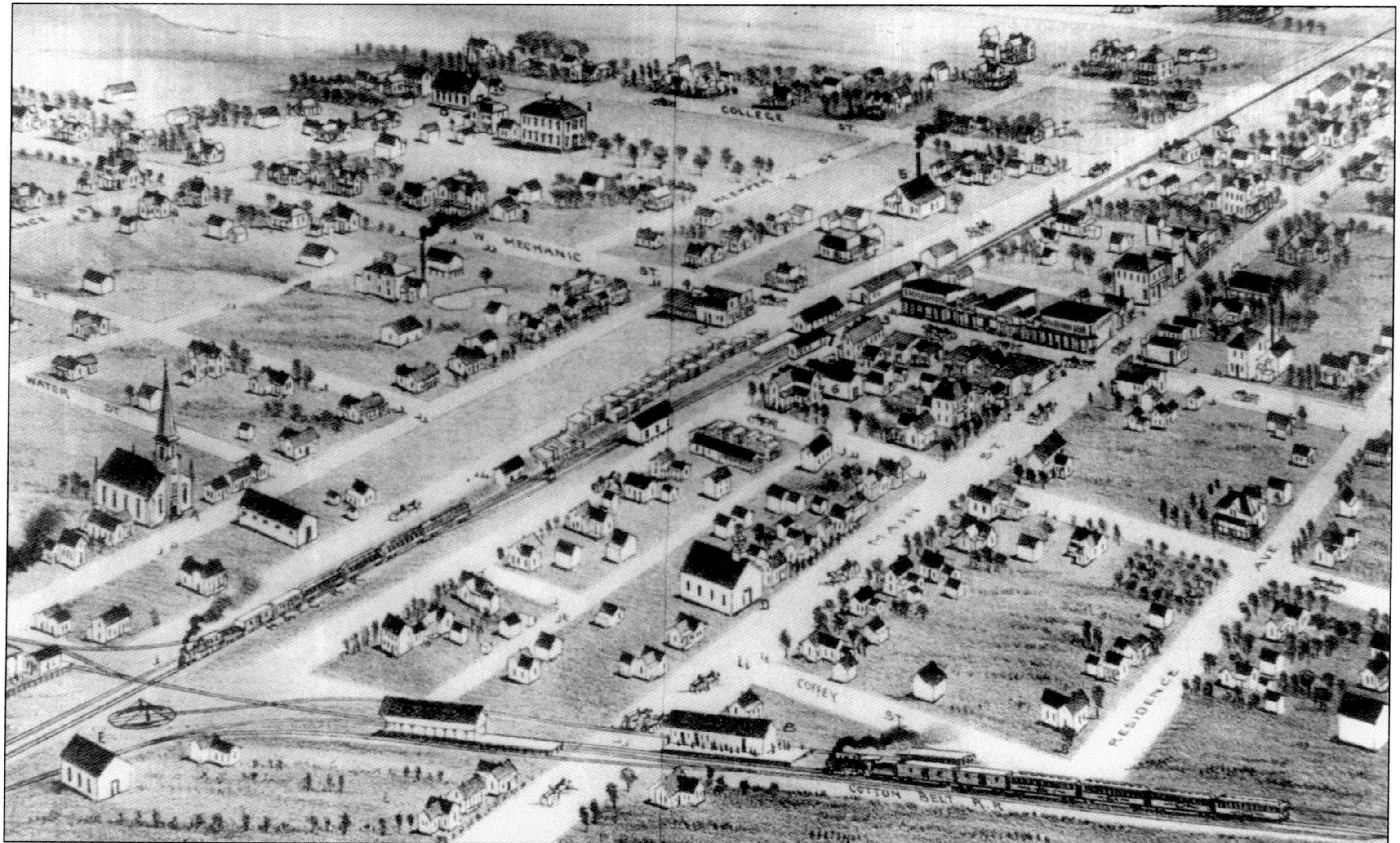

Plano, Late 1800s. (Courtesy of the Francis Wells Collection.)

Three

Homes and Buildings of the Past

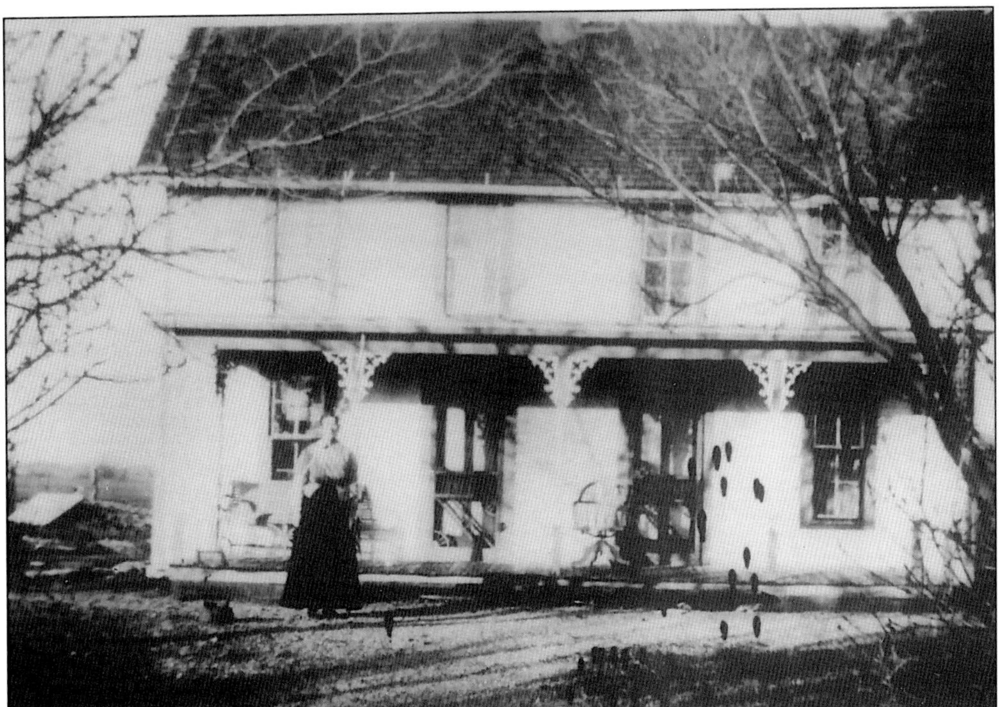

J. Will Haggard Farm. J. Will Haggard and Mariah Texanna Haggard lived in this house.

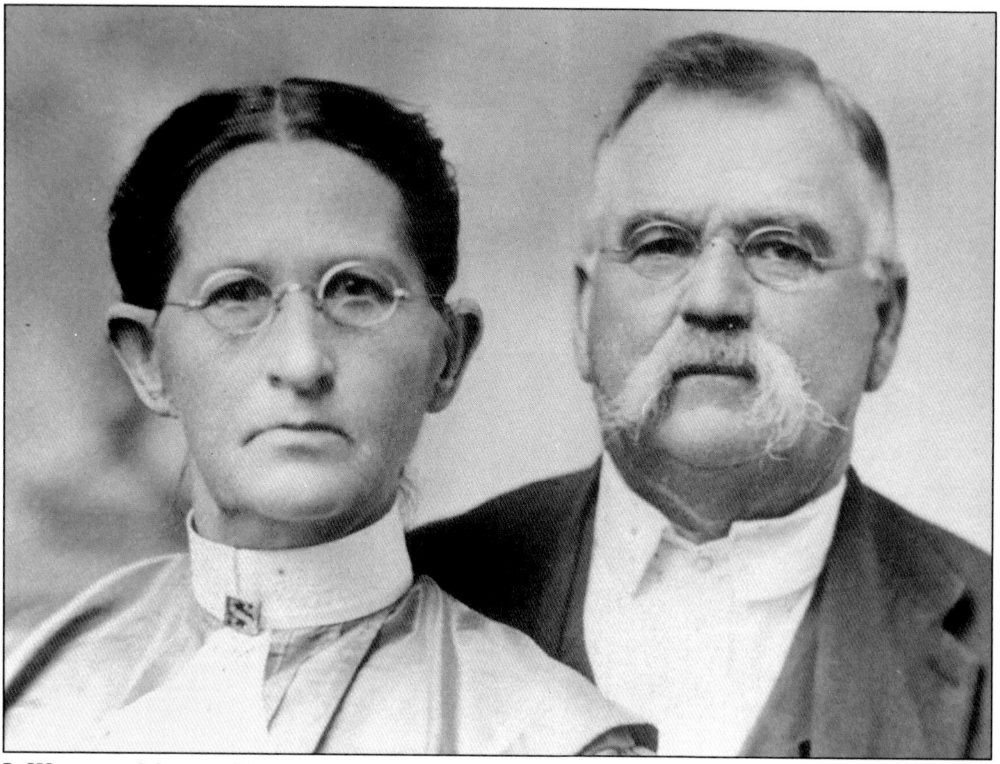

J. Will and Mariah Texanna Haggard. The couple was married in 1872.

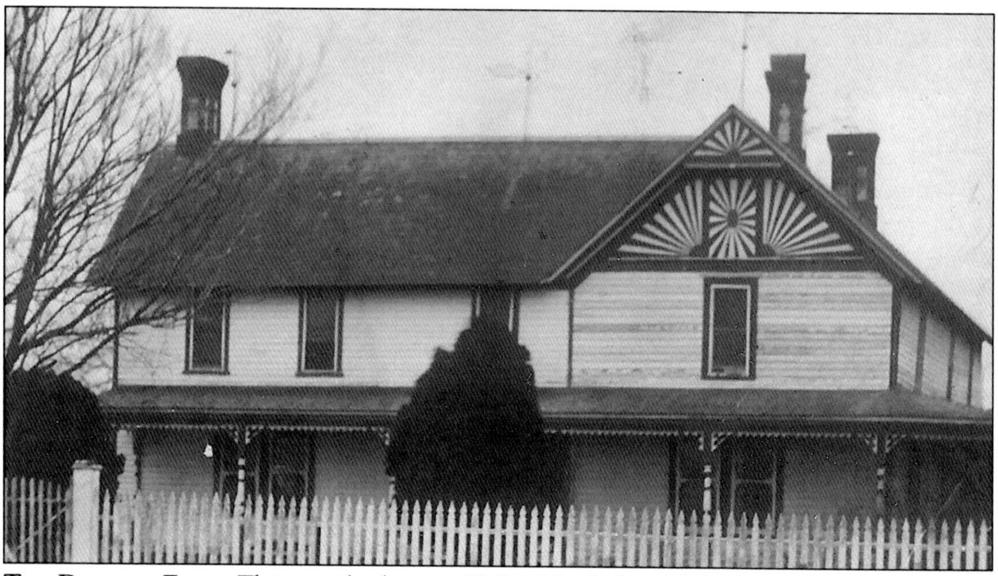

The Daffron Farm. This was the home of John Marshal and Maude Salmon Daffron. The Daffron Farm was located between present-day Park Boulevard and Yeary Road, west of Preston Road. The family raised turkeys.

Mr. Daffron bought a 1916 Maxwell automobile. He was attempting to park the car in the carriage house after driving into town when he took his foot off of the brake to stop it, and the car lunged forward. Out of habit, he yelled, "Whoa."

The Daffron Family. Mr. Daffron would take his family to Plano in a wagon where they would catch the Interurban to ride into Dallas. There they would visit the fair, spend the night, and go home the next day.

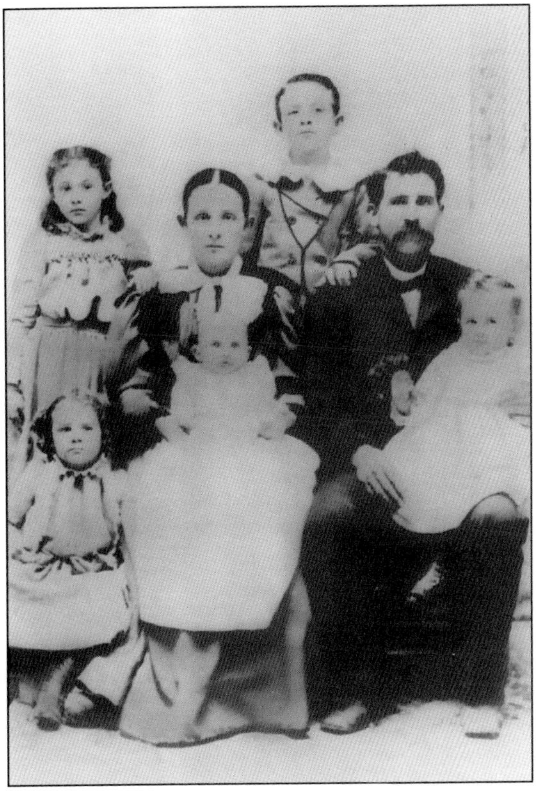

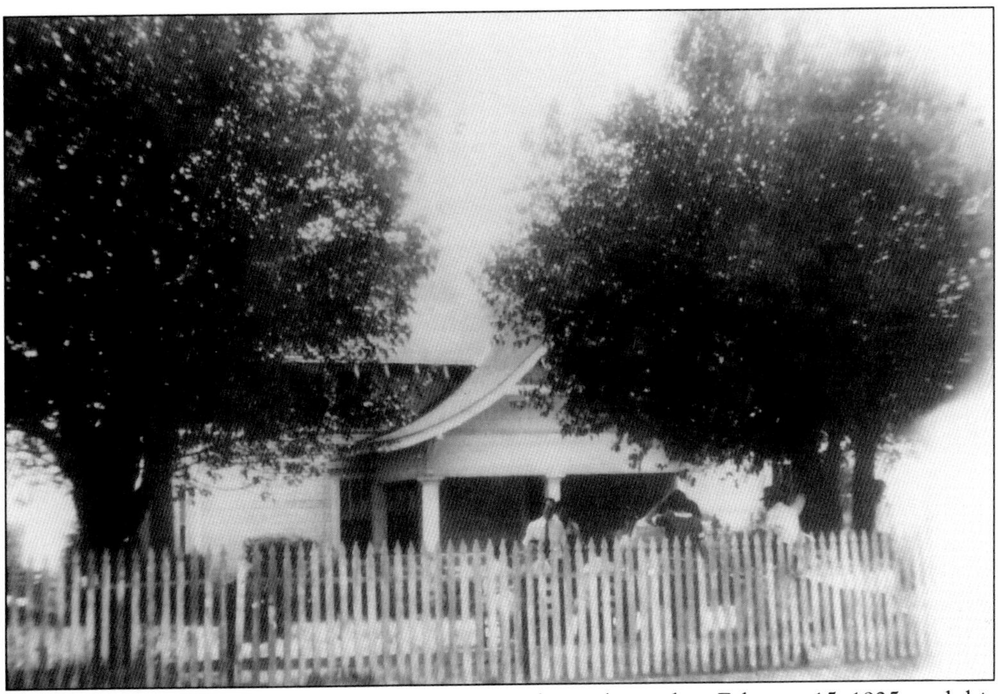

The New Daffron Farmhouse. The original farmhouse burned on February 15, 1925, and this new house was built in its place.

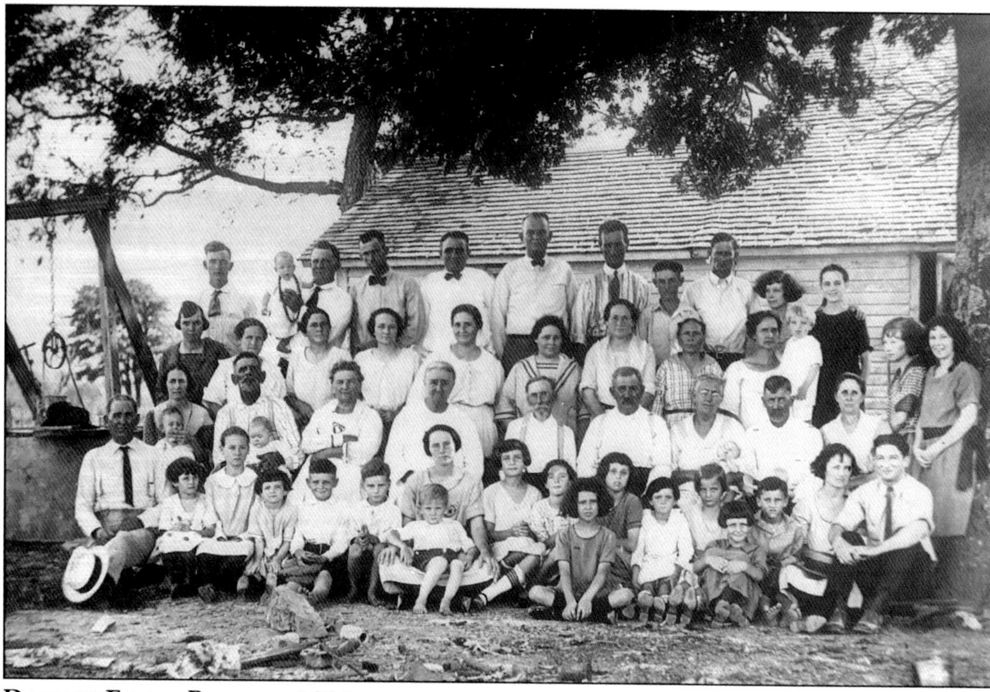

DAFFRON FAMILY REUNION, 1920.

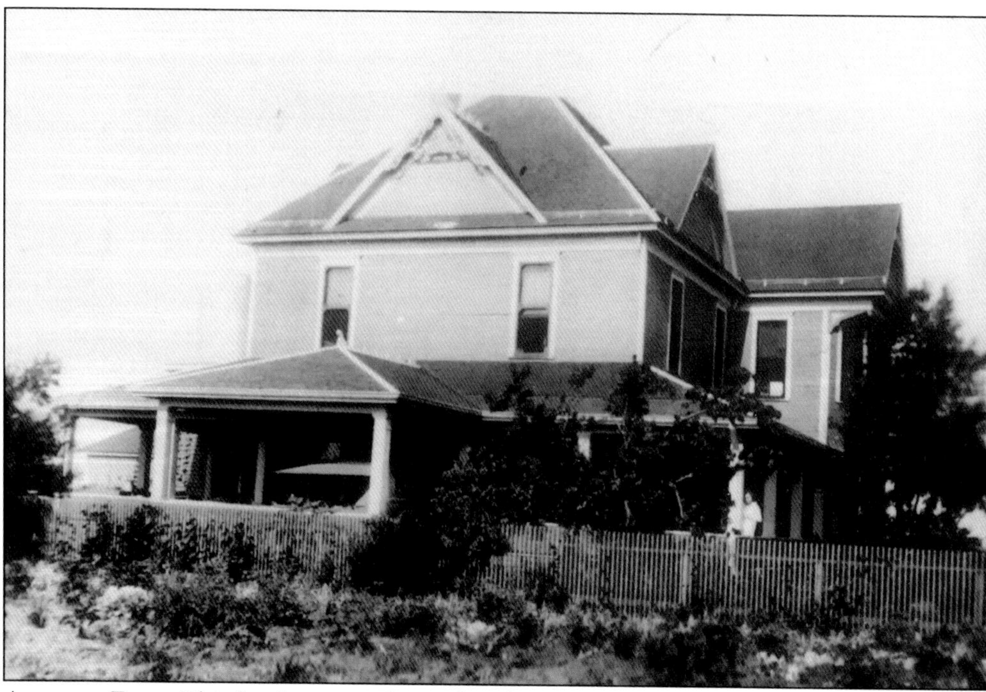

ANDREWS FARM. This farmhouse was located at the corner of present-day 15th and Coit Streets on the southwest corner behind the present-day office building at 4100 West 15th Street.

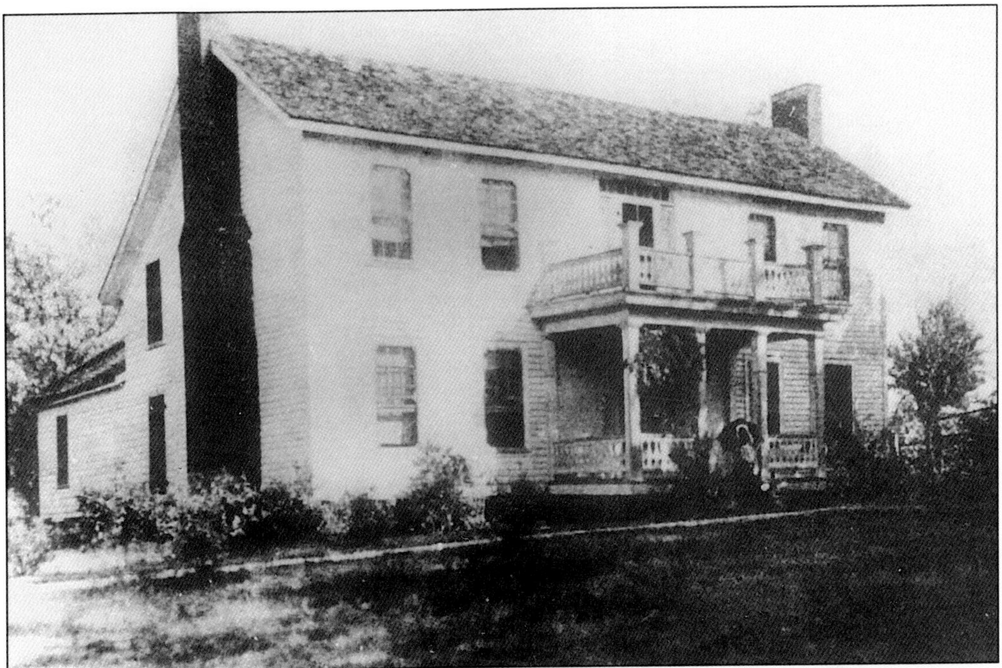

THE ROUTH HOME. This house was located north of Richardson overlooking Spring Creek and east of Central Expressway. Jacob Routh began building it just before the Civil War. Construction ceased during the war and was completed afterwards. This home was remodeled in 1907. (Courtesy of the Frances Wells Collection.)

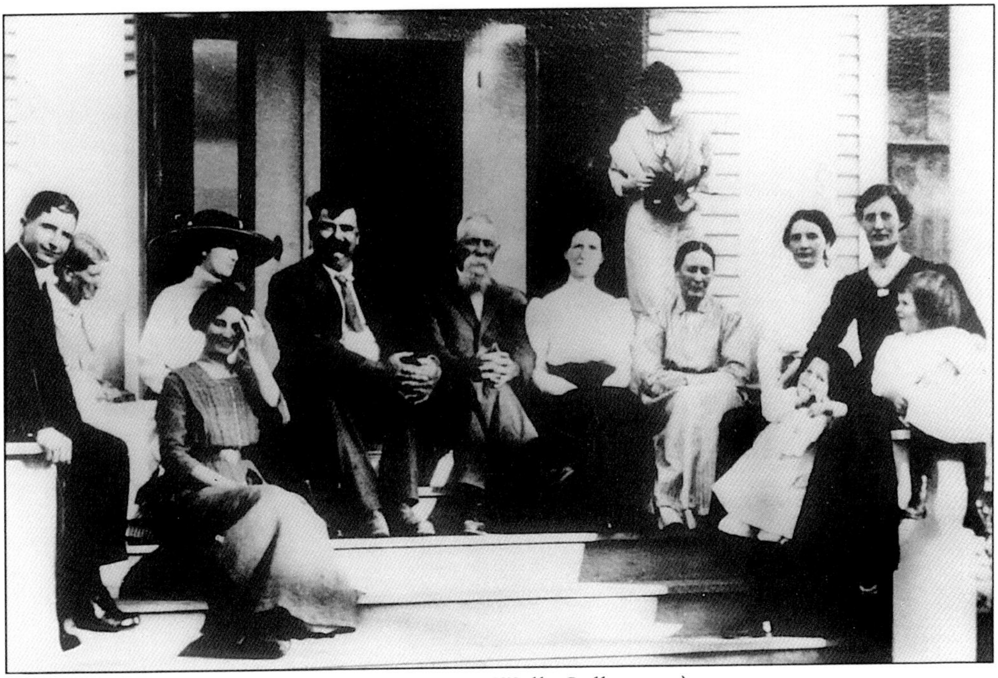

THE ROUTH FAMILY. (Courtesy of the Frances Wells Collection.)

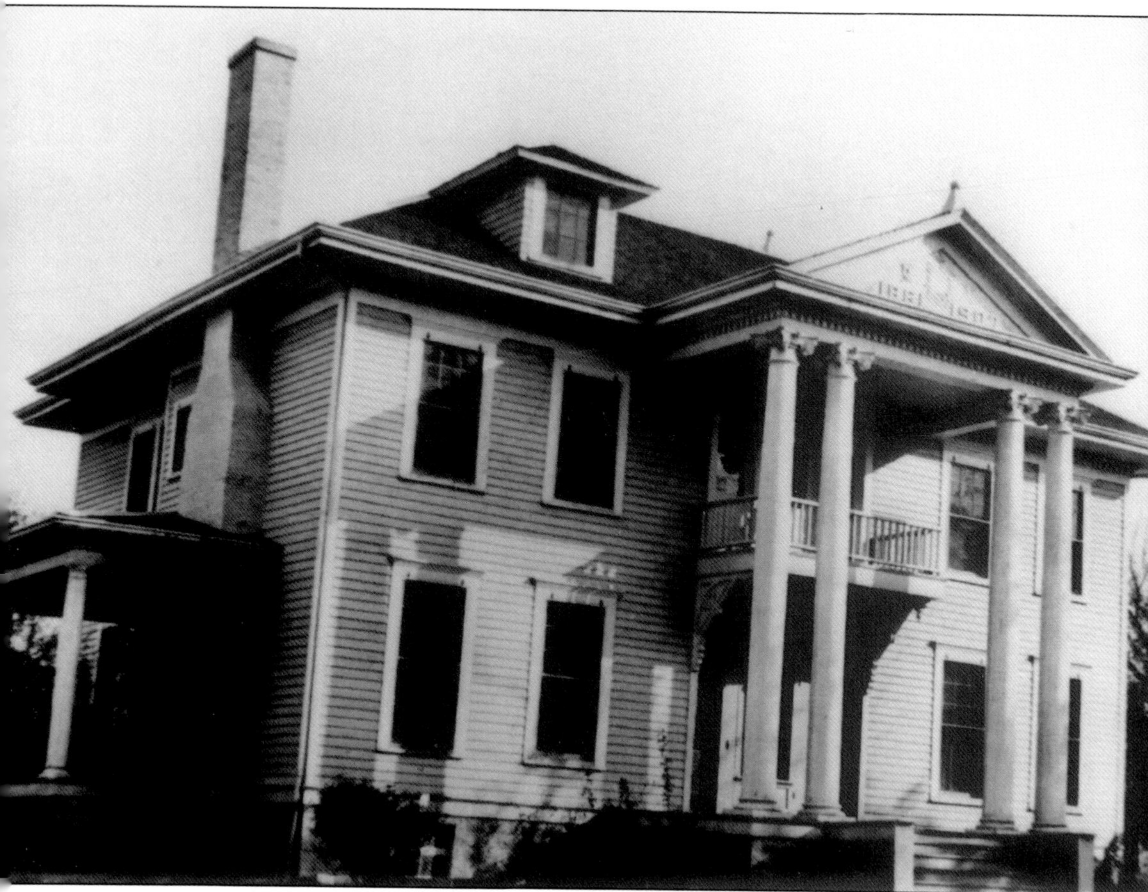

THE ROUTH HOME AFTER REMODELING IN 1907. The Routh's house burned in 1963. (Courtesy of the Frances Wells Collection.)

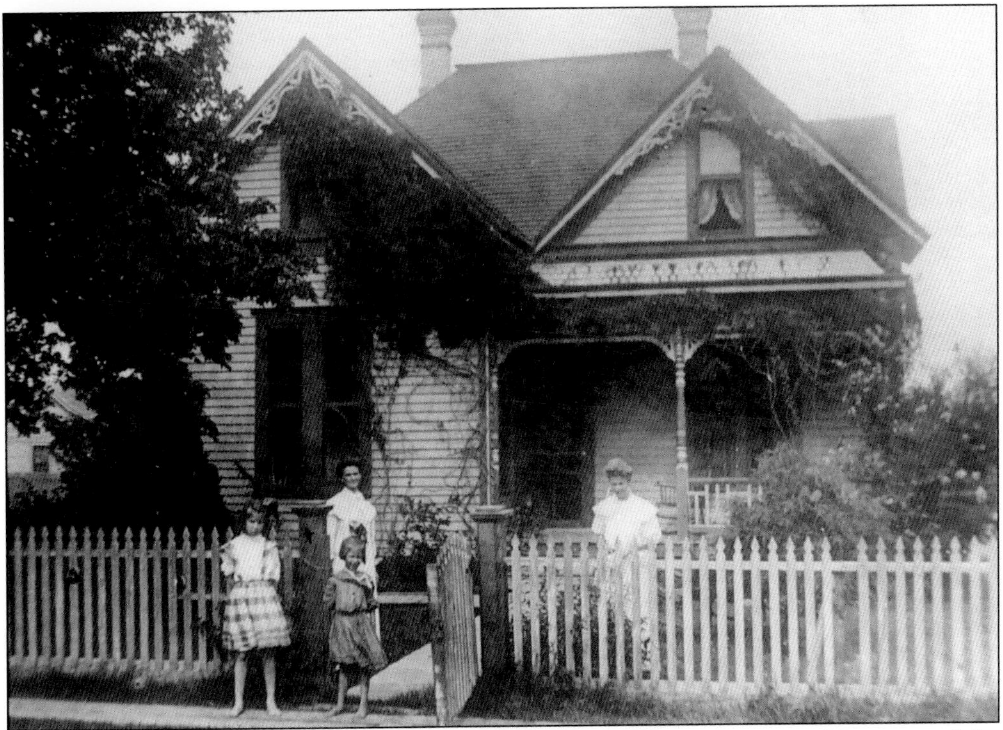

The Dudley House. This house was located on present-day 15th Street. (Courtesy of the Frances Wells Collection.)

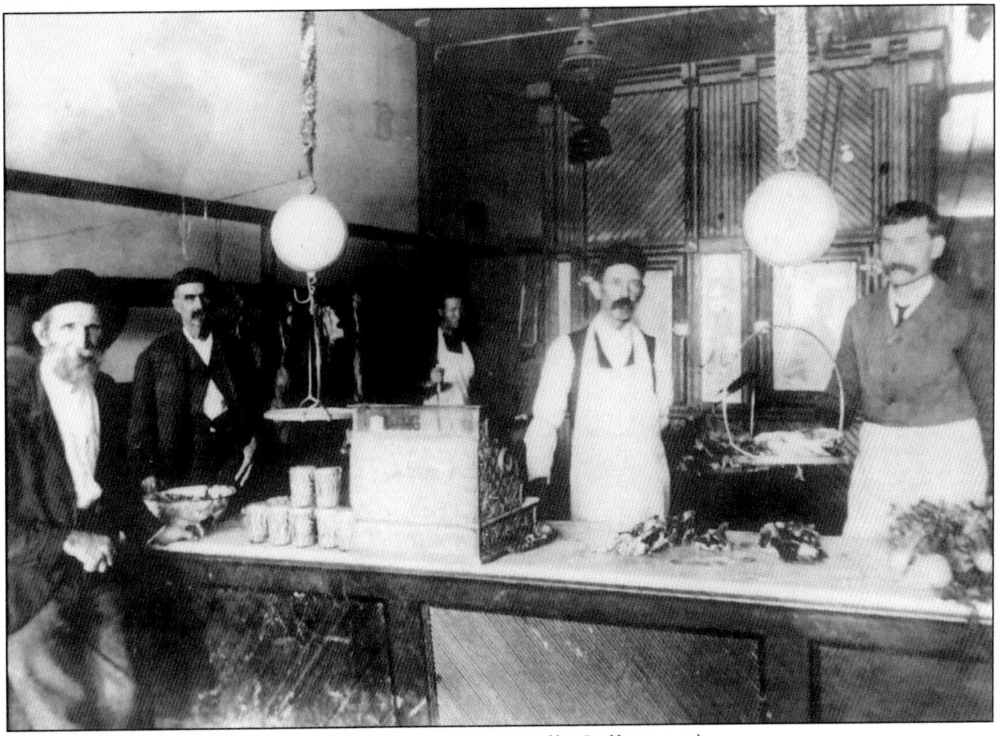

The Dudley's Store. (Courtesy of the Frances Wells Collection.)

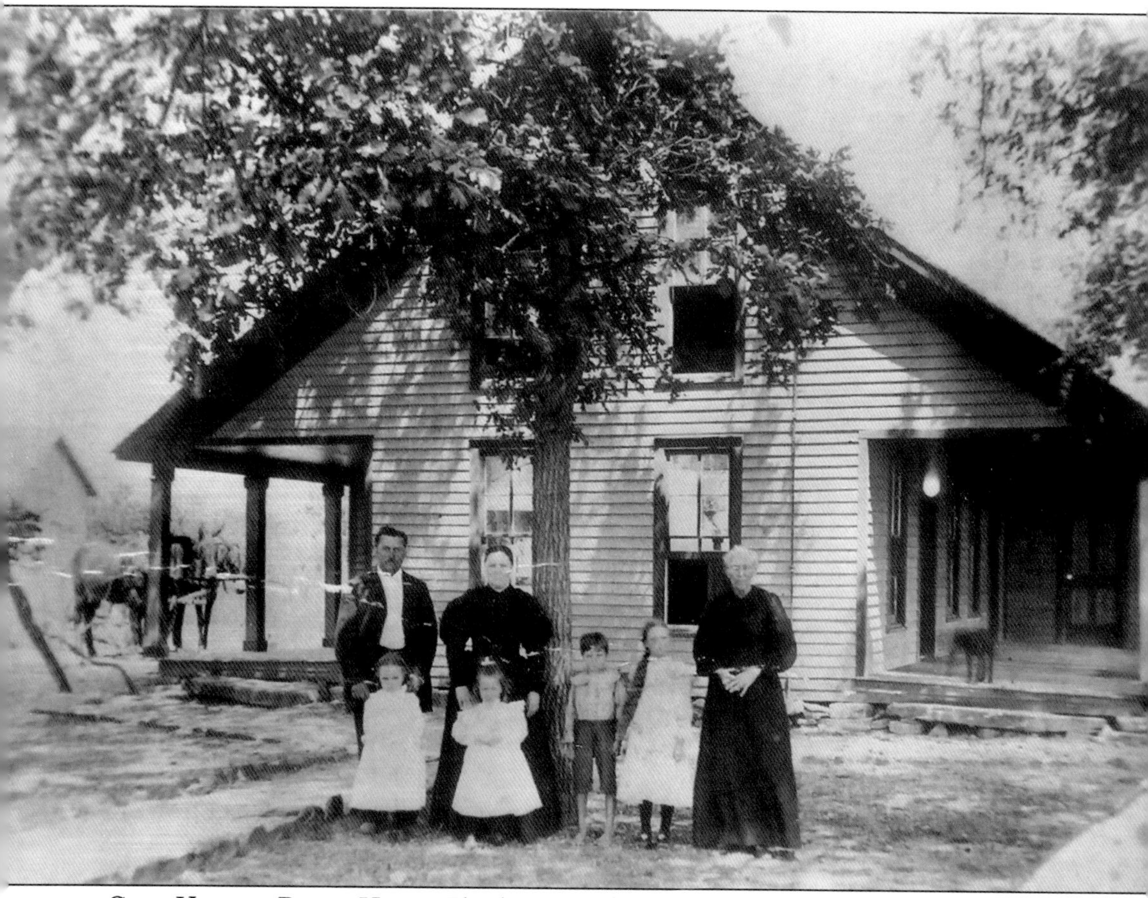

Cook-Heustiss Bishop House. This house was located near present-day Legacy Drive and the Tollroad. (Courtesy of the Frances Wells Collection.)

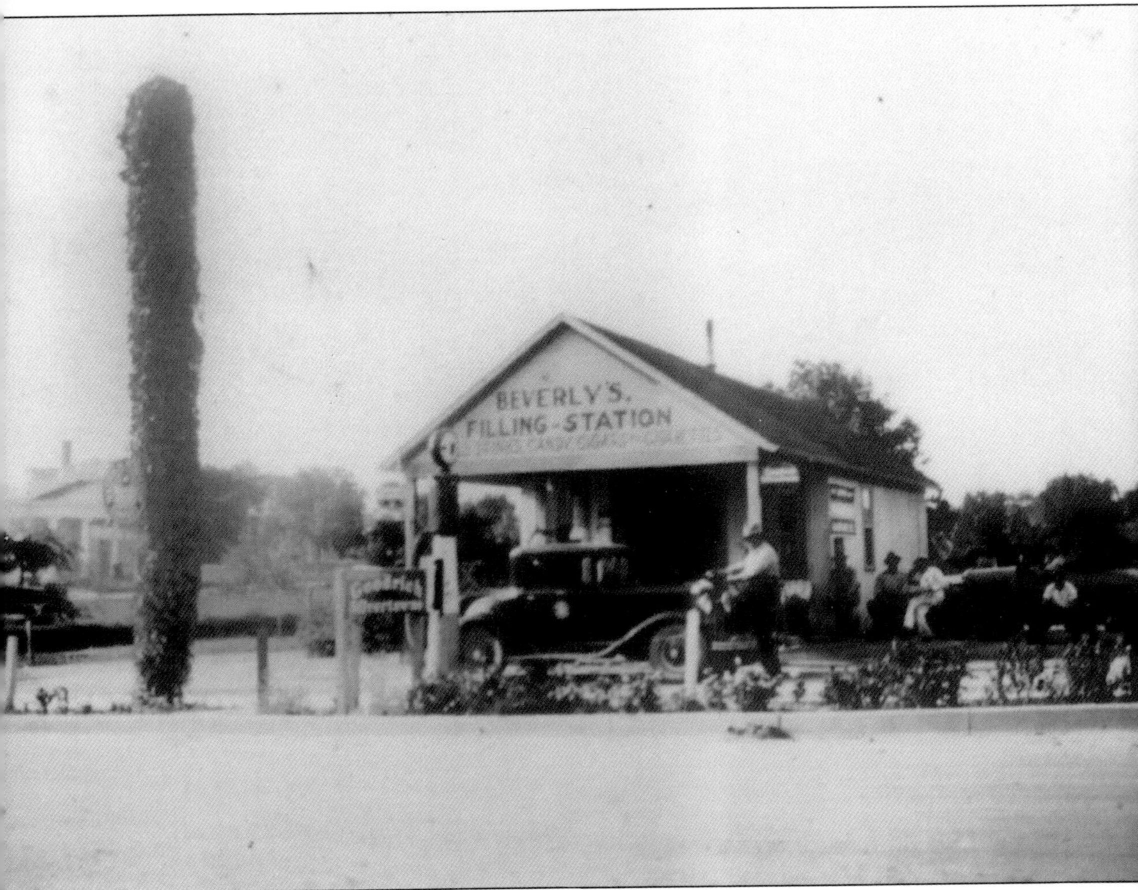

BEVERLY'S FILLING STATION. This station was located on present-day 15th Street, just west of the Interurban Station.

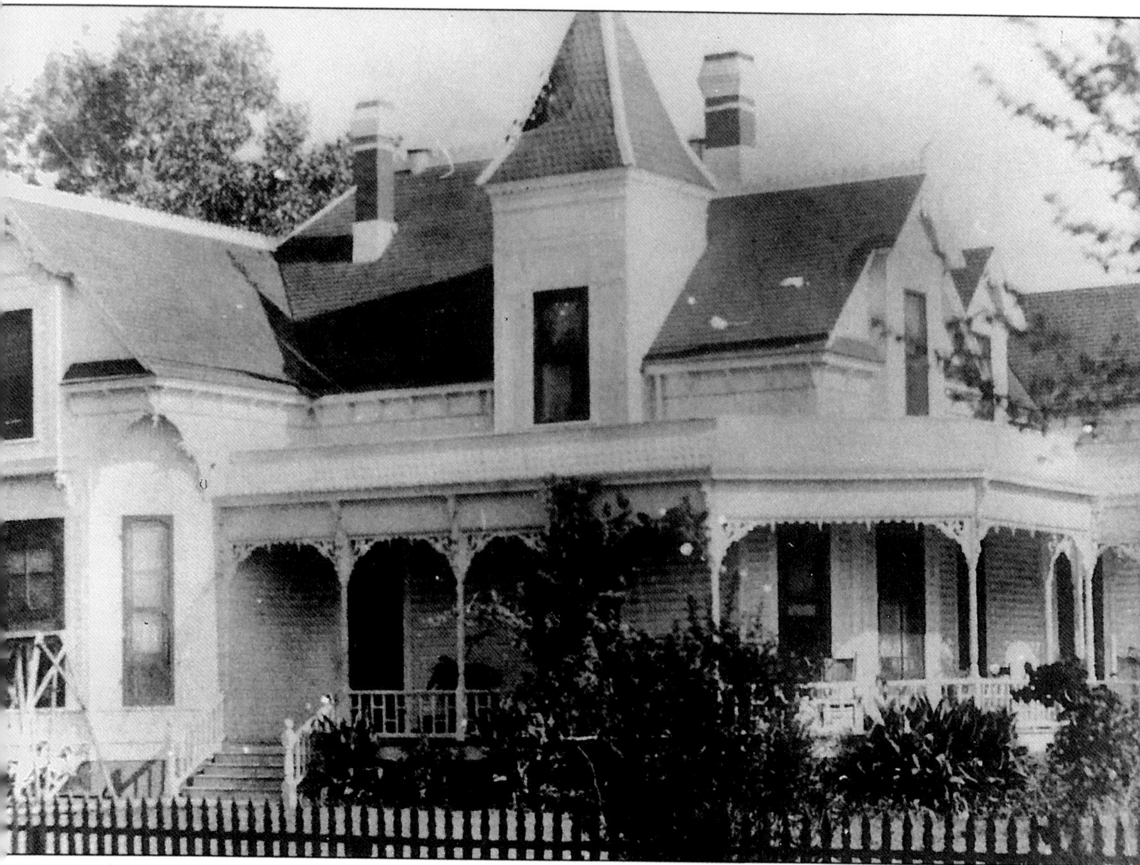

Silas Harrington Home. (Courtesy of the Frances Wells Collection.)

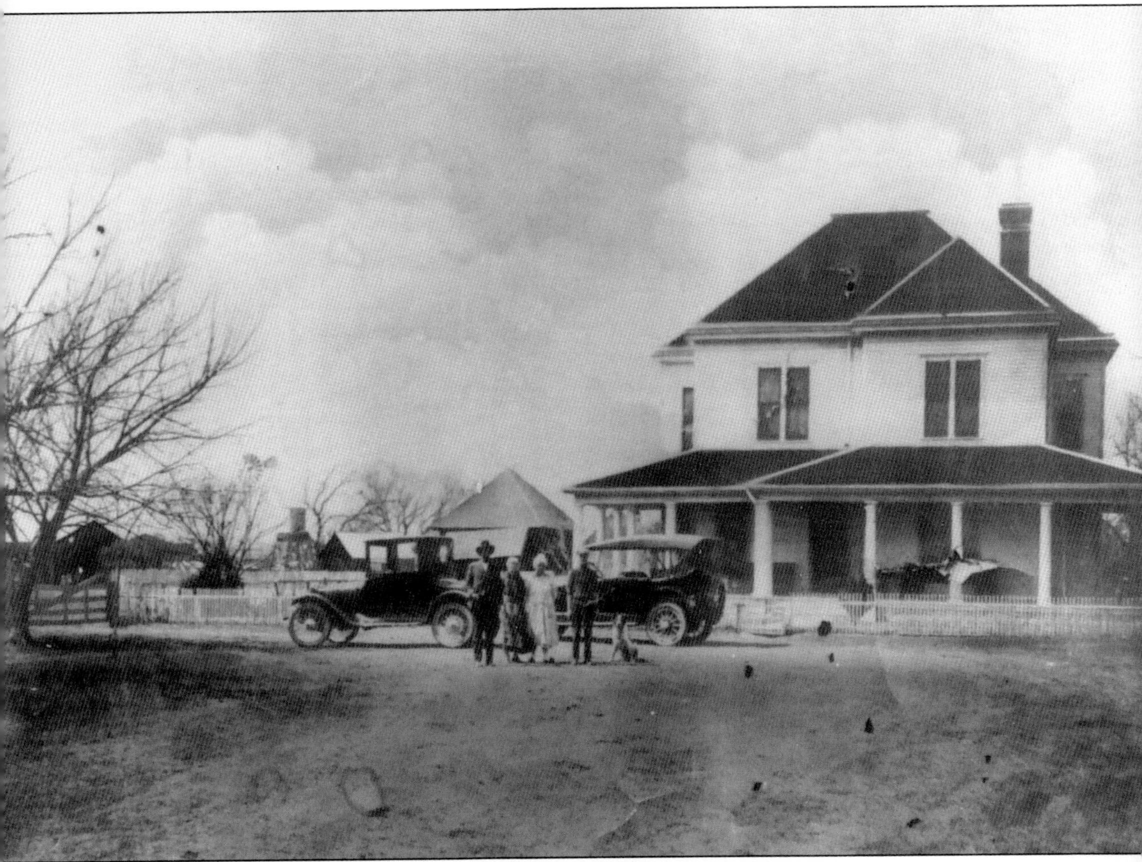

John Harrington Home. (Courtesy of the Frances Wells Collection.)

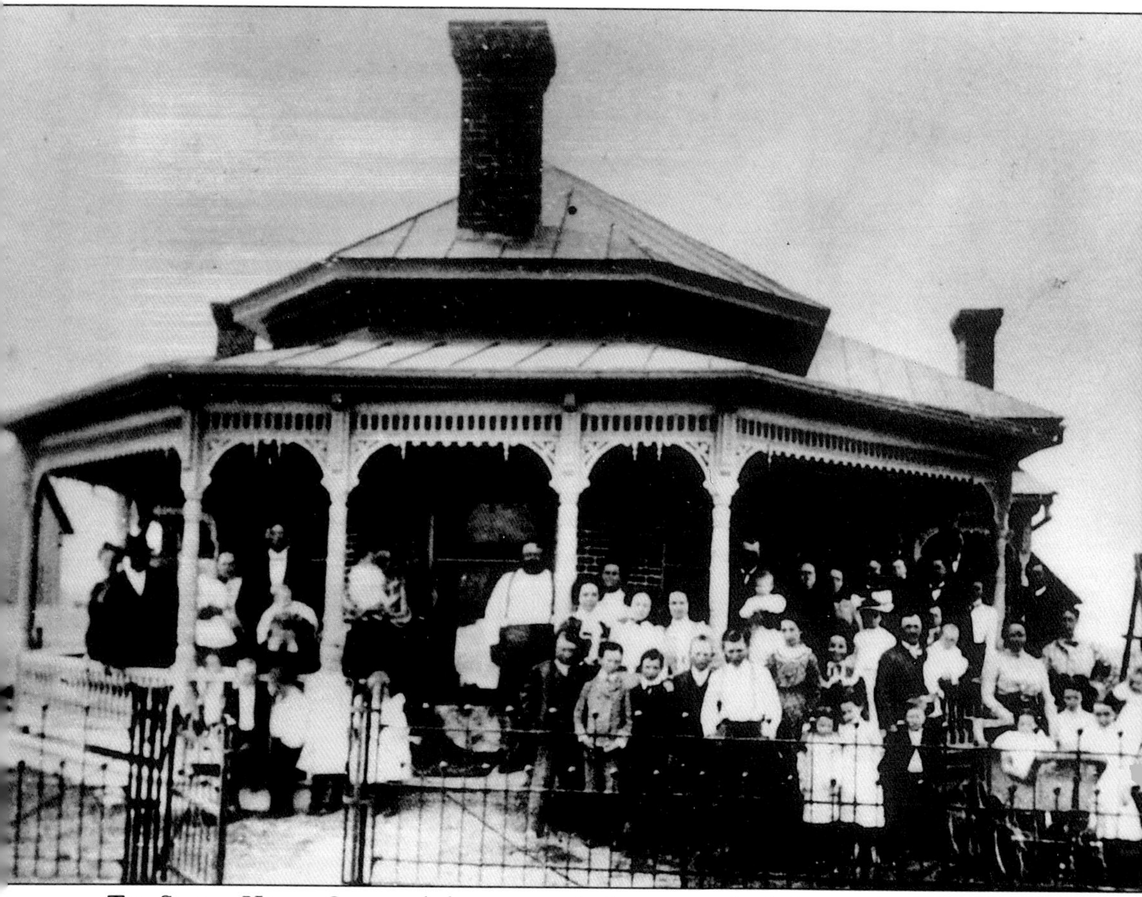

The Sachse House. Some early homes were built in a circular fashion such as this one for easy defense against Indians. (Courtesy of the Frances Wells Collection.)

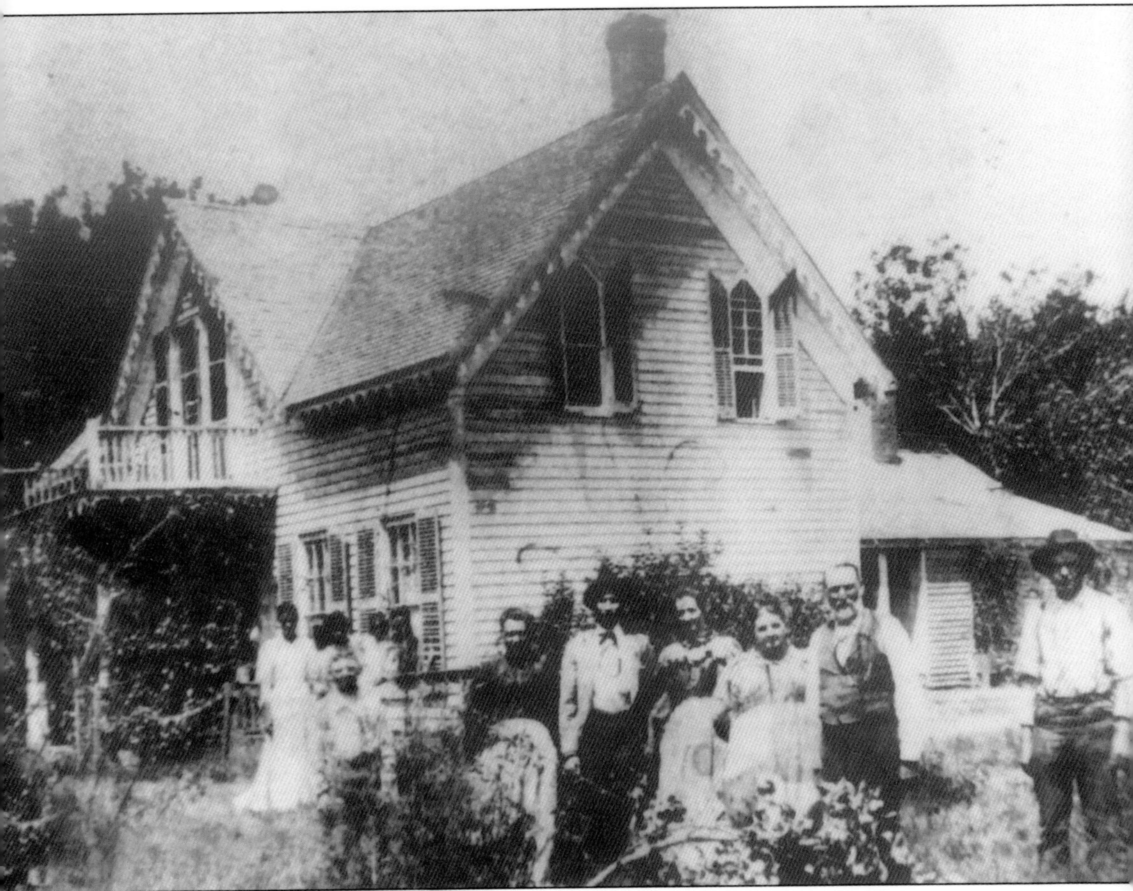

R.W. CARPENTER HOUSE. This house was built around the original log cabin. Robert W. Carpenter was married to Lizzie Carpenter, who kept a diary that many refer to today for information on early Plano life. R.W. Carpenter loaned money to help start Add-Ran College, which later became Texas Christian University. He was repaid with receipt of land. The Carpenters of early Plano are all descendants of R.W. Carpenter. (Courtesy of the Frances Wells Collection.)

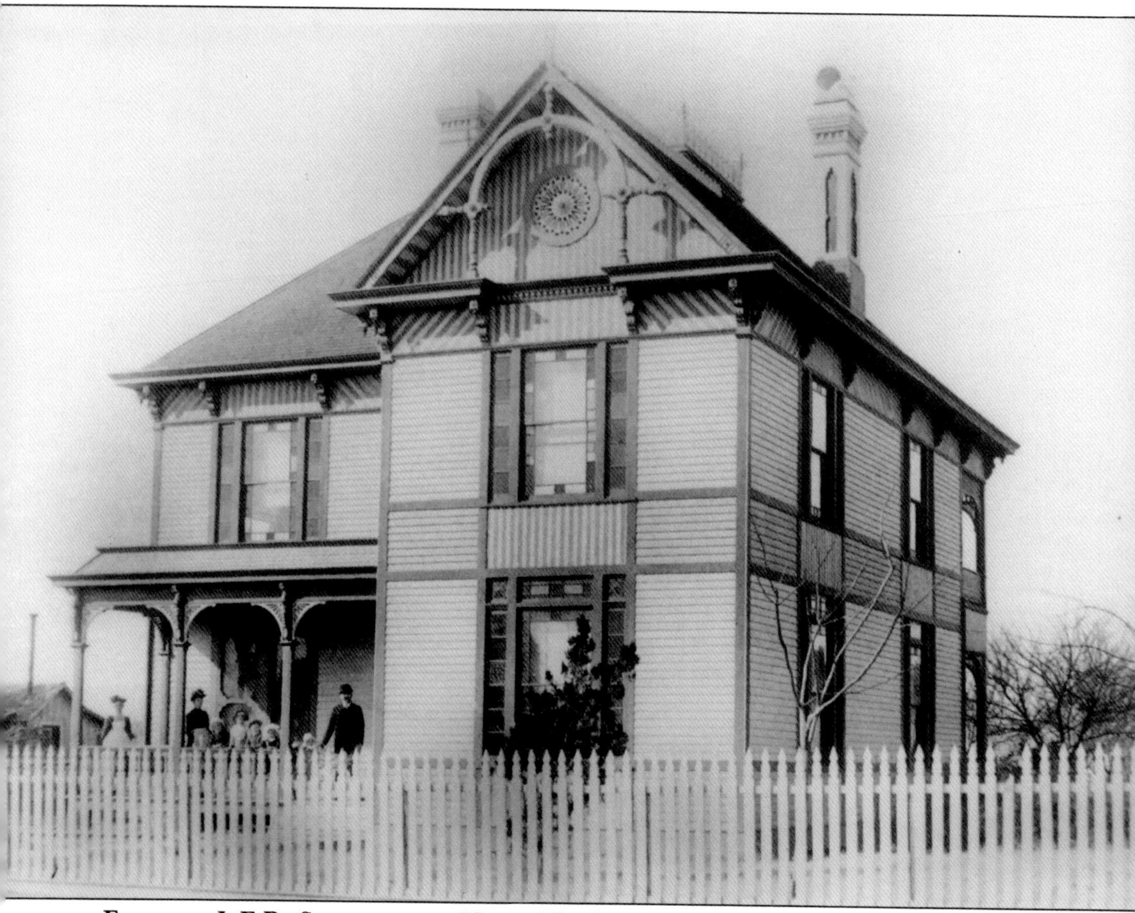

FRED AND L.E.R. SCHIMELPFENIG HOME. This home was located at the present-day corner of 14th Street and Avenue K. Fred and L.E.R. (Louise Ernestine Rammer) Schimelpfenig brought up their family in this home. The children used to go out on the roof of the second story of the house. The girls would tie their ankles to the house with a rope for fear of falling off.

Fred Schimelpfenig maintained stores in downtown Plano which were both destroyed in the downtown fires of 1881 and 1895. L.E.R. fought against the many saloons in downtown Plano. The cause of the fires was blamed on all of the flammable alcohol in the many saloons. L.E.R. won her fight at about the same time Fred became mayor of Plano. (Courtesy of the Frances Wells Collection.)

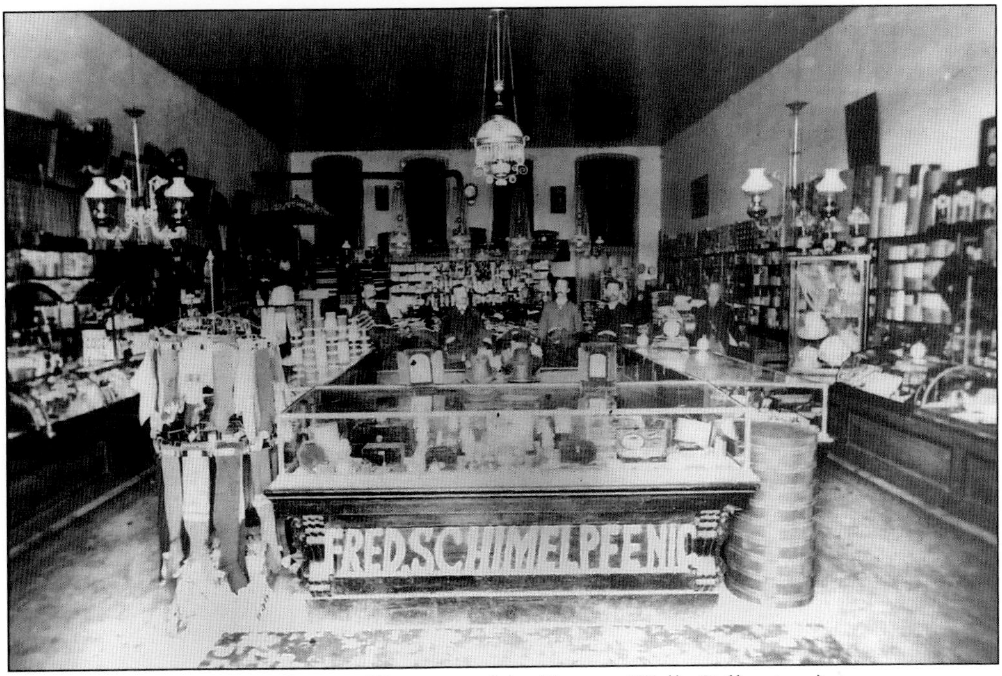

THE FRED SCHIMELPFENIG STORE. (Courtesy of the Frances Wells Collection.)

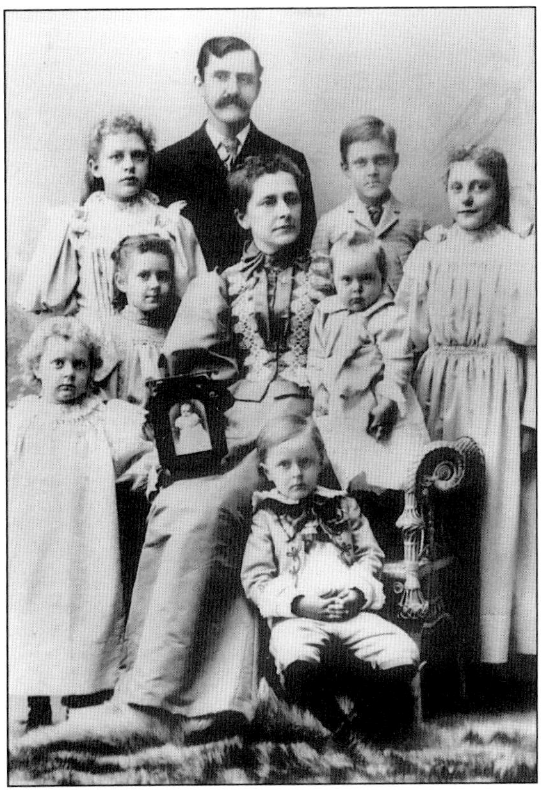

THE SCHIMELPFENIG FAMILY. (Courtesy of the Frances Wells Collection.)

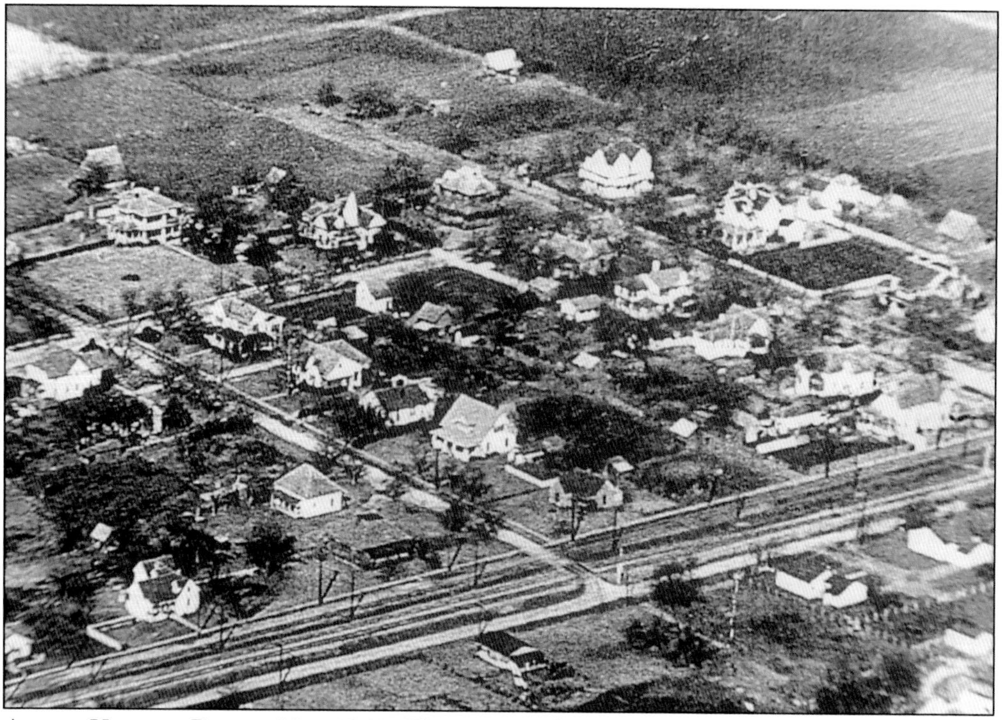

Aerial View of Plano, Mid-1940s. This picture depicts an aerial view of the area around Avenue G and 17th and 18th Streets in the 1940s.

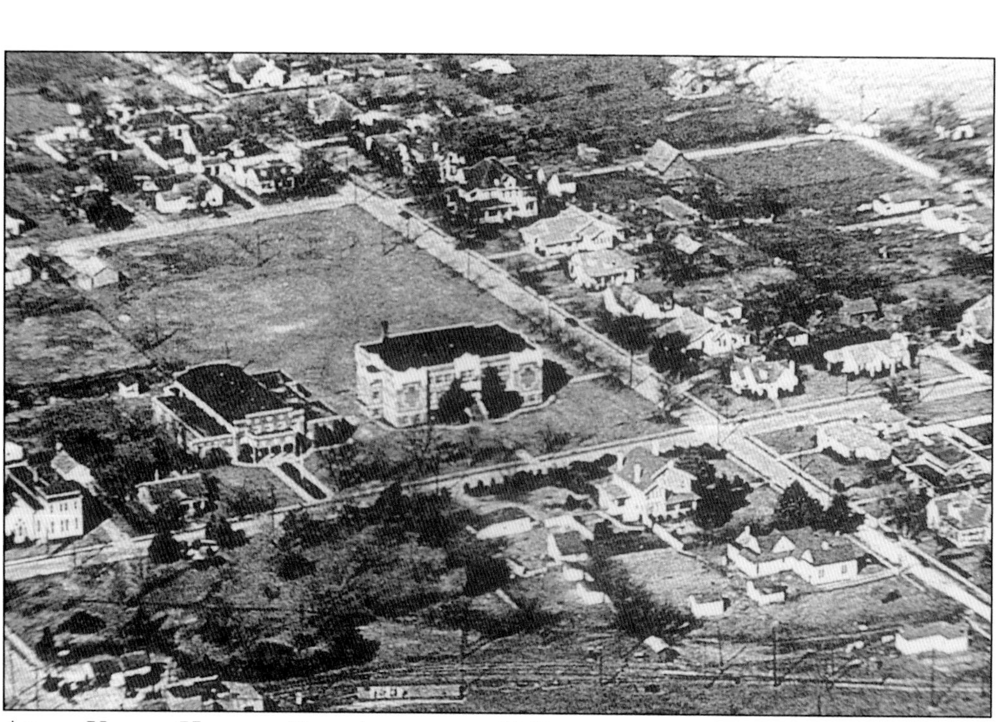

Aerial View of Haggard Park Area in the 1940s.

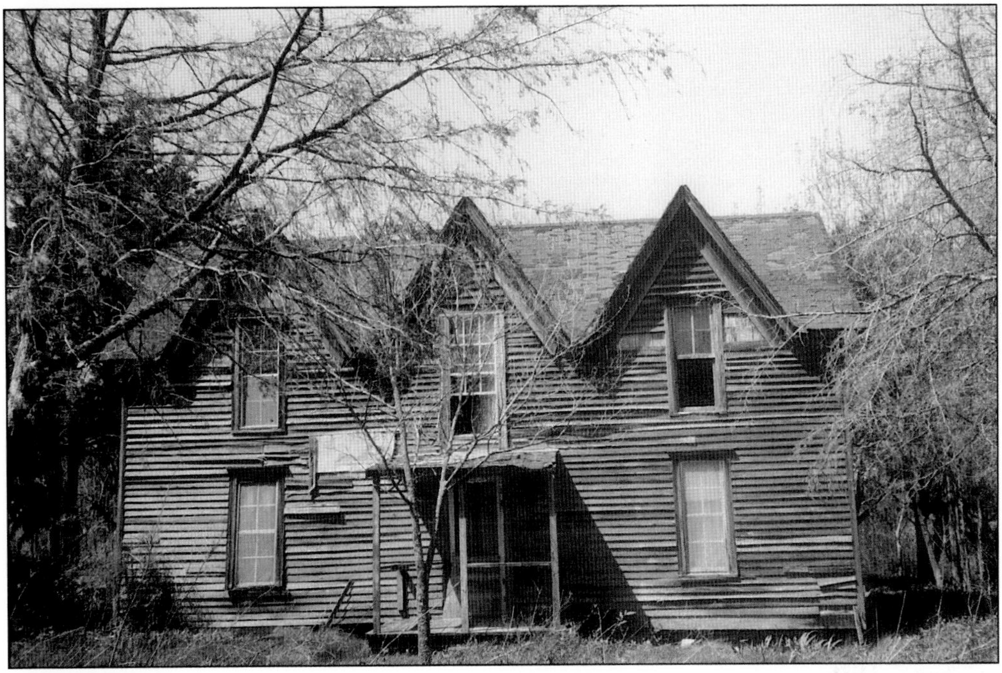

YOUNG HOUSE.

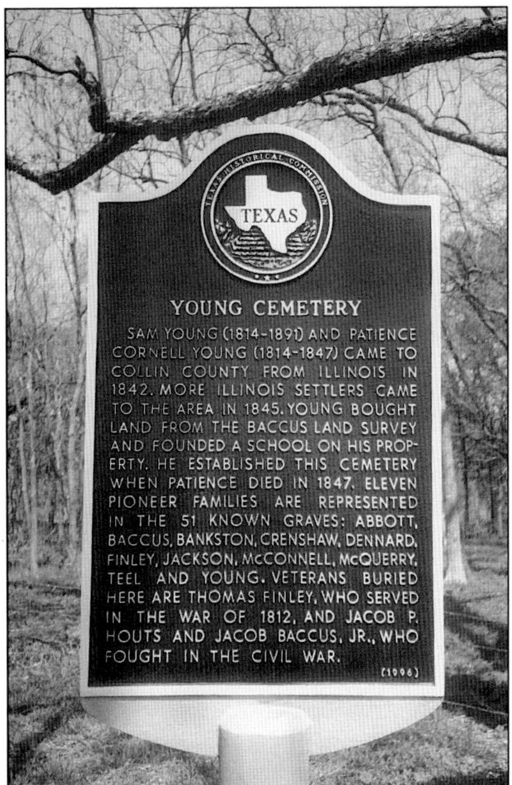

YOUNG FAMILY CEMETERY MARKER NEARBY.

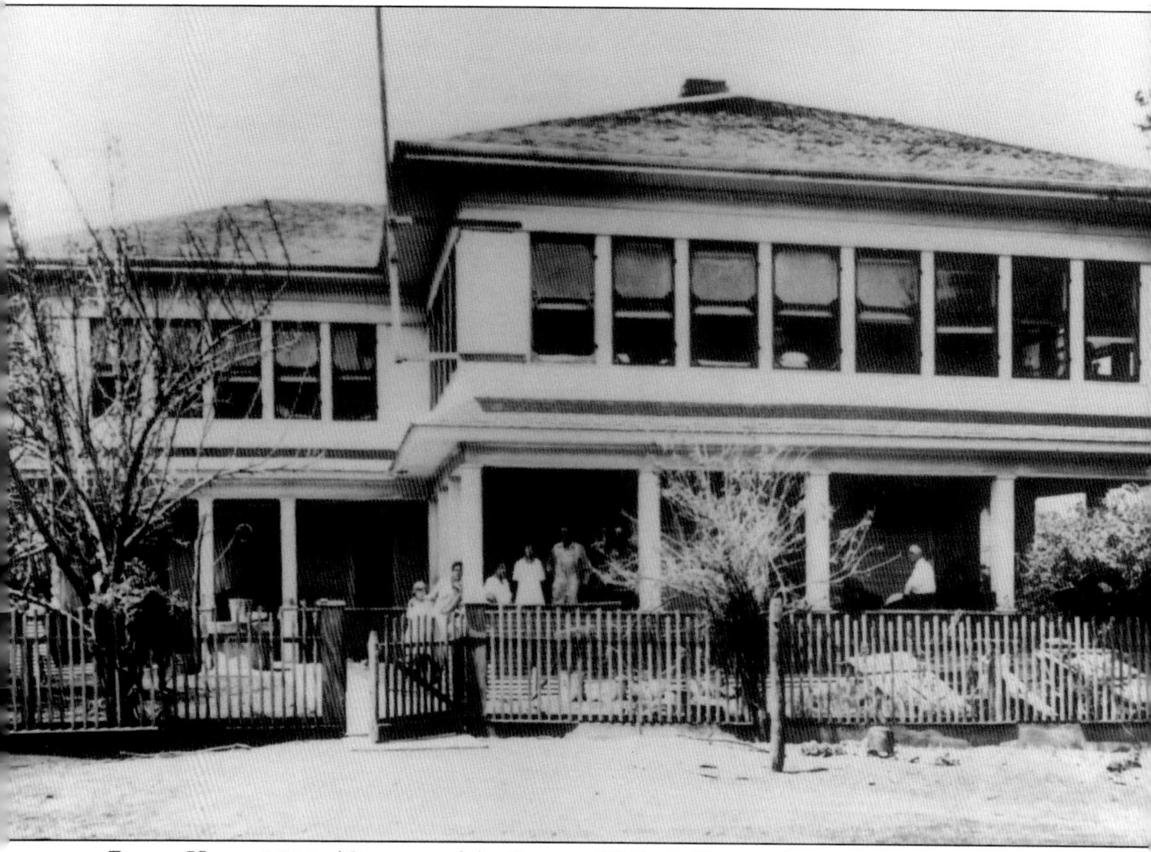

RASOR HOME, 1918. (Courtesy of the Frances Wells Collection.)

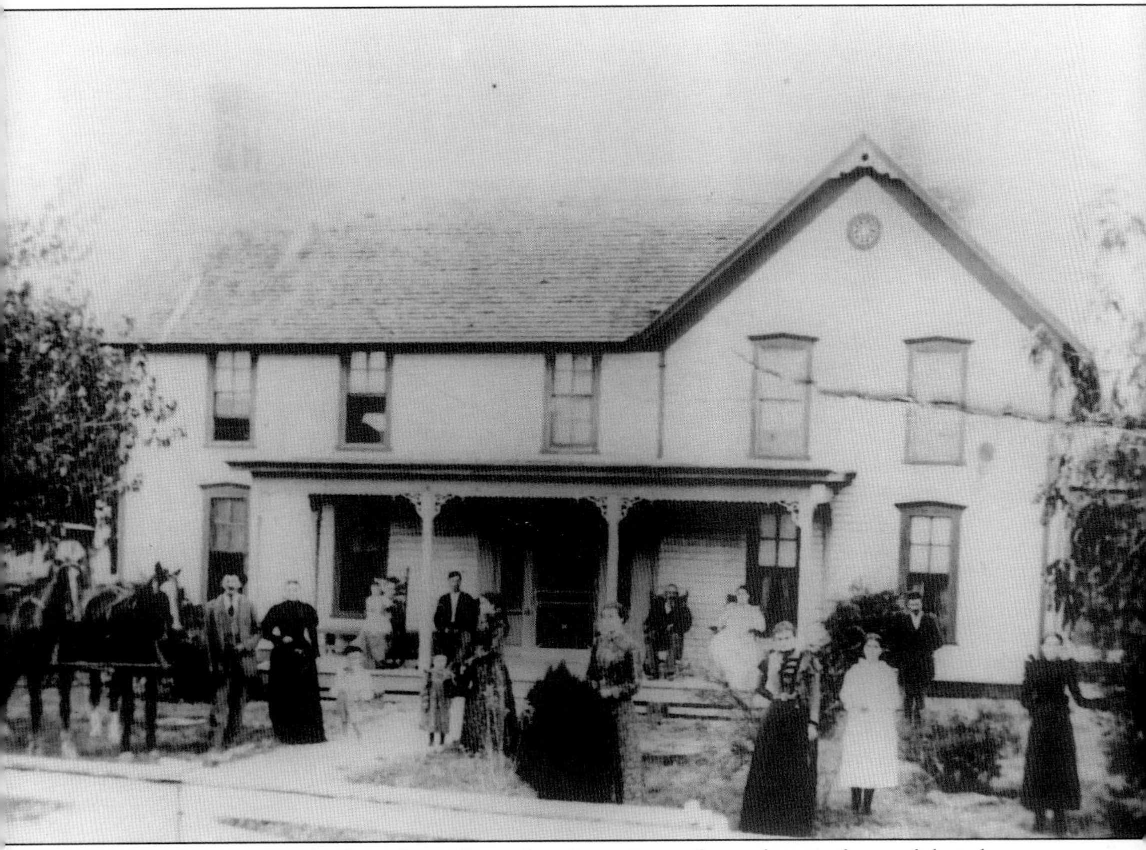

Spring Glade, 1897. The Joseph Huffman family is pictured standing in front of their home. (Courtesy of the Frances Wells Collection.)

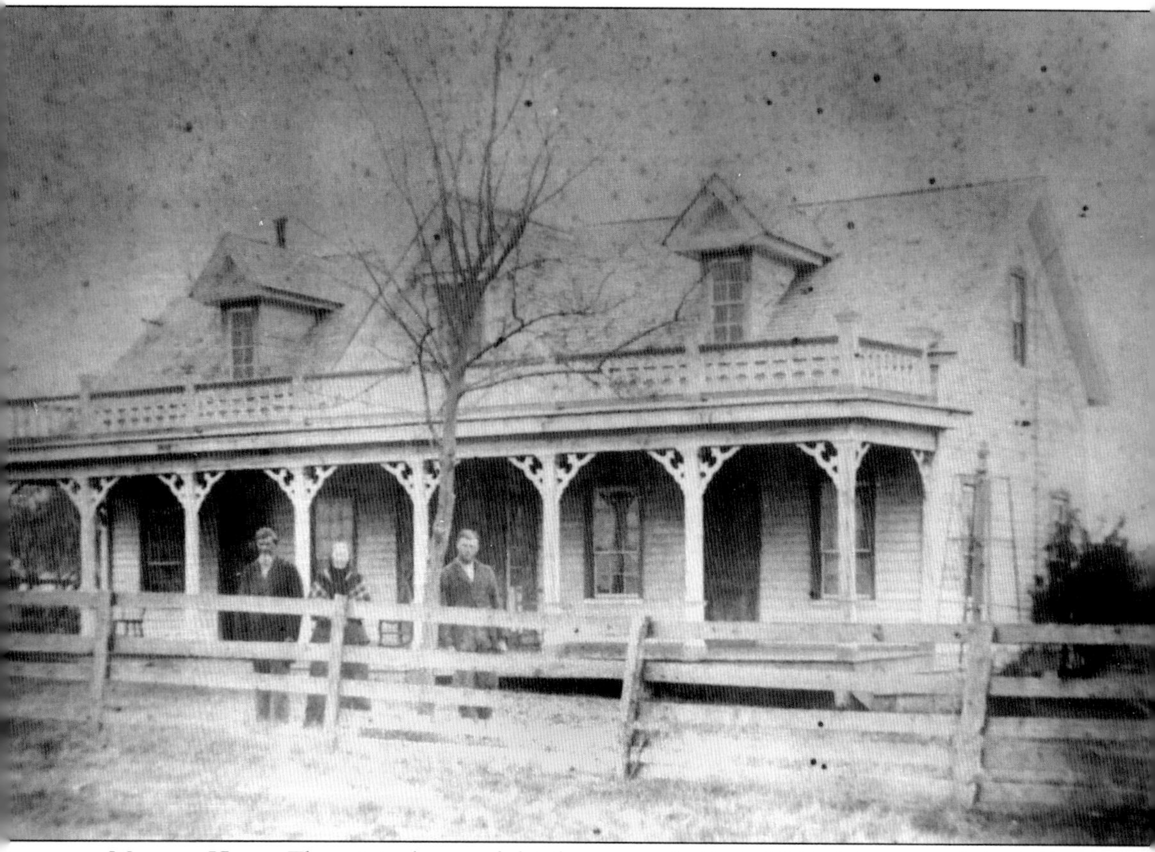

Murphy Home. The original part of this house was built in 1874. (Courtesy of the Frances Wells Collection.)